A History of Seafaring in the Classical World

Fik Meijer

ST. MARTIN'S PRESS
New York

Scholarly & Reference Division,
St. Martin's Press, Inc., 175 Fifth Avenue, New York, NY 10010
First published in the United States of America in 1986
Printed in Great Britain

Library of Congress Cataloging-in-Publication Data

Meijer, Fik.
    A history of seafaring in the classical world.

    Bibliography: p.
    Includes index.
    1. Navigation — Mediterranean Region — History.
2. Mediterranean Region — History, Naval. I. Title.
VK.16.M45 1986   623.89′091822   86-17854
ISBN 0-312-00075-8

Contents

Figures

Preface

The Mediterranean, the centre of the Classical world, was sailed by Greeks and Romans from the third millennium BC until the sixth century AD. This book offers a survey of ancient seafaring from the beginning in Crete and the Aegean islands until the Byzantine period. Various aspects are discussed: the invention and development of warships and freighters, the extent of trade, the social position of all those concerned with seafaring, Greek and Roman naval policy and the significance of numerous naval battles, which were sometimes decisive for the balance of power.

This book is intended for all those with a serious interest in ancient maritime history. Greek and Latin words are used only if they are technical terms. In names of persons, cities and regions Latin or Greek orthography is used, unless a more common English equivalent seemed preferable. The book being a survey, all references to both ancient and modern sources have been placed in the notes. Passages from Thucydides and Herodotus are cited from the Penguin Classics translations by Rex Warner and Aubrey de Selincourt, respectively.

My debts to others are manifold. First of all, my colleagues in the departments of Greek, Latin, Ancient History and Classical Archaeology greatly stimulated my work. My debt to three of them is profound: Professors C.J. Ruijgh and J.M. Hemelrijk each read several chapters and provided much helpful criticism; Professor P.J. Sijpesteijn meticulously read the entire typescript and offered a great number of useful suggestions. Most of all, acknowledgement should be made to the authors of the books and articles which I consulted while writing this book. I trust they will not find that violence has been done to their ideas.

The book was originally written in Dutch. Norman Giles started on the translation, but his untimely death prevented him from completing this task. I am especially indebted to Hotze Mulder who not only finished the translation and edited the book as a whole but also called my attention to many an

vii

error. I should also like to thank Hetty de Schepper for her assistance in preparing the typescript and the staff of the computer centre of the Faculty of Arts of the University of Amsterdam for their patience with those uninitiated in the art of word processing. Many thanks are also due to Jack de Vries, who accomplished the difficult task of producing clear drawings from often vague originals.

Finally, I am grateful to the Allard Pierson Foundation for providing financial support for the translation of the book.

Fik Meijer
Amsterdam

Chapter One

The Aegean: 3000–1100 BC

Little is known about the earliest history of seafaring in the Classical world. When and how people first ventured to sea in prehistorical times is uncertain. No remains of boats have been discovered and the earliest representations date from after 3000 BC; maritime objects such as knives, scrapers and fish-hooks constitute the only evidence. The oldest specimens (*c.* 8000 BC) are made of obsidian, a hard volcanic stone, found on the island of Melos. By comparison with the early history of seafaring in other parts of the world, it may be conjectured that the Mediterranean peoples first ventured to sea to catch fish, and later on to conduct small-scale barter and to wage piracy. The appearance of the earliest boats is not known, but we can assume that in the beginning they consisted mainly of simple hollowed-out trees. In a later phase planks were added to widen and lengthen the dug-out. A subsequent development was the reshaping of the dug-out itself; with the aid of fire and water, the sides were softened and stretched, following which they were reinforced by thwarts and frames. Using the same techniques, the extremities were raised so that they were higher than amidships. The result was an elegant curved shape similar to that of a plank-built boat. Finally strakes were sewn to both sides of the dug-out base. In turn the dug-out itself was reduced to a keel-like axial beam that was lengthened by the sewn planks, and the freeboard height was increased by adding washboards to the gunwale. This change marks the transition to the plank-built boat.

This transition did not come about in the same manner everywhere. The earliest representations from the Aegean are from the Cycladic islands of Naxos and Syros. A lead model found on Naxos and dating from before 2500 BC shows a long ship with a gently rising stem and a markedly raised forefoot (Fig. 1.1). The same goes for the ship portrayed on a terracotta 'frying pan' from Syros (after 2500 BC). It is straight and low and displays in the bows a projecting forefoot; this, namely the lengthening of the

1

keel beyond the stem, was a structural feature. At the stern the bottom turns upward more slowly (Fig. 1.2). In both cases the general picture is clearly one of swift, sizeable galleys with a frame made from a dug-out to which planks were added on both sides in order to achieve a higher freeboard. No mast is shown on these representations, which indicates that the ships were propelled by oars or paddles.[1] Ships of this type sailed from the Cycladic islands to Asia Minor, Crete and the mainland of Greece. Traces of Cycladic exports are found even on the Dalmatian coast and on Sicily.

Figure 1.1 Lead Model from Naxos

Drawings and models from the third millennium BC in Egypt portray a different kind of ship. Unlike the long, narrow-oared ships of the Aegean, both rivercraft and seagoing ships have a spoon-shaped hull. A ship of this type is that found alongside the pyramid of Cheops (about 2650 BC) with a length of 43.5 m and a width of 5.53 m, flat-bottomed and without a keel. A similar description is applicable to the ships on a relief in the temple of King Sahure at Abusir near Cairo (about 2500 BC). They have a gently rising stem and stern and a bipod mast which slants back towards the stern. A number of stays fore and aft support the mast. From stem to stern ran a hogging truss of rope that was tightened in the middle with the aid of a spar which was drawn through the strands of the rope truss and turned to shorten the latter. The intention was to support the two ends so that they did not collapse under a wave amidships.[2]

With these ships the Egyptians went in a southerly direction in the Red Sea as far as Punt in Somalia and in a northerly direction from the Delta along the coasts of the Levant from where they imported cedar-wood for shipbuilding. In the second millennium BC these ships developed into oared merchant vessels with rising bow and stern, twin rudder oars, ten to 20 oarsmen on either side, masts with single poles supported by stays and shrouds and sails

Figure 1.2 Terra-cotta 'Frying Pan' from Syros

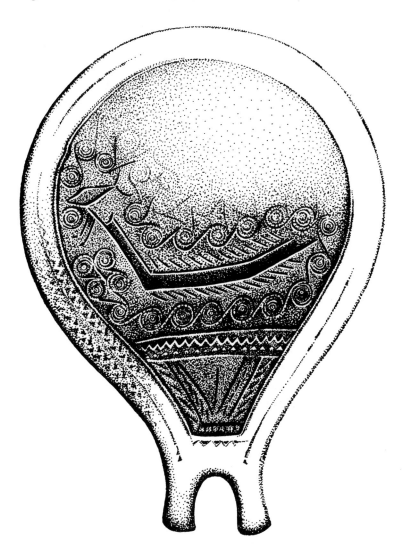

that were rigged with yard-arm and boom. Even in the third millennium BC the Egyptians had already voyaged by sea as far as a number of Greek islands, including Crete, from which they imported various objects. The similarity between the Egyptian and Cretan ships leads one to suppose that the Egyptians also passed on their knowledge of shipbuilding. Most of the portrayals on Cretan seals show rounded hulls with symmetrically rising bow and stern. The rig consists of a massive pole mast, supported by stays fore and aft and with a single broad sail (Fig. 1.3). But some seals depict ships which more closely resemble the Aegean shipbuilding tradition: asymmetrical with forefoot.[3]

Figure 1.3 Vessels on Minoan Seals

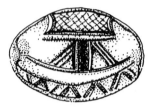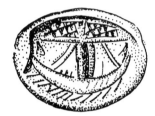

From 2000 BC the Cretans extended their influence over great areas of the Mediterranean; in a southerly direction as far as Egypt and Libya; in a westerly direction to Sicily, Apulia and the Lipari Islands; and in a northerly direction to Thrace. Expansion of their sphere of influence to the east was halted by the Hittites. Thucydides, the fifth-century Greek historian, maintains that the Cretans even exercised a thalassocracy over the neighbouring islands as a result of their naval supremacy. From their open, unfortified palaces, he writes, they dominated the Cyclades. The opposing view holds that Cretan dominion or overlordship could only have come about gradually and relatively peacefully and that forms of control could have been exercised without the stationing of a garrison. Crete was the dominant power that provided security for sea-borne trade. The evidence points to an intensive trade in metals, luxury goods and many other items, often accompanied by Minoan traders. This latter view is reinforced by the fact that Minoan seals portray ships with an almost identical prow and stern, a feature not of warships but of merchant vessels, which had to be easily manoeuvrable in harbours and narrow channels.[4]

How various building traditions were mingled in the second millennium BC can be seen from a miniature fresco depicting a great array of ships and boats on the walls of a room in the Western House at Akrotiri, Thera (mod. Santorini), dating from the second half of the sixteenth century BC (Fig. 1.4). The extremities of the basically symmetrical hulls are differentiated by structural and ornamental additions. The bows have an elongated end with floral symbols. The sterns are more solid and provided with a substantial jutting structure and compact figures or the skins of large feline predators. The placement of the mast in the centre of the deck structure and the rolled-up sails on a line of elevated beams strongly resemble the vessels of the Egyptian New Kingdom. All the ships on the fresco have steering oars on the starboard quarter only, not on both quarters as was the custom later in antiquity. They are manned by armed warriors and are paddled by half-naked men (in the best preserved one there are 21 paddlers on the starboard side), which leads one to suspect that a ceremonial procession is portrayed but that the ships were used both for military and for commercial purposes. Seeing that other features of the Akrotiri settlement give clear evidence of a significant Minoan presence on the island during the sixteenth century BC, it may be assumed that the ships are Cretan.[5]

Figure 1.4 Ship on a Fresco from Thera

In the second half of the fifteenth century BC, the Cretans lost their position to invaders after large parts of Crete had already been devastated by either earthquakes or the volcanic eruption of

Thera. The invaders put an end to the authority of the palace of Knossos and introduced their own customs. From that time on the so-called 'Warrior Tombs' appeared on Crete. We do not know how the invasions from the north came about or whether, and if so, where, a military confrontation occurred. It may well be that the Cretan fleet had been damaged by the natural catastrophes to such a degree that it could not put up any resistance. But it cannot be ruled out that the Minoan round ships were simply not a match for the fleet of the Greek newcomers, who used ships built according to the Aegean building traditions.

The invaders were the Mycenaeans. On the Greek mainland vast changes had come about from *c.* 2100 BC as a result of the influx of tribes from the north. This migration is generally referred to as 'The coming of the Greeks'. By about 1600 BC Mycenae had become a warrior civilisation and a centre of wealth and power; other centres arose in central and southern Greece, on the Aegean islands, on the coasts of Asia Minor and Syria, in southern Italy and on Sicily. The unity characterising these centres gave rise to the concept of 'Mycenaean civilisation'. Their widespread geographical distribution indicates that seafaring must have played an important role.[6]

The abundance of Mycenaean luxuries and pottery in the eastern Mediterranean illustrates the extent of the trade between Syria and Egypt on the one hand, and the Mycenaean centres on the other. Precious metals probably formed important items of commerce, since, for lack of natural resources, Greece was dependent on imports. Presumably the metals were obtained from eastern Turkey or Syria. G. Bass, who excavated a boat wrecked off Cape Gelidonya in south-west Turkey, concluded that the copper and tin ingots on board were of a type traded by Syrian merchants in the fourteenth and thirteenth centuries BC. In his opinion, the Semitic seafarers played a larger role in maritime commerce during those centuries than has generally been accepted. Other archaeologists believe that the Cape Gelidonya ship must have been Mycenaean, since the Mycenaeans were lords of the Mediterranean. The wreck itself was not preserved. All that can be said is that it must have been a freighter not longer than 9 m. Perhaps the excavation of a recently discovered shipwreck at Kas (not far from Cape Gelidonya), loaded with ingots, *pithoi* (large storage jars) and amphoras of a well-known Canaanite type, can help in the discussion about Mycenaean and Syrian trade in the eastern part of the Mediterranean. If parts of the hull are preserved, questions about ship construction can better be answered.[7]

Until then the shape of the Mycenaean ships has to be guessed from representations on a clay box found in Pylos (Fig. 1.5) and on a vase from Asine (Fig. 1.6), both dating from the twelfth century BC. In broad lines the shape resembles the Aegean models from the third millennium BC. The ships have a straight low hull with a sharply rising high stem and a short stern-post to add some height aft. In addition there were bulwarks to screen the bows and quarters. The ships were propelled by oars. A list was found at Pylos containing the names of 30 persons who were to proceed to Pleuron as rowers. Another list contains the names of 569 rowers. It is possible that the ships, like the largest of the Thera ships, had 42 or even 50 rowers, prototypes of the later penteconters mentioned by Homer. The poet, whose Iliad and Odyssey are the culmination of a long tradition of oral poetry, relates how in the heroic age the Greeks fitted out 1186 ships to attack Troy, which was situated on a hill a few miles from the Aegean and the Hellespont. Although much of the information in both epics seems to refer rather to Homer's own time, namely the eighth century BC and the Dark Ages preceding it, it is probable that the catalogue of ships in the second book of the Iliad is based on general notions about the Mycenaean thalassocracy: the most powerful states furnished the greatest contingents; Nestor, king of Pylos, for instance, commanded 90 ships. It is remarkable that the ships play no active role in the struggle against the Trojans: they serve only as troop transports. No mention whatsoever is made of a Trojan fleet although Troy was situated close to the sea.[8]

Figure 1.5 Clay Box from Pylos

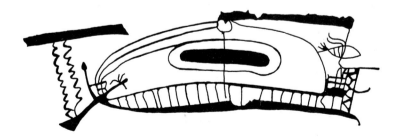

Figure 1.6 Vase from Asinè

Whether the siege of Troy really took place or is merely an oral tradition based upon Greek raids on enemy settlements is still a matter of dispute. Round about 1200 BC, the time when the siege and capture of Troy are supposed to have taken place, the Mycenaeans were themselves under pressure from invaders from the north. These were composed of various ethnic groups known as the Sea Peoples, who left their mark on history particularly in the eastern basin of the Mediterranean. They arrived in Greece by land and by sea, the western Peloponnese with its important centre of Pylos forming a prime target. It is possible that the above-mentioned list of 569 rowers is connected with a threatening invasion. In that case, the rowers were in all likelihood called up to resist the Sea Peoples' fleet, as were the 800 look-outs named on another tablet. The ships had neither offensive weapons nor rams, so that the tactics had to be limited to overtaking and boarding enemy craft.[9]

That the Sea Peoples had good ships at their disposal can be observed on an Egyptian relief from Medinet Habu depicting a naval battle in which Ramses III defeated a coalition of Sea Peoples in *c.* 1185 BC (Fig. 1.7). The ships were probably built under the influence of Aegean building traditions. They have a gently curved hull, ending in high stem- and stern-posts decorated with duck heads. Forecastles and aftercastles were raised at bow and stern. The ships are undecked and mostly depicted without oars and with sails furled. The absence of oars is remarkable, because one may well wonder how they could reach the Nile Delta without them.[10]

Figure 1.7 Ships of the Sea Peoples on a Relief in a Temple at Medinet Habu

The victory of Ramses III was an exception. In Asia Minor, Syria and Greece, the Sea Peoples were more successful and overcame the ruling powers. For Greece the result was catastrophic. The palaces and their fortress complexes disappeared and there was an overall decline in population. Some centres, such as Pylos, were abandoned completely; others, such as Athens, remained inhabited but on a smaller scale. The population, in particular the upper classes, were reduced to poverty and saw no use for prestige projects as in the Mycenaean period. Apparently, a change for the better was considered unlikely: great numbers of people crossed the Aegean and settled on the offshore islands and the coast of Asia Minor. Initially, this migration was a refugee movement rather than a form of planned colonisation. The most northerly immigrants, traditionally known as Aeolians, moved across to Lesbos and the stretch of coast between Cyme and Pitane. Those now known as Dorians settled on the more southerly part of the coast of Asia Minor and the islands of Melos, Thera, Rhodes and Cos. Between the Dorians and the Aeolians, the Ionians settled on the Cyclades and the central part of the coast of Asia Minor. Twelve cities sprang up of which Miletus, Ephesus, Phocaea and Samos are the best-known. The whole of the Aegean was now Greek, but there was no central authority to guarantee safety at sea. Sea trade sank to a low level and ships that ventured to maintain trade links became an easy prey for pirates.

Notes

1. AEGEAN SHIP CONSTRUCTION: Casson, 1971, pp. 30–2; De Graeve, 1981, pp. 99–100.
2. SHIP ALONGSIDE THE PYRAMID OF CHEOPS: Jenkins, 1980.
3. CRETAN SEALS: Betts, 1973, pp. 325–9.
4. CRETAN THALASSOCRACY: Thuc. 1.4; 1.8. The various aspects of the thalassocracy are treated in Hägg and Marinatos (eds.), 1984.
5. THERA SHIPS: Raban, 1984, pp. 11–19; cf. Casson, 1975, pp. 3–10; Gillner, 1978, pp. 125–34.
6. MYCENAEAN SEAFARING: Chadwick, 1977, p. 173; cf. Marinatos, 1933, pp. 170–235; Guglielmi, 1971, pp. 418–35.
7. SHIPWRECK AT CAPE GELIDONYA: Bass, 1967, pp. 163–7; contra: Muhly, 1977, pp. 73–82. SHIPWRECK AT KAS: Bass, Frey and Pulak, 1984, pp. 271–9; Pulak and Frey, 1985, pp. 18–24.
8. MYCENAEAN SHIPS: Casson, 1971, p. 32. LISTS OF ROWERS: PY An 1; PY An 610; cf. Chadwick, 1977, p. 173. CATALOGUE OF SHIPS: Hom. *Il.* 2.494–779; cf. Hope Simpson and Lazenby, 1970; see for different opinions about the catalogue Heubeck, 1974, pp. 59–64.
9. SIEGE OF TROY: Finley, 1977, pp. 61–3; cf. Heubeck, 1974, pp. 160–4. SEA PEOPLES: Sandars, 1978, pp. 180–1.
10. SHIPS OF THE SEA PEOPLES: Wachsmann, 1981, pp. 187–220.

Chapter Two

The Dark Ages

After the migrations of the twelfth and eleventh centuries BC, centralised monarchies such as Mycenae disappeared and in their place small and relatively poor communities sprang up consisting of scattered villages. In each of these communities political power was concentrated in the hands of a king, surrounded by a council of aristocrats, or in the hands of the aristocracy as a body. This was a small group of large landowners. The people, small farmers, labourers and artisans, obeyed them unconditionally.

In the period 1100 to 800 BC, the Dark Ages, contacts with the outside world were sparse. Trade, which in the Minoan and Mycenaean periods had been of great importance, sagged to a low level but did not disappear completely. The development of proto-geometric and early geometric pottery in the tenth and ninth centuries BC and the diffusion of this pottery and other products over a large area indicate that there was still some overseas trade. Maintaining trade lines cannot have been easy, for pirates, profiting from the power vacuum in the Aegean, formed a continuous danger. They attacked villages adjacent to the sea and fell upon merchant ships. Piracy was not considered a base occupation, as Homer informs us: when, at the court of the king of the Phaeacians, Odysseus tells the story of his wanderings, he describes an attack on the town of Ismarus. He laid waste to the town, killed the men and took away their women and possessions. In another passage, the meeting of Odysseus with the swineherd Eumaeus immediately after his return to Ithaca, the typical pirate is portrayed. Odysseus poses as the bastard son of a wealthy Cretan who has survived the Trojan war. Longing for excitement and adventure, he had left home once again, this time to sail to Egypt in search of booty. That subsequently everything got out of control — many of his crew were killed and others taken away as slaves — is not important in this connection. The fact that Odysseus dares to tell such a story illustrates that piracy was considered a respectable martial activity, in which many indulged.

11

The expeditions of Menelaus, king of Sparta, along the coasts of Cyprus, Phoenicia and Egypt also yielded great quantities of booty. Nobody thought any the worse of him for that. The respectability of the profession of pirate in the Dark Ages was much later expressed by Thucydides as follows:

> The leading pirates were powerful men, acting both out of self-interest and in order to support the weak among their own people. They would descend upon cities which were unprotected by walls and indeed consisted only of scattered settlements; and by plundering such places they would gain most of their livelihood. At this time such a profession, so far from being regarded as disgraceful, was considered quite honourable. And in the old poets we find that the regular question always asked of those who arrive by sea is 'Are you pirates?' It is never assumed either that those who were so questioned would shrink from admitting the fact, or that those who were interested in finding out the fact would reproach them with it.[1]

The ships with which these plundering expeditions were undertaken and commerce conducted are briefly described by Homer and depicted on a number of late geometric vases (Fig. 2.1). The poet calls the ships fast, spacious and open and compares the crooked bows and stern-posts with the horns of cattle. The vase paintings with open galleys — aphracts — correspond with Homer's description. There is one difference; Homer nowhere mentions rams but the galleys on the geometric vases do have one. It was probably introduced sometime during the Dark Ages but did not become significant before the eighth century BC (see p. 23).[2]

Homer's galleys are low and have no superstructure. He relates how in a Trojan attack on the beached Greek ships Hector could prize off ornaments attached high up on the stern-posts. He also tells how with one mighty heave of a puntpole Odysseus managed to get his ship clear of the shallows near the island of the cyclops Polyphemus, from which the conclusion may be drawn that his ship could not have been very heavy. In place of a deck there were only short platforms fore and aft. The open construction indicates that the ships were beached during the night. It is not clear from Homer how they were constructed, because he mentions two different shipbuilding traditions. In the Iliad it is related how the

Figure 2.1 Mixing Bowl (First Half Eighth Century BC) with a Warship Attacked on Shore

planks of the Greek ships had rotted after nine years and how the ropes, made of Esparto grass, had lost their stitching effect. But another type of ship construction is mentioned, the basic principles of which remained the same throughout antiquity, the mortise and tenon joint. The garboard strakes were fixed into a rabbet in the keel and the succeeding planks were edge-joined with a number of mortises and tenons (in the description of Greek freighters of the fifth and fourth centuries BC this method will be treated in greater detail; see p. 77). The hull was constructed from a keel, bow- and stern-post, timber frames, strakes, gunwales and cross-beams, which possibly could have served as rowing benches. The usual sorts of timber employed were oak, poplar and pine. The colour was usually black but it is not clear whether black paint or a sort of pitch was applied.[3]

The dimensions of the Homeric ships can only be estimated from the number of rowers. The most usual type of ship was the *eikosoros* (20-oared), in which ten men could be seated on each side and which was used mainly as a freighter. The ship must have been about 16 m long. It had no military significance. The penteconter, a 50-oared ship of *c.* 39 m in length, on the other hand, is repeatedly mentioned as a troop transport, but not as a 'real' warship. This is not surprising because naval warfare was a later development. Presumably, the Greeks also had triaconters, 30-oared ships of *c.* 23 m in length. Homer also relates that the Boeotians used galleys which had room for 120 men. These ships were possibly rowed at two levels; rowed at one level, they would have had to be about 75 m long and, therefore, unmanageable.[4]

The ships were propelled by rowers. From their benches, they pressed the oars against tholepins. The oars were attached to the tholepins by a leather strap which held the oar in place when the rower bent forward for the stroke or even when he lost his grip. Oars were also used for steering. Homer mentions only one steering oar, but a bowl from Thebes from the second half of the eighth century BC very clearly shows two. How exactly this 'rudder' functioned is obscure; it is surmised that it could be moved to and fro in a lateral and longitudinal direction. It is equally unclear whether the two oars were used separately or in combination.

If the wind was favourable, the rowers could take it easy and the square sail could be hoisted. By hauling on the two forestays, the mast was lifted from the crutch on the stern and placed in a tabernacle situated above the keel. The forestays did not run as far as the bow but were fastened at a distance of about a quarter of the ship's length from the bow, thereby securing a certain stability. There was only one backstay. The sail was secured to a yard, a long cross-beam that was hoisted aloft by means of two halyards. The rest of the running rigging comprised braces, sheets and brails. The remaining gear (mooring ropes, stone anchors and other requisites) was, together with the sails, stowed under the decks and benches.[5]

Although the ships were usually hauled ashore at night, it was far from exceptional to sail through the night. After his visit to Aeolus, the king of the winds, Odysseus sailed for nine days and nights at a stretch. And in the story he tells Eumaeus (see p. 11) he relates that he sailed directly from Crete to Egypt in five days. The last item of information provides an indication of the speed which the ships could attain. On the basis of a distance of 400 sea miles this means an average speed of almost 3.5 knots per hour. Even if we assume that there was a favourable north-westerly wind, this is still a high speed (cf. p. 227).[6]

Notes

1. PIRACY: Hom. *Od.* 4.80–90; 9.32–52; 14.199–313; 16.424–44; Thuc. 1.5; cf. Ormerod, 1924, p. 61; pp. 88–9.

2. QUALIFICATION OF SHIPS: according to Morrison and Williams, 1968, p. 45 the epithet *thoè* is mentioned 50 times in the Iliad and 52 times in the Odyssey; *okeia* occurs once in the Iliad and twice in the Odyssey; *okuporos* occurs nine times in the Iliad and twice in the Odyssey; the epithets *glaphurè* and *koilè* indicate that the ship was open; *koronis* and *orthokrairaoon* suggest that the stern and probably also the bow were curved. Casson, 1971, p. 49 distinguishes the open galleys and the galleys with an elaborate structure. RAM CONSTRUCTION: Morrison and Williams, 1968, p. 7 suggest that the Mycenaean ships were equipped with a ram.

3. LOW SHIPS: Hom *Il.* 15.704; 15.716–17; *Od.* 9.487–8; 9.546. SHIP CONSTRUCTION: Hom *Il.* 2.135; *Od.* 5.244–57; see for a treatment of the construction of Odysseus' boat Casson, 1971, pp. 217–19.

4. EIKOSOROS: Hom. *Il.* 1.309; *Od.* 1.280; 4.669. PENTECONTER: Hom. *Il.* 2.718–20; 16.169–70. TRIACONTERS: Casson, 1971, pp. 44–5. Hom. *Il.* 2.509–10 relates that a Boeotic galley was manned by 120 rowers; cf. Thuc. 1.10.4; see Morrison and Williams, 1968, p. 46 and p. 88.

5. STEERING OAR: Hom. *Od.* 3.281; 5.255; 5.315. SUPERSTRUCTURE OF THE SHIP AND RUNNING RIGGING: Casson, 1971, pp. 43–58; Morrison and Williams, 1968, pp. 47–61.

6. LONG DISTANCE VOYAGES: Hom. *Od.* 10.28; 14.257–8.

Chapter Three

The Age of Expansion

At the beginning of the first millennium BC, conditions on the coasts of the Levant became sufficiently stable to encourage a growth in trade. The inhabitants of the most important coastal cities, Sidon, Berytus, Tyre, Byblus and Aradus, were the main exploiters of the new commerce. The cedars of the mountainous Lebanon supplied wood for good merchantmen. With these, generally spacious, ships the Phoenicians crossed the Mediterranean in a westerly direction and founded colonies on the coasts of northern Africa, Sicily and Spain. Most of the settlements remained factories but some developed into cities such as Utica, Carthage and Gades. There, the Phoenicians traded merchandise of their own manufacture and also products which the Aramaeans brought to the coastal cities from Mesopotamia. Thus, bronze objects, ivory, wood and textiles found their way across the Mediterranean.

For about two centuries the Phoenicians controlled the searoutes to the west. In the ninth century BC the Greeks, too, realised the importance of expanding their sea trade. The elite began to show an interest in goods from the east but the extent to which they could obtain these luxuries depended upon their capacity to provide the Near Eastern centres with raw materials. Although the aristocrats regarded trade, which anyway did not fit in with their idea of autarky, as below their dignity, they temporarily turned to it to satisfy their desire for luxuries and their need for metals particularly for the purpose of warfare. The trade slowly increased; by about 800 BC Greeks from Chalcis and Eretria set up a small settlement, Al Mina, on the Syrian coast. The interest in voyaging increased further when it was realised that new land could be found overseas in order to cope with the overpopulation in many cities. Cities such as Corinth, Chalcis, Eretria, Megara, Miletus and Phocaea colonised on a large scale and an exchange of trade took place between the mother and daughter cities. The upper classes for the most part occupied themselves with their estates and left trade to men of meaner background, although they did maintain an interest in it.

In some cities commerce caused such rapid social changes that political conflicts arose between the aristocrats, who had always been in control, and those who profited from the economic revival and now wanted their share of political power. Disputes inevitably resulted. Sometimes a tyrant emerged who put an end to the disorder by establishing absolute power with the support of merchants and/or farmers. Sometimes a section of the population, having unsuccessfully attempted to assert its influence, had to take ship and set up a new settlement elsewhere in the name of the mother city. But most of those who set out from the harbours of the homeland did so voluntarily. In good harmony with the authorities they went to sea in order to explore other coasts, both for reasons of trade and to found colonies which could relieve the population surplus.[1]

This wave of colonisation which drastically extended the Greek world in the eighth and seventh centuries BC spread over the whole of the Mediterranean and Black Seas, from the Crimea to Spain. In north-north-easterly direction, the northern part of the Aegean, the Thracian coast, the coasts of the Hellespont and the Black Sea were colonised. The colonies founded here were principally trading factories which exported iron, lead and copper from Thrace, timber from the Balkan, fish from the rivers of Russia and grain from southern Russia to Greece in exchange for wines, olive oil and Greek ceramics. In northern Africa colonisation was limited because of the presence of the Egyptians and Carthaginians. The two best-known colonies are Cyrene and Naucratis; in *c.* 625 BC the latter was designated by Pharaoh Psammetichus as a trading-centre for all Greeks conducting commerce with Egypt. Most of the Greeks went west in the wake of the Phoenicians, who had been using these routes for some centuries already. The oldest settlement in the west was Pithecussae (Ischia) on the Gulf of Naples, which was founded in *c.* 800 BC and quickly grew into a prosperous city with its own pottery works and iron foundry. In the following 100 years many other settlements in southern Italy and Sicily came into existence. In the seventh and sixth centuries BC some of the new cities, Syracuse, Acragas and Selinus in Sicily, and Cumae, Puteoli, Sybaris, Croton, Paestum and Tarente in southern Italy, gained such influence that the region became known as *Magna Graecia* (Greater Greece).[2]

Another important reason for this expanding colonisation was the shortage of metals as a result of the suspension of the deliveries of iron by the Phoenicians, who needed it themselves to combat the aggression of the invading Assyrians. The Greeks went further afield, thus coming closer and closer to the very sources of the Phoenician merchandise. The inhabitants of Phocaea, an Ionic city in Asia Minor, were the first to discover the sea-route to the far west where they founded Emporium in Spain and, later, Massilia (Marseilles) in southern France.

The problems facing the Greek seamen at the time of colonisation were far from negligible. First there was the problem of rations. Drink, both wine and water, they took with them in great quantities. Food was also taken on board, but on long exploratory journeys the Greeks developed a method which reduced the amount of foodstuffs to be taken along. During their voyages in unknown territory they continuously searched for strategic points with a fertile hinterland. There they went on shore, bivouacked for some time and, just like in Greece, sowed wheat and barley. Then they took to their ships once again, continued their voyage and finally returned after a few months to gather in the harvest and spend the winter.[3] In addition to the wheat and barley which were turned into bread and thick porridge, the Greeks ate large amounts of fish, which they caught during their voyages. No mention is found of fruit and vegetables, which were consumed in great quantities at home, but it seems probable that non-perishable dried fruits, such as figs, appeared on the daily menu.

The further the Greeks ventured to sea and the longer the journeys lasted, the stronger the ships had to be, not only the merchantmen but also the warships which sometimes accompanied them in order to protect them from attacks by pirates or other enemies. Until the eighth century BC ships were open and without a deck, but then, in the eighth century BC, they were provided with a deck that was laid about 70 cm above the rowers. This covered the entire length of the ship, from bow to stern, but not the whole breadth. From this platform marines, at first only archers and javelin-throwers, could operate. This innovation ushered in a new method of warfare at sea. The time for grappling and boarding an enemy was over. From then on victory depended upon the combined action of oarsmen and marines, and would be gained by the best trained crew.

In the Dark Ages all ships were rowed from the gunwale. The platform mentioned above allowed the rowers to row from there as well, using longer oars. Therefore, the raised deck was not only a fighting deck, but could accommodate the rowers when no enemies were near. Whenever the ship had to come into action they resumed their position at the gunwales, leaving the deck to the marines. The small space above the rowers' heads was open, or, at the most, closed off by open latticework, in order to give the rowers fresh air and allow them to leave the ship in emergencies.

The notion that ships could be rowed both from the gunwales and from the deck brought shipbuilders at the end of the eighth century BC to design ships which could be rowed from both levels at the same time (Fig. 3.1). It is difficult to discover whether the Greeks or the Phoenicians first hit upon this idea, because the traditions of both peoples ran parallel. From Greek as well as Phoenician sources early portrayals of biremes are known. At any rate, in the eighth century BC many efforts were made to increase the speed of ships without making them too large to manoeuvre. According to the numbers manning the Homeric galley, 20, 30 or 50, the rowers were placed permanently both on the upperdeck and along the gunwales. At first, this type of ship closely resembled the older type, which had been provided with a fighting platform. The essential difference was that the choice between the upper and lower level no longer existed: the rowers manned all

Figure 3.1 Oarage of a Bireme

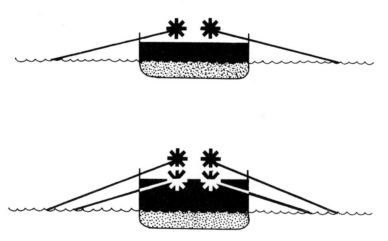

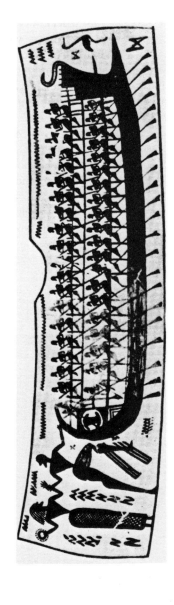

Figure 3.2 Bireme on a Bowl from Thebes (Second Half Eighth Century BC) with Upper Level Manned

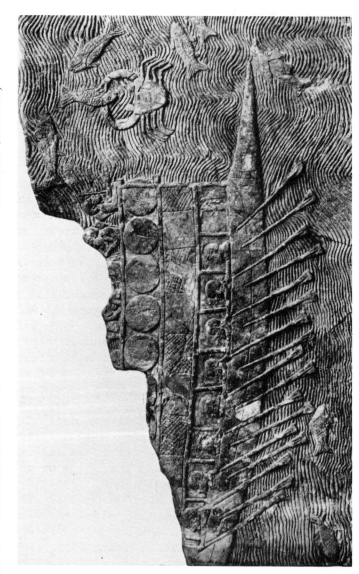

Figure 3.3 Phoenician Bireme on a Relief from the Palace of Sennacharib (c. 700 BC)

available places at the same time (Fig. 3.2). This meant that the penteconter was rowed by two rows of twelve rowers on either side. As a result, ships became much shorter (presumably *c.* 21 m) while accommodating the same number of rowers.[4]

In the seventh century BC the principle of rowing on two levels was further elaborated. The first biremes, with their high construction, were top-heavy vessels. Presumably the two rowing levels were adjusted on the initiative of the Phoenicians. The upper row of rowers was placed at the height of the gunwales, the lower row stuck their oars through holes in the hull just above the waterline. Furthermore, the rowers no longer sat right above each other, but in such a way that the upper rower step-wise filled the space between the two under him (Fig. 3.3). In all likelihood the rowers of the Greek biremes were placed more to the outside than their colleagues on the Phoenician ships. It cannot be stated for certain if they occupied a *parexeiresia*, an outrigger construction, as did the uppermost tier of rowers in fifth-century triremes (see p. 37). As a result of these alterations stability increased and the ships became more manoeuvrable (Fig. 3.4). People began to reconsider the function of the ram, with which all warships were equipped. An unplanned attack on an enemy ship was no longer a feasibility, because the smallest error of judgement or a slight change of course by the adversary could abruptly change the situation. Rather it was a matter of careful manoeuvring into the right position, while the archers and javelin-throwers tried to rattle the enemy, after which there was a choice between fighting at close range or ramming. Using the ram in such a way that the vulnerable parts of the enemy ship were directly hit required increasingly greater skill and long training for helmsman and rowers; for instance, the latter had to be practised in reversing direction. By placing the oars more or less in the middle between the rowing benches the rower could step over his oar, sit on the bench of the rower behind him and then row in the opposite direction (Fig. 3.5).[5]

Even less is known about freighters than about warships. The aristocratic writers' disapproval of trade and traders is, of course, one of the causes of this lack of information. In the Mycenaean and in the pirate-dominated Dark Ages, there was little difference between warships and merchantmen. The upsurge of commerce, however, demanded a type of ship that could make journeys to distant lands profitable. The first deviation from the uniform war-

Figure 3.4 *Parexeiresia*

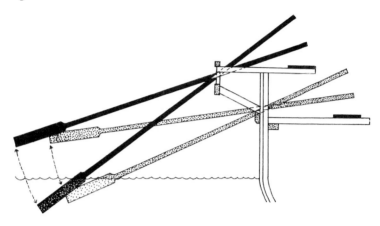

Figure 3.5 Reconstruction of the Bow of a Warship from the End of the Eighth Century BC

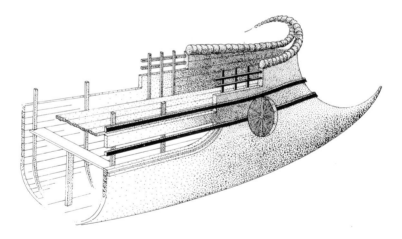

ships/merchantmen was that ships specially constructed for commercial purposes became heavier and more spacious. Concessions had to be made with regard to speed and manoeuvrability. The main change came in the seventh century BC, a change which unmistakably shows Phoenician influence. The round hull, which was used by the Egyptians and the Cretans in the second millennium BC, appeared once again in the Greek harbours. If the

Figure 3.6 Athenian Black Figure Cup with a Two-levelled Warship (perhaps a Pirate Ship) Attacking a Merchantman (Second Half Sixth Century BC)

Greeks were to compete with the leading seafarers, the Phoenicians, they had to have ships that could carry an equal load. Therefore, they imitated the construction technique of the Phoenicians and, after almost 800 years, reintroduced the round hull, which was to become a lasting feature for these ships. A black figure cup from the second half of the sixth century BC neatly illustrates the difference between the round ships and the long ones (Fig. 3.6). Judging by the length of the long ships with two levels of oars, probably penteconters with two rows of twelve rowers above each other and two steersmen, the length of these freighters may be put at 18 m. In spite of the purpose-built merchantmen, the penteconter was still used as a freighter. Herodotus relates that the Phocaeans, who sailed to distant lands long before the other Greeks, did not travel in round ships but in long ones. When in 543 BC the Persian Harpagus attacked the Ionian cities, the Phocaeans launched their penteconters, put in their wives, children and all their goods and chattels and sailed to Chios. In the sixth century BC, according to Plutarch, the Samians, whose reputation as seafarers matched that of the Phocaeans, had a kind of super-penteconter, the *Samaina*, which could transport larger cargoes. From both these testimonies it appears that the introduction of specialised merchant ships took place gradually and that particularly for long and dangerous journeys with a precious cargo penteconters were often preferred.[6]

The rigging, especially of the round ships, was considerably improved. The huge square sail that was secured to a single long yard made of two spars remained standard. A parral secured the yard to the mast. The sail was made of lightweight cloth, which with the wind aft gave a clear bellying effect. On the edges of the sail vertical hem-ropes served as reinforcements; horizontally too, the edges were reinforced. The mast was generally composite, joined by wooldings and secured in the keel. A forestay and a backstay formed the standard rigging. The yard and the sail were hoisted by two separate halyards and held in the right position by lifts that ran from masthead to yard-arms. Braces from yard-arms to deck took care of a lateral adjustment of the yard. The sail could be shortened or furled by means of brails, lines which were secured to the lower edge of the front of the sail and ran up over the yard down to the deck aft (Fig. 3.7). The basic principles of this rigging system were maintained throughout antiquity.[7]

Figure 3.7 Standard Square Sail

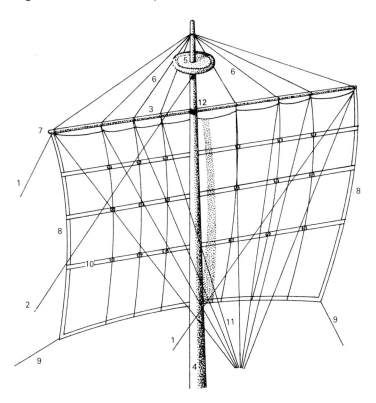

1 brace   2 halyard   3 yard   4 mast   5 fitting for the halyard   6 lift
7 leather patch   8 bolt rope   9 sheet   10 strips of leather   11 brail   12 parral

Now that the horizon of the Greeks included the entire Mediterranean more geographical and climatological knowledge was needed. Greek seafarers learned that during the summer the winds in certain regions blow in a certain direction. Quite early on they had divided the sea into a number of zones with specific climatological characteristics. Roughly speaking there were three zones. The western basin from the Pillars of Hercules (the Strait of Gibraltar) to the Balearic Islands was regarded the domain of the easterly winds. In the central zone, between the Balearic Islands and Sicily, Sardinia and Corsica the winds were predominantly south-westerly, with the exception of the dreaded *mistral*. In the Tyrrhenian the wind blew from the north-west but in the southerly part from the north. The eastern basin also had a northerly wind, which in the autumn alternated with the *bora*, the storm-wind blasting from the Dalmatian coast into the upper Adriatic, and the *sirocco* which from the deserts of northern Africa descended into the Aegean with gale force.

As a result of colonisation, knowledge of currents had also increased. The currents in narrow straits were feared; the most dreaded were the Strait of Messina, which acquired the name of Scylla and Charybdis, and the passage of the Euripus near Chalcis on Euboea. Calm currents along the coasts, on the other hand, were carefully studied. Particularly where with only a few rowers on board ships had to sail against a head wind, the seamen endeavoured to make optimal use of them. After the Spanish east coast had been reached by the Phocaeans, it became known that there is a difference in water-level between the Atlantic Ocean and the Mediterranean which causes an easterly current reaching as far as the Aegean. This current largely determines the water circulation in the whole Mediterranean. Off Sicily the current splits in two; one branch turns to the north, runs along the western coast of Sicily and Italy and continues its way to the north-west along the coast of southern France and southwards along the Spanish coast; the other branch pursues its way along the south coast of Sicily in the direction of the African coast down to Libya and is then deflected in a northerly direction along the Levant and Asia Minor. Half-way along the Turkish coast it hits a counter-current from the Black Sea which produces a split: one branch going along the Illyrian coast as far as the bosom of the Adriatic and southwards along the east coast of Italy; the other part passes southern Italy and Sicily and is finally taken up again in the mother stream (Fig. 3.8).[8]

By the end of the sixth century BC there was a network of Greek colonies from the Black Sea coasts in the north-east to Cyrene in Libya in the south and Massilia and some settlements on the Spanish coast in the west. An ever increasing variety of products was carried by sea. The cargo no longer consisted of only raw materials which were offered for processing, but more and more of manufactured and processed items. Nothing can be said about the extent of the trade. Data are lacking and no wrecks from this

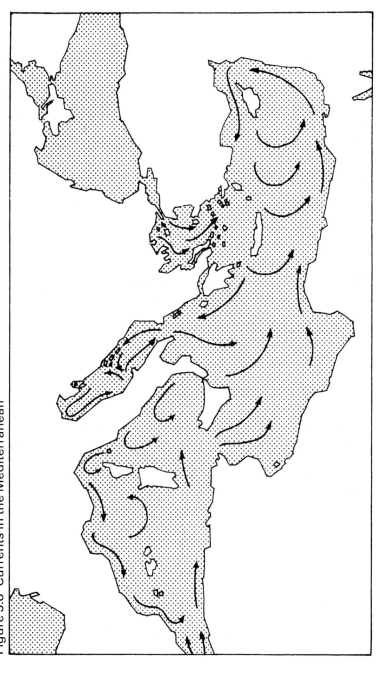

Figure 3.8 Currents in the Mediterranean

period have been investigated. Since from the fifth century BC onwards the minimum carrying capacity of merchantmen on the transmediterranean route was 70 tons, it may be assumed that at the end of the archaic age, when the shipbuilding experiments had been more or less finalised, many ships had a similar tonnage. Even less is known about the intensity of the traffic. But the construction of a causeway (*diolkos*) across the Isthmus of Corinth at the beginning of the sixth century BC so that ships could be hauled over and were not obliged to sail round the Peloponnese, shows that transportation by sea had become quite important. This is corroborated by the construction of large harbour works, both in the old mother cities and in the colonies.[9]

In spite of the increase and the importance of commerce, the standing of those engaged in it remained low. The aristocratic pattern of thought in the Greek cities condemned participation in trade and industry. Herodotus relates that traders and artisans had little repute except in Corinth.[10] In the Greek cities no powerful new economic element arose that could organise itself and could harness politics in its own favour. The traders and craftsmen were dependent on the upper classes and had to make their products fit in with their standards. Nevertheless there were opportunities because overseas and internal demand continued to grow.

Notes

1. ARISTOCRACY AND TRADE: Starr, 1977, pp. 26–7 and p. 77; see for a debate on trade and politics Cartledge, 1983, pp. 1–15. MOTIVES FOR COLONISATION: Graham, 1964.

2. COLONISATION: Boardman, 1964; Littman, 1974; Jeffery, 1976; Starr, 1977.

3. Wallinga, 1965.

4. INVENTION OF BIREMES: according to Casson, 1971, p. 58 biremes were invented by the Phoenicians.

5. DEVELOPMENT OF BIREMES: Morrison and Williams, 1968, pp. 73–81; Casson, 1971, pp. 53–60; Morrison, 1980a, pp. 13–16; cf. Basch, 1969, pp. 139–62.

6. INTRODUCTION OF ROUND SHIPS: Morrison, 1980a, p. 52. MAINTENANCE OF PENTECONTERS: Hdt. 1.163.2; Plut. *Per.* 26.3–4; cf. Snodgrass, 1983, pp. 16–17.

7. RIGGING: Casson, 1954a, pp. 214–19; Casson, 1971, pp. 68–70; Rougé, 1975, pp. 55–64.

8. INCREASING MARITIME KNOWLEDGE: Cary and Warmington, 1929, pp. 19–28; Thomson, 1948, pp. 44–64.

9. TONNAGE: Casson, 1971, pp. 170–3; *contra*: Hopkins, 1983, pp. 99–100. HARBOURS: Lehmann-Hartleben, 1923, pp. 50–65.

10. REPUTATION OF TRADERS AND ARTISANS: Hdt. 2.167; cf. Cartledge, 1983, pp. 3–5.

Chapter Four

Greeks versus Persians: The Invention of the Trireme

In the sixth century BC the destruction of the Assyrian empire brought about a radical change in the political and economic situation along the eastern coasts of the Mediterranean. For a long time the Assyrian despots had enslaved the conquered peoples of the Near East from Armenia and eastern Anatolia to Egypt, deported their leaders and destroyed their cities. In 612 BC the hated rulers were defeated. Niniveh, the capital of the Assyrian empire, was reduced to ashes by the combined armies of the Chaldaeans (New Babylonians) and the Medes from the Zagros mountains in Iran. The Near East was divided into four great kingdoms: New Babylonia, Egypt, Media and Lydia. Media in particular experienced great prosperity under its ruler Cyaxares, whose expansionist policies constituted a continual threat to Lydia in the western highlands of Anatolia. Cyaxares' successor, Astyages, a less energetic personality, had to face a rebellion from Cyrus, a Persian prince, the son of a certain Cambyses, satrap in Pasargadae. Cyrus succeeded in taking over power in 550 BC and in establishing the dynasty of the Achaemenids.

This marked the beginning of the Persian empire. Like his Median predecessors Cyrus had, in the first instance, set his sights on prosperous Lydia. In a rapid campaign ending with the capture of the capital Sardes, Lydia was in 546 BC incorporated in the Persian empire. Immediately after the defeat of Lydia, the New Babylonian empire fell into Persian hands (539 BC) after the destruction of the capital Babylon; Phoenicia, Syria and Egypt also came under Persian domination. After the surrender of the Phoenicians, the Persians had not only gained access to the Mediterranean, but had also got hold of a good fleet and first-class sailors.

The conquest of Lydia had unfavourable consequences for the Greek cities on the coast of Asia Minor. Relations between the

31

Greeks and the Lydians had been good. From the start the Lydians had been receptive to Greek influences and the Greeks had in turn taken over the Lydian currency system, which simplified trade. The defeat of Lydia exposed the Greek cities to the Persian aggression, but they were unable to take collective action. Though a certain weak sense of community did exist, expressed, for instance, in the religious and ethnic festival of Panionium, attempts to set up a single Ionic council with plenipotentiary power for the twelve centres failed. A request for help to Sparta immediately after the capture of the Lydian capital Sardes, made by all cities except Miletus, came to nothing. Finally, nothing could prevent the Persians from also taking over the Ionian cities. The Persian satraps did not exercise direct rule but left the administration to collaborating tyrants. One of these, Aristagoras of Miletus, fell into disfavour in 500 BC after he had had difficulties with Megabates, the Persian commander, during a joint expedition to establish a plutocratic oligarchy on Naxos. The venture was a failure. Fearing that Megabates' reports might bring him into discredit, Aristagoras abdicated his tyranny and began a revolt against the Persian domination. Open hostilities began when the Ionians seized the Persian fleet which had just returned from Naxos and was docked at Myous. They arrested the commanders who were on board the ships.[1]

Herodotus does not elaborate on the motives which may have induced the Ionian cities to take this step. Unfortunately so, for what were Ionian cities in comparison with the Persian empire? It is true that trade was unfavourably influenced by the arrival of the Persians. They controlled the Hellespont and the Bosporus as well as the coasts of Egypt. The consequences for the four principal centres of the revolt, Lesbos, Chios, Samos and Miletus, were indeed considerable but to challenge the Persians over this appears a very risky undertaking. Perhaps the Ionians expected the states on the Greek mainland to come to their help, so that their revolt would grow into a confrontation between Greeks and Persians. This was an error of judgement, for their mission to Greece resulted in a disappointment. Sparta, at the time the leading state in Greece, was not prepared to plunge into such a risky adventure: recently their naval adventures against Athens and Samos had failed. The inhabitants of Aegina rejected the request for reasons of competition. Like the Samians, Chians and Milesians, they were interested in trade with Naucratis. The call for help from fellow Greeks carried no weight against the prospective commercial advantages which would follow the disappearance of the Ionian cities from international commerce. The Corinthians also competed with the Ionians on the eastern markets but they had another reason for not offering support: if they helped the Ionians but failed, their dominant position on the western markets might be endangered.

Only in Athens and Eretria did the appeal of the Milesians not fall on deaf ears. The Athenians promised 20 ships and the Eretrians 5. The latter did this to repay an old debt; the Milesians had in the past helped the Eretrians. Unfortunately, Herodotus does not tell us why the Athenians offered their aid but it is plausible that, faced with a refusal from Sparta, they saw a chance to increase their political influence. The fact that the Athenians allotted 20 of the 50 warships at their disposal makes this idea all the more credible.[2]

The fifth book of Herodotus is fairly detailed on the Ionian revolt. Initially the Ionians were successful. Sardes was recaptured by the insurgents, as well as the whole of the Hellespont. But when Cyprus also joined the Ionians the Persians began to take serious countermeasures. From 496 BC on the balance was clearly in favour of the Persians. Within one year Cyprus, Caria and the cities of the Hellespont were conquered. Both sides felt that only a naval campaign could bring about the decision. The Milesians, because in the past they had survived a twelve-year siege by the Lydians thanks to their access to the sea and because a confrontation on land precluded success in advance; the other Ionian cities because they were more vulnerable and because the searoutes could only be safe if the Persian fleet was eliminated. They also took heart from the victory of a combined Ionian-Cypriot fleet over the Persian-Phoenician fleet a few years earlier. The Persians were likewise eager to settle the conflict in a decisive confrontation at sea, because the destruction of the Ionian fleet would silence the insurgents for good.[3]

The fleets that faced each other in the bay between Miletus and the island of Lade in 494 BC were of considerable size. The Persians put to sea 600 ships chiefly built in Phoenician and Cilician harbours and financed by means of a tribute which had been imposed upon the subject nations. The Greek total amounted to 353 ships: Miletus contributed 80 ships; Priene and Myos twelve and three respectively; from Teos there were 17 ships; from Chios 100 and from Erythrae eight; Phocaea could only supply three ships but Lesbos managed to contribute 70 and Samos 60.[4] Not only the numbers were exceptional but also the ships themselves. Herodotus speaks of triremes (the Greek term is *trieres*, which literally means 'three-fitted'), a type which hitherto had not been met with in the Greek fleet although they were known to exist. A result of extensive experiments in Phoenician and Greek harbours, this type of ship was to occupy a central place in all navies in the fifth century BC. For this reason, before discussing the battle between the Ionians and the Persians, it seems worthwhile to devote some attention to the development of the trireme.

There are various theories concerning the invention of the trireme, which can be traced back to Thucydides' remark. Some scholars accept Thucydides' version in its entirety. It runs as follows:

> The Corinthians are supposed to have been the first to adopt more or less modern methods in shipbuilding, and it is said that the first triremes ever built in Hellas were laid down in Corinth. Then there is the Corinthian shipwright, Ameinocles, who appears to have built four ships for the Samians. It is nearly 300 years ago (dating from the end of this present [that is, the Peloponnesian] war) that Ameinocles went to Samos. And the first naval battle on record is the one between the Corinthians and the Corcyraeans: this was about 260 years ago.

Concerning the further development of the trireme in the seventh and sixth centuries BC Thucydides offers as little information as Herodotus. He merely states that the Ionians had a strong fleet at the time of Cyrus and his son Cambyses and were masters of the sea along the coasts and that Polycrates, who at the time was tyrant of Samos, subjected a number of neighbouring islands to his hegemony through the power of his fleet, statements which might point to a possible presence of triremes.[5]

Other scholars have grave doubts about the inventions ascribed to the Corinthian Ameinocles and suggest that the trireme was not used by the Greeks until the end of the sixth century BC. Their scepticism is supported by some passages from Herodotus. In a description of the evacuation of Phocaea in face of the Persian threat in 540 BC, he relates how the inhabitants transported their families and possessions in pentaconters. Likewise, in the naval battle in 535 BC at Alalia on Corsica, in which the Phocaeans had to face the Etruscans and the Carthaginians, the masters of the western Mediterranean, only pentaconters were used. Herodotus first mentions triremes in reference to Polycrates. Having rapidly established a powerful position in 539 BC, he had 100 traditional pentaconters at his disposal. In 525, however, he sent 40 triremes in support to Cambyses who was preparing for an expedition against Egypt. This is the first mention of Greek triremes. The supporters of the theory that the trireme was introduced in the last quarter of the sixth century BC base their views on the change in Polycrates' fleet. They consider it extremely unlikely that a type of ship that was invented before 700 BC only came into use 200 years later, while it was superior to the pentaconters.[6]

If it was not Ameinocles who designed the first trireme, then its inventor must be looked for in one of the Phoenician harbours, as Clement of Alexandria maintains in the second century AD. According to him the trireme was invented in Sidon and taken over by others, Greeks and Egyptians, in the last decade of the seventh century BC. Since Sidon was laid waste by the Assyrians in 676 BC, the trireme must have been put into service before that time. Implicit arguments in favour of this theory can be found in Herodotus. He relates that the Egyptian pharaoh Necho, the son of Psammetichus, wanted to construct a canal in order to secure a passage from the Mediterranean to the Red Sea. This canal had to be wide enough for two triremes to sail next to one another. Necho died in 593 BC and the triremes, which he had built in great numbers, were thus almost three-quarters of a century older than the oldest Greek triremes. The supporters of the Ameinocles-theory are of the opinion that Necho, in order to construct the triremes, summoned the help not of Phoenician but of Greek shipbuilders. They cite the presence of the Greeks in Naucratis, about ten miles from Necho's capital, and the links between Periander, the tyrant of Corinth, and Necho's father Psammetichus. Periander allegedly called his own son Psammetichus after him.[7]

The invention in Phoenicia is not in contradiction with Thucydides' statement that Corinth was the first place in *Greece* where triremes were built. This means that the priority of the Phoenicians can remain unchallenged.[8] That there must have been experiments in both countries can be inferred from the essential differences between the triremes which were the results of these experiments. The Phoenician triremes were more spacious and higher than the Greek ones and did not have an outrigger construction.

Few concrete data are known about the trireme; about the oldest types of the sixth century BC, none at all. Regarding the length and breadth we have information from the boathouses of Zea in the harbour of Piraeus. The dimensions of these docks, in which the triremes were drawn over the slips with the aid of winches or rollers, have become known through excavations: on the average they were 37 m long and a little less than 6 m broad. From these figures the length and breadth of the triremes can be deduced; the length is estimated at 35 m and the greatest breadth at 4.8 m (see p. 71).[9]

The oarage of the trireme has been uncertain for a long time due to the scarcity of representations, most of which are vague and offer few concrete data. The most informative representation is the Lenormant relief (*c.* 400 BC), which is the starting point for the study of the oarage of the Greek trireme (Fig. 4.1). There are two main theories. According to the first theory the three categories of rowers named in the sources were divided over foreship, the thalamites, middle ship, the zugites, and aftership, the thranites. Like on the Genoese galleys of the fifteenth century AD, three rowers sat on one thwart, both on port and starboard, each with their own oar, the so-called *zenzile* formation (Fig. 4.2). This view is difficult to maintain. First of all it seems impossible that six rowers could row on the selfsame level with complete freedom of movement in a ship scarcely 5 m wide. In addition there is Aristophanes' remark that rowers understood the art 'of farting in the face of the thalamite', which clearly shows that the latter sat in a lower position than the other rowers. It is incorrect to brush aside this remark as a typical Aristophanic joke, since also a scholium on Aristophanes shows that the thalamites sat below, the zugites in the middle and the thranites above (Fig. 4.3).[10] This is also the view generally held by scholars who have studied the oarage of the trireme and have interpreted the design of the trireme from the bireme. The development of the bireme had introduced the placing of the rowers at different levels. Experience had shown that speed and manoeuvrability were increased. Why then should the ancient shipbuilders have abandoned this principle and returned to the old way of rowing? The natural course in the development of shipbuilding was to introduce a third level. The hull needed not to be altered drastically but only to be modified. The Phoenician ships presumably had wider hulls than the Greek ones and could accommodate all the oarsmen. They all sat beneath a full upper deck. The more narrow Greek ships had to be adapted to take in the top rank of rowers. The 170 rowers who manned the triremes were placed as follows: the 54 oarsmen of the lowest row, the thalamites, worked their oars through oarports 40 cm above the waterline. They sat about 92.5 cm from each other, exactly as the rowers on the other levels. To keep out the water the oarports were provided with leather bags that fitted closely round the oars. The 54 oarsmen of the middle row, the zugites, sat on thwarts above and slightly forward of the thalamites and worked their oars through ports just below the gunwale. The upper row of oarsmen, the 62 thranites, rowed from benches which were slightly higher than those of the zugites (Fig. 4.4). Because they could not be placed too high on the slender galleys, they were set outboard of the other rowers. To solve the problem the shipbuilders devised the *parexeiresia*, an outrigger construction along the hull, which jutted out 60 cm from the sides of the ship (Fig. 4.5). The thranites' task was the hardest — they were sometimes paid extra — since, their oars being of the same length (*c.* 4.18 m) as those of the other rowers, they had to row at a sharper angle than the others.[11]

Figure 4.1 Lenormant Relief

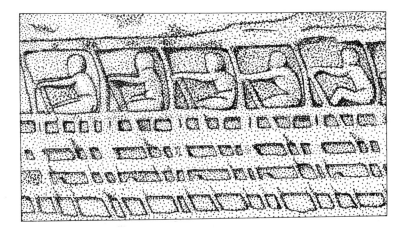

Figure 4.2 Zenzile Oarage

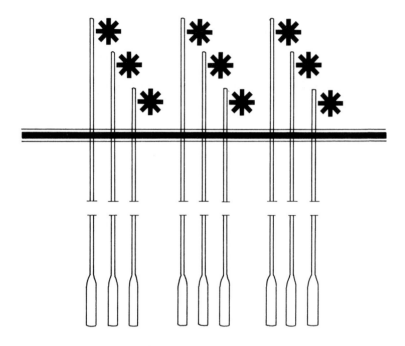

Figure 4.3 Oarage of the Trireme

Apart from the 170 oarsmen there were another 30 crew members, including five officers, the *trierarchos*, the *kubernetes*, the *proreus*, the *keleustes* and the *pentekontarchos*. The *kubernetes* (helmsman) was *de facto* commander of the ship, since the captain (*trierarchos*) was a political figure who seldom came on board. The *proreus* supervised the front of the ship and kept a look-out for

Figure 4.4 Sketch of a Trireme

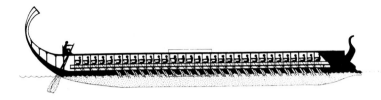

Figure 4.5 *Parexeiresia*

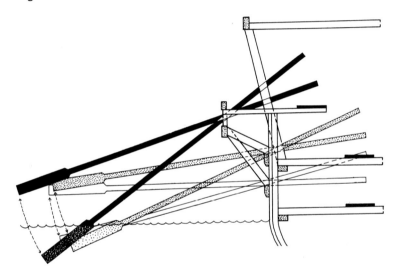

possible enemies and submerged rocks. The *keleustes* supervised the rowers, their training and feeding. To encourage the rowers in a fighting situation the *keleustes* was assisted by a *trieraules* who piped the time on a flute. The lowest in rank was the *pentekontarchos* (presumably, this term originally designated the commander of a penteconter) who had all sorts of odd jobs. The other 25 crew members included a carpenter, marines and archers.

Judging by the velocity and manoeuvrability required, the trireme must have been slender, almost arrow-like in appearance. But its sturdiness was unimpaired; the keel, for instance, was fashioned from hard wood, probably oak. Under the keel a metal strip was attached in order to prevent it from damage if the ship was beached or drawn into a boathouse. Timbers ran from the keel, usually made of fir, but if this was not available, of pine, which was heavier. The strakes were joined to each other by dowelled joints. Round the hull ran horizontal wales to reinforce its strength.

The weapon of the trireme was the ram, designed to penetrate the flanks or quarters of the enemy ship. Unlike the single-pronged rams of the archaic galleys, it was two-pronged. The cutwater was reinforced by massive horizontal beams which joined together into a bronze-coated core, to which the ram was attached. The bronze layer or even the whole ram could be removed for repair. Above the ram there was sometimes a subsidiary ram. Just behind the ram vertical beams ran upward which both supported and protected the outrigger and prevented the ram from digging too deeply into the enemy ship, which might make withdrawal difficult and the ship itself a target for other ships.

The rigging had not undergone any radical changes. A single mast carrying a large square sail was also part of the equipment of the triremes. Ancient sources offer little information about the sailing qualities of the trireme; representations of triremes under sail are not known. Consequently we still do not have full knowledge of the use of the sail. Presumably the main sail was only used on patrol trips, whereas in battle situations the mast was lowered and left behind on the beach. Only a small mast and a small sail were carried, in order that the speed might be increased during flight or pursuit.[12]

These ships were abundantly represented in the Greek and Persian fleets facing each other at Lade. Initially the Persians were reluctant to join battle with the Ionian fleet. Though they knew that the Phoenician contingents were adequately trained and equipped, they assumed that their opponents were well-trained, confident sailors. That, in reality, they overestimated their enemy appears from the following passage from Herodotus:

The Ionians agreed to take orders from Dionysius, who at once got to work. Every day he had ships and crews out for training, making the fleet sail in line ahead, arming the troops on board, practising the oarsmen in the manoeuvre of 'breaking the line' (*diekplous*), and insisting that all ships, for the remainder of the day, should lie to their anchors instead of being hauled ashore.

Thus the men got no rest from morning to night. For seven days they continued to obey orders; but after that, being unaccustomed to such hard work and worn out with toiling away under the hot sun, they began to grumble. 'This', they said to each other, 'is as bad as doing penance. Why, we might have committed some fearful sin! The whole thing is crazy: we must have taken leave of our senses, to have put ourselves into the hands of this swollen-headed Phocaean, a fellow who couldn't provide more than three ships for the fleet! Yet here he is, taking complete charge; the way he treats us is outrageous: we shall never recover from it — many of us are ill already, and many more expect to be on the sick-list before long. Anything would be preferable to the misery we now endure — if it's a choice between two sorts of slavery, then the one we are threatened with, however bad it turns out to be, could hardly be worse than what we are putting up with now. I'll tell you what — from now on, let us refuse to obey his orders.' It was no sooner said than done. Every seaman in the fleet refused duty. Like soldiers they pitched tents on the island, lounged about in the shade all day, and refused to go aboard their vessels or to continue their training in any way whatever.[13]

A factor contributing to all this was the fact that the Ionians had no central organisation. The administration of the fleet, which consisted of contingents from eight Ionian cities and Lesbos, was left entirely to the individual contributors, nor was there any kind of central tribute system to finance the fleet.

Badly prepared though they were, the Ionians did not initially seem to stand no chance at all. The Milesians held the right wing (the land side), the Chians took the centre and the Samians the left wing. For about a week the two fleets held each other in balance, but then the situation changed through the desertion of the Samians and the Lesbians. Why they turned their back on the Ionian fleet and went home cannot be established, but the possibility of diplomatic pressure from the Persians cannot be ruled out. The Samians must surely have realised that a victory at Lade was no guarantee for the future. Chios and Miletus continued to fight. Despite the immense numerical superiority of the Persians they held out for a long time. The Chians even took the offensive, broke through the enemy lines — *diekpleontes* Herodotus says — but, though they rammed many enemy ships, they had to give up the struggle.[14]

The *diekplous* of the Chians is not without significance. It is the first time in Greek maritime history that we hear of this tactical manoeuvre, which was to develop into one of the most important fighting methods. It could only be carried out if by raising the beat the rowers made such speed that the ship could attack the enemy before countermeasures could be taken. It was the intention to ram amidships or stern quarters and then to rejoin their own ranks quickly. Another tactic, probably not suitable at Lade but carried out in many other sea-battles in the fifth century BC, was the *periplous*, an encirclement of the enemy ships. The connection of this tactic with the *diekplous* is quite clear. In order to be able to defend themselves against a possible *diekplous*, the fleet-leaders could form a circular formation (*kuklos*). The next step was to take the offensive by sailing at high speed along the flanks of the enemy and attacking from the rear.

The Ionian fleet had no opportunity to pursue these tactics. The Chians lost many of their ships and a remnant of the fleet was able finally to escape. Dionysius, the Phocaean, also escaped. He did not sail home but first to Phoenicia and then to Sicily where he attacked a number of merchantmen and acquired a lot of booty. The Milesian fleet was destroyed, perhaps to the last trireme.

After the battle at Lade the Persians besieged Miletus both from land and sea. Within a short time the city was taken and the inhabitants deported to the city of Ampe at the mouth of the Tigris. The Persians were not satisfied with the capture of Miletus and the Apollo temple of Didyma, but reimposed their rule in other Greek cities of Asia Minor. Subsequently the coasts of the Hellespont were again placed under Persian authority. Mardonius, Darius' son-in-law, who had been given command of the army and the fleet, intended to proceed through Thrace to Greece, but part of the Persian fleet perished in 492 BC during a violent northerly storm which surprised them when rounding the Athos mountain range in Thrace. Thus the punishment of Eretria and Athens, which had helped the Ionians on a modest scale, had to be postponed. Herodotus reports that in total 300 ships and 20,000 men perished. Assuming that the total Persian fleet at Lade had consisted of 600 ships, it is not difficult to see that this was a loss of some gravity which compelled the Persians to return.[15]

Two years later the Persians made another attempt. In the summer of 490 BC the Persian fleet set sail from Cilicia. The Persian forces, consisting of the warships, the army and merchant vessels for transport of horses and chariots, were commanded by Artaphernes and Datis, a Mede by origin. In his account Herodotus speaks of 600 ships, including a maximum of 200 triremes, and 80,000 men. Later authors give absurd numbers of 200,000 to 600,000 men. Modern commentators estimate the total number of men that embarked at 25,000, a small number by Persian standards.[16]

The slender triremes described earlier were not suitable for transport. Presumably the Persians had special transport triremes. We know from Thucydides that at the time of the Peloponnesian war the Athenians had special triremes which could transport some 100 soldiers, the *stratiotides*. They were propelled by fewer oarsmen. Other ships were specially fitted out to transport horses, the *hippagogoi*; the capacity was sufficient for 30 horses. Sometimes old triremes were converted for this purpose. The rowing benches of the lowest rows of oarsmen, the thalamites and the zugites, were removed and only 62 thranites retained their rowing position. Although these types of ship were only recorded at the time of the Peloponnesian war and there are no reports of this kind with regard to earlier expeditions, it can nevertheless be assumed that the converted trireme quickly became known as a freighter probably already at the time of the Persian wars.[17]

This fleet of triremes, penteconters and very diverse kinds of freighters sailed, via Rhodes and Samos, to Naxos, which was laid waste. The next objective was Eretria. Despite assistance from Athens the city was taken and the inhabitants sold as slaves. Now it was Athens' turn. The Persians landed at Marathon, 40 km from Athens by land and about 90 km by sea. A sheltered bay served as a mooring place for the triremes.

The Athenians had not been idly sitting back waiting for the Persians to appear before the city. In 493 BC the Athenian citizens had elected Themistocles, an astute politician, archon for the following year. He immediately initiated a programme of defence and reconstruction. In his judgement the confrontation with the Persians would turn out favourably for the Athenians if the harbour of Piraeus, which consisted of three natural bays, could be walled in and if at the same time the existing small fleet would be drastically enlarged.

Yet, by no means all Athenians were in agreement with Themistocles. The aristocrats with their large estates and the small-scale farmers saw no advantage in Themistocles' plan to abandon the land around Athens. Only the thetes, who earned a meagre living as day-labourers, harbour workers and oarsmen, supported Themistocles. The naval development programme was rejected and only the fortification of the harbour won the approval of the Assembly. A policy based on the citizen army was preferred. When the arrival of the Persians was announced, Miltiades, the spokesman of the aristocrats, insisted that the citizen army should move to meet them and fight. On his advocacy troops were raised in all haste in order to check the onward march of the Persians. Herodotus does not give the numbers of the Greek army at Marathon, but later authors mention a number of about 10,000 men: 9,000 Athenians and 1,000 soldiers from Plataea. Of the Persians who had set out from Cilicia probably about 15,000 men actively fought against the Greeks. In all likelihood the Athenians took the initiative by attacking on the morning of 12 September 490 BC. On the flanks everything went smoothly; the Athenian hoplites pushed the Persians back. In the centre some ground was lost, but then the Greek wings gave up their pursuit, wheeled inwards and caught the enemy in a pincer movement, killing many. In all, the Persians lost 6400 men, the Athenians no more than 162.[18]

Only the fleet could save the Persians now. This the Athenians realised too; they tried to set the ships on fire or to put them out of order. Only seven fell into their hands, and with the rest the Persians set sail, not to the home ports as would be expected after such a defeat, but along Cape Sunium to Phalerum. They intended to capture Athens before the Athenian army returned. In itself it was a good plan to occupy the city by surprise. Theoretically the triremes with a complete crew of oarsmen and under sail could reach the city before the return of the rejoicing Athenians. Plutarch (first to second century AD) says that the stiff breeze prevailing at the moment gave the Persians a good chance of success. Miltiades, however, saw through this tactic and rapidly marched his troops back to the city while the Persian fleet was still on the open sea. On hearing this the Persians changed their tack and sailed back to Asia Minor.[19]

Yet the Greeks were not confident about the future, largely because of the Persians' numerical supremacy. They had indeed been beaten on land, but it had not escaped the Greeks that they could raise new troops and return until one day they would win. In the long run land battles with the Persians could well have a disastrous outcome. Even Miltiades shared this view but an error of judgement on his part prevented him from continuing to play a role in politics. He undertook an expedition against some islands in the Aegean which he suspected of having too readily chosen the side of the Persians. In reality his aim was the quest of booty. The island of Paros successfully resisted and Miltiades sailed back to Athens. A short time later he died in prison of wounds incurred in the futile siege. The way was now open for Themistocles, who left no stone unturned in order to add to Athens' naval reputation. The Persians wanted to take revenge for the defeat they had suffered and likewise commenced preparations for a new campaign which was to put an end to, in Persian eyes, the provocative attitude of the Greeks. In this way the time became ripe for a conflict that would profoundly affect the whole of the Aegean world.

Notes

1. PLANNING AND COMMENCEMENT OF THE IONIAN REVOLT: Hdt. 5.36–8; the prelude of the revolt has been analysed by Lateiner, 1982, pp. 129–44; see also Wallinga, 1984, pp. 426–30.

2. IONIAN MISSION TO GREECE: Hdt. 5.49–50; 5.97; 9.106; *FGrH* III A 262 F 10. SPARTAN ATTITUDE: Larsen, 1932, pp. 136–50. ATHENIAN ATTITUDE: Gomme, 1944, pp. 321–30; Lateiner, 1982, pp. 137–8 gives further literature; see also Haas, 1985, pp. 44–5 who suggests that the Athenians did not send triremes but penteconters.

3. DECISION TO UNDERTAKE A NAVAL CAMPAIGN: Burn, 1962, p. 209; Lateiner, 1982, p. 147.

4. STRENGTH OF THE FLEETS: Hdt. 6.8–9.

5. Thuc. 1.13; POLYCRATES' FLEET IN 539 BC: Hdt. 3.39. The invention of the trireme is ascribed to Ameinocles by Morrison and Williams, 1968, pp. 128–31; Morrison, 1979, 53–62; Morrison, 1980a, pp. 19–20; Lloyd, 1975, pp. 45–61; Lloyd, 1980, pp. 194–8.

6. EVACUATION FROM PHOCAEA: Hdt. 1.164. BATTLE AT ALALIA: Hdt. 1.166; Gras, 1972, pp. 698–716. POLYCRATES' HELP TO CAMBYSES: Hdt. 3.44. The opponents of the Ameinocles-theory are mentioned in note 7.

7. INVENTION IN PHOENICIA: Clem. Al. *Strom.* 1.16.76. NECHO'S TRIREMES: Hdt. 2.158–9; cf. Morrison, 1979, p. 53. Invention of the trireme is ascribed to the Phoenicians by Davison, 1947, pp. 18–24; Basch, 1969, pp. 139–62 and pp. 227–45; Basch, 1977, pp. 1–10; Basch, 1980, pp. 198–9.

8. Torr, 1894, p. 4, note 8; Casson, 1971, p. 81, note 17.

9. DIMENSIONS OF THE TRIREME: Morrison and Williams, 1968, pp. 181–3; Casson, 1971, p. 364.

10. ZENZILE OAR SYSTEM: Tarn, 1905, pp. 137–56 and pp. 204–24; Amit, 1965, p. 14 and pp. 99–102. ARISTOPHANES' REMARK: Ar. *Ran.* 1074–5; cf. *Schol.* Ar. *Ran.* 1106.

11. The Phoenician triremes have been reconstructed by Basch, 1969. pp. 139–62, spec. pp. 157–60. The Greek triremes have been reconstructed by

Morrison, 1941, pp. 14–44; cf. Gille, 1965, pp. 36–71; Morrison and Williams, 1968, pp. 268–71; Casson, 1971, pp. 82–4.

12. SHIP'S COMPANY: Jordan, 1975, pp. 117–52; Morrison, 1984, pp. 48–59. HULL, RAM AND RIG: Morrison and Williams, 1968, pp. 279–309; Casson, 1971, pp. 85–91 and pp. 235–7. KINDS OF WOOD: Theophr. *Hist. Plant.* 5.7.1–3; Meiggs, 1982, pp. 118ff.

13. Hdt. 6.12.

14. BATTLE AT LADE: Hdt. 6.6–17; cf. Myres, 1954, p. 50–5; Lateiner, 1982, pp. 149–57.

15. SHIPWRECK AT ATHOS: Hdt. 6.44–5.

16. NUMBER OF SHIPS: Hdt. 6.96. SIZE OF THE PERSIAN ARMY: Hammond, 1968, p. 32 suggests 25,000 men.

17. TRANSPORT TRIREMES: Thuc. 6.43; cf. *IG* 1^2 22; Thuc. 1.116; 8.82; Morrison and Williams, 1968, pp. 247–8; Casson, 1971, pp. 92–4; Wallinga, 1982, pp. 463–82.

18. BATTLE AT MARATHON: Hdt. 6.94–120. TRUSTWORTHINESS OF LATER SOURCES: Hignett, 1963, pp. 7–25. COURSE OF THE BATTLE: Burn, 1962, pp. 236–52; Hignett, 1963, pp. 55–74.

19. PERSIAN SURPRISE ATTACK: Plut. *Arist.* 5.

20. EXPEDITION TO PAROS: Hdt. 6.132–6; Haas, 1985, p. 44 suggests that Miltiades used penteconters.

Chapter Five

Greeks versus Persians: The Decisive Confrontations

After their setback at Marathon the Persians spent three years assembling the greatest army of all time for the decisive campaign. When everything looked promising and departure was imminent, serious delay was caused by revolts in Egypt and Babylonia and the death of King Darius. His son Xerxes undertook a campaign against the two insurgent peoples and oppressed them. Then he began anew to recruit levies from the whole empire for the expedition against Greece (Fig. 5.1).

The delay of the Persian attack was not unwelcome to the Greeks. In Athens disputes hampered preparations for war and more attention was given to the local conflict with Aegina than to a renewed invasion by the Persians. The other Greek city-states did not react very energetically either. Some states minimised the Persian threat and others such as the Thessalians, Locrians and Thebans offered the Persian envoys 'earth and water' as a token of subjection.

It was only when the preparations of the Persians were in full progress and an immense force was being assembled in Asia Minor that a number of Greek cities agreed to form an army to meet the expected Persian invasion. How the Hellenic League was organised is not known; we do not even know where the first meeting in 481 BC was held. At this first session it was decided to end the wars in progress between its members, including that between Athens and Aegina. No decisions were taken concerning future strategies.[1]

The Persian forces must have been enormous. Herodotus enumerates all the manpower included in the army. His remark 'what people from Asia has not Xerxes swept into his force against Greece' speaks for itself, but the astronomical numbers mentioned by him, 1,700,000 foot-soldiers, 80,000 cavalry, 20,000 chariots and camels and 30,000 Thracians and Greeks pulled in *en route* are

Figure 5.1 Persian
Invasions in Greece

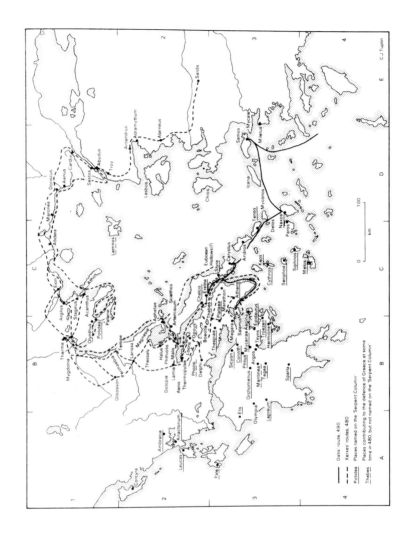

Datis' route, 490

Xerxes' routes, 480

Potidea   Places named on the 'Serpent Column'

Thebes   Places contributing to the defence of Greece at some
                time in 480, but not named on the 'Serpent Column'

C.J.Tuplin

so excessively high that they cannot represent the real military force. Later writers give figures of 700,000 to 800,000 men and modern estimates run from 80,000 to 200,000.[2]

The fleet, too, must have been rather impressive. Aeschylus and Herodotus list the number of ships: a total of 1207 triremes, supplied by Phoenicia (300), Egypt (200), Cyprus (150), Cilicia (100), Pamphylia (30), Lycia (50), Caria (70), Ionia (100), the Asiatic Dorians (30), Aeolia (60), the cities of the Hellespont (100) and the Cyclades (17). According to Herodotus, 120 ships from Thrace and the northern islands must be added to this number. There were a further 3000 transport ships, ships of old-fashioned types such as triaconters and penteconters, freighters and triremes converted to troop transports. It is difficult to say whether the number of triremes is realistic, but it is certain that at the first confrontation with the Greeks at sea at Artemisium the number was much lower (see p. 52). The difference cannot be ascribed only to losses as a result of shipwrecks in storms. Rather, the original number of triremes was probably of the order of 600 to 800.[3]

Yet, this number was still significantly higher than that of the Greek ships. Thucydides speaks of 400 triremes, Aeschylus of 310 and Herodotus writes that at the battle of Salamis there were 378 triremes and at the battle of Artemisium there were 271 triremes. These were raised by the city-states as follows: Athens 127, Corinth 40, Megara 20, Aegina 18, Sicyon 12, Sparta 10, Epidaurus 8, Eretria 7, Troezen 5, Styra 2, Ceos 2. Chalcis itself provided no ships but supplied the crews for 20 ships placed at its disposal by Athens. From this list it is clear that only the Athenians contributed an impressive force (127 + 20) to the total capacity. In 483–482 BC Themistocles had convinced the Athenians that the extra income flowing into the city from the proceeds of the recently discovered silver-lode at Laurium should be invested in the construction of warships. The ship construction programme was to yield 200 vessels. Herodotus says that Themistocles won over the Athenians by stressing the war with Aegina, but it may be conjectured that Themistocles foresaw that he would need the vessels against the Persians.[4]

By 481 BC the Persian preparations were complete. In the spring of the following year the army moved to the Hellespont, which was crossed at Abydus. To do this an improvised bridge was made of 674 penteconters and triremes, after the original bridge had been destroyed by a storm. Both land and sea forces were subject to a last inspection at Doriscus. From there army and fleet travelled side by side along the Thracian coast to Acanthus and the Chalcidic peninsula. Here army and fleet temporarily parted company. The army marched to Therma, while the fleet sailed through the canal dug through the Athos mountains. They were reunited in Therma, after which the army marched diagonally through lower Macedonia and Thessaly to Trachis on the Malian Gulf. The fleet remained in Therma for another eleven days and then sailed to the coast between the city of Kasthnaia and Cape Sepias, not far from the city of Magnesia. The first vessels to arrive were beached, the others were anchored with their bows facing the sea, in eight ranks. During the night the weather remained calm but the following morning the ships were surprised by a heavy storm which caused the anchored vessels to break adrift and cast them on the nearby coast. In total the Persians are supposed to have lost more than 400 ships and countless men. This estimate is probably too high.[5]

The actual cause of the Persian shipwreck is a matter of dispute, due to the divergent reports of Herodotus and Pausanias, a travelling geographer (second century AD). In Herodotus' account only the storm is responsible for the destruction of part of the Persian fleet. Pausanias, on the other hand, relates how the diver Scyllias from Scione on the Chalcidic peninsula, together with his daughter, cut through the anchor cables of the Persian triremes. The story of Pausanias cannot be set aside as pure imagination, since Scyllias did in fact play an important role in the events of 480 BC, in Herodotus' version too. After the shipwreck he had collected a large number of objects from the Persian fleet and shortly afterwards defected to the Greeks by swimming underwater from Aphetae, where the Persian fleet had subsequently sailed, to Artemisium, a distance of 80 stadia (*c.* 1500 m). Scyllias, who was rated the best diver of his time, presumably did cut through the anchor cables of the Persian fleet, thereby giving the northerly storm free play. This also explains his 'defection' to the Greek forces at Artemisium.[6]

In spite of the loss of a great number of ships the Persians, still numerically superior, decided to proceed to a confrontation with the Greeks. The army advanced through the plain of Malia right to the pass of Thermopylae. A part of the fleet (*c.* 200 ships) sailed round Euboea to prevent the Greeks from withdrawing and the rest of the fleet proceeded to Aphetae opposite Artemisium where they cast anchor.

The Greeks were compelled to take countermeasures. They too opted for a combined strategy involving both fleet and army. On land the pass of Thermopylae, the corridor from Thessaly to central Greece, was chosen as the place of action. The Hellenic League sent the Spartan king Leonidas with 7000 hoplites to defend the pass. The fleet was dispatched to Artemisium. Unfortunately, Herodotus and later historians say nothing about a co-ordinated attack at Thermopylae and Artemisium. But everything points in that direction. Both at Thermopylae and at Artemisium the Persians took the offensive and throughout the whole operation maintained meticulous contact between the land and sea forces. But the Greeks, too, had mapped out their strategy on the basis of a co-ordination of fleet and army.

Herodotus relates that the battles of Artemisium and Thermopylae took place at the same time. There was a lapse of four days between the arrival of the Persian army at Trachis and the first attack on the pass. Herodotus' explanation, that Xerxes had expected the Greeks to flee as soon as they saw the might of the Persian army, is unacceptable. The army was probably waiting for the fleet which, carrying the greater part of the supplies, had reached its destination later as a result of the shipwreck at Sepias. On the fifth day Xerxes sent Median and Kissian soldiers to the pass. They were, however, beaten off by the defenders. A new attack by Persians selected from the corps of the ten thousand Immortals was equally unsuccessful. The sixth day brought no change. Once again the attackers were beaten off. Only after the Persians surprised and overpowered the thousand Phocians guarding a concealed path which allowed them to bypass Thermopylae did the tide turn. Leonidas did not withdraw but decided to give battle with 300 Spartans, 700 Thessalians and 400 Thebans. This unequal struggle was speedily settled and on 20 August 480 BC the gateway by land into central Greece lay open to the Persians.[7]

The events at Thermopylae had important consequences for the strategy of the Persian and Greek fleets. A distinction must be made between the naval activities before Thermopylae and after. Initially the Persian fleet held back. But there was danger for the Greeks, not so much from the squadron that monitored the movements of the Greeks in Artemisium, but especially from the

200 ships which were sailing around Euboea and could attack the Greeks in the back during a withdrawal. For the Greeks the threatening clash was a test case. After the battle of Lade no Greeks had measured their strength against the Persians at sea. The Persians had the advantage in the number of ships and trained crews; the Greeks in their knowledge of the sea: shallows and sunken rocks did not have the same mysteries for them as for the Persian sailors. It must not be overlooked that the crews of the Persian fleet consisted of Phoenicians, Egyptians and Ionians, of whom the latter two were still resentful. Finally, an important factor was the fact that the Persians were the aggressors but the Greeks defenders: for them, any false step could have fatal consequences.

The confrontations at Artemisium are difficult to reconstruct because Herodotus' description is rather summary. So much is clear that the Greeks, on the instigation of Themistocles, made a surprise attack on the Persians before the outcome of the battle at Thermopylae had become known. They were induced to make this move by the information of Scyllias about the shipwreck at Cape Sepias and the squadron sent round Euboea. Initially the Greeks thought of sailing to meet this part of the fleet but realised that it would weaken their position at Artemisium. Instead they decided on a surprise attack on the Persian fleet at Artemisium, to the great consternation of the marines and officers of Xerxes' fleet who considered the Greeks completely mad to attack a fleet which was so much greater than their own. The reply of the Persians was the *periplous*, the encirclement, which the Greeks parried by setting up a *kuklos*. With the sterns together and the bows projecting outwards like the spokes of a wheel they made a stand. Neither of the parties could gain a decisive advantage but the Greeks did capture 30 enemy ships.

The following day the Greeks adopted the same tactics. After it became known that part of the Persian squadron cruising round Euboea had run onto the rocks the Greeks summoned up courage for a new attack, reinforced by the arrival at Artemisium of 53 new Athenian triremes, sent directly from the shipyards in order to check the advance of the Persians. The late arrival of these ships may be explained by the fact that the ship construction programme in Athens was only just beginning to bear fruit. This time the objective of the Greek surprise attack was the Cilician flotilla. How many ships were destroyed or captured is not mentioned by any of our sources. It seems improbable that the greater part of the 100 Cilician ships was destroyed. In such a case Herodotus would have devoted more lines to this 'battle' than he did.

The Persians took the initiative on the third day. In their ranks it must have been considered a great scandal that the Greek ships could damage their mighty fleet. But they had been warned by the events of the previous days. Consequently they did not proceed in line ahead with the objective of forcing a break through the Greek ranks but formed a *kuklos*, precisely as the Greeks had done on the first day. The counter-strategy, the *periplous*, could not be applied by the Greeks in view of the numerical superiority of the Persians. Instead the Persians themselves attempted an encirclement, which, however, came to nothing. The ships got into each other's way in the comparatively small bay and the fight finally led to a battle in which the marines were the decisive factor. In this respect the Persians had the advantage, since the decks of their ships were large and on the quarters only a very small space was open. The Greek ships, on the other hand, had large undecked areas both at the prow and stern as well as on the quarters. Thus, the Greek marines had much less room to defend their ships. Both sides fought bitterly. Since they were evenly matched and the one would not yield to the other, the losses of ships and men were great. It is impossible to give the exact result of the battle but the Greek fleet left Artemisium and retreated in a southerly direction.[8]

Taken together the battles at Thermopylae and Artemisium were a Persian success. Their aim had been reached: central Greece lay open before them. Resistance on land was slight and many cities opened their gates for the Persians. The next goal for the Persian advance was Athens. The army moved via Boeotia and Phocis to Attica, the fleet sailed from Aphetae via Artemisium to Histiaea on Euboea and subsequently through the Euripus to the bay of Phalerum. Presumably the Persians thought that their advance would terrify the Athenians; but it was the Athenians' own decision to withdraw the fleet from Artemisium to Salamis, not only because of its strategic location but also because a great part of the non-combatant Athenian population had taken refuge on the island. On the evacuation from Athens there are two versions. Herodotus relates that the evacuation to Troezen, Aegina and Salamis was not the implementation of a worked-out plan, but the result of an *ad hoc* decision. A different kind of strategy may be seen in the so-called Troezen-inscription from the third century BC which purports to be a copy of a plan drawn up by Themistocles and approved by the Athenian Assembly. It stresses the premeditated character of the evacuation to Troezen and Salamis. There is mention of the manning of the ships, of which 100 were to be sent to Artemisium and another 100 to guard Salamis and the Attic coast. In contrast to Herodotus' version, the Themistocles decree makes the evacuation plan a part of a clear strategy, put into effect when the Greek fleet was still at Artemisium. If the text of the Themistocles decree is authentic one may well wonder that the evacuation plan was executed at such a late stage. After the battle of Artemisium the Athenians had only a few days to bring women, children and the aged into safety before the Persians reached Attica.[9]

At the request of the Athenians the whole Greek fleet cast anchor at Salamis. A council of war was held, during which it was reported that the Persians had reached Attica and had taken and devastated Athens. Some Greek commanders were so panic-stricken that they left the council and ran off. The rest wanted to leave Salamis and build up a defensive line on the Isthmus. At this point Themistocles threatened to evacuate the Athenian population to Siris in Italy, in which case the numerical inferiority of the Greeks as compared to the Persians would become excessive. Faced with this, the other commanders changed their mind and began preparations for a sea-battle.[10]

In the Persian camp at Phalerum the decision to attack the Greek fleet was adopted by a great majority of votes. If they could eliminate the Greek fleet before winter, the conquest of Greece would be settled quickly. If the Greek fleet should escape them, it would remain a permanent threat. Aided by Greek contingents from the west, it would be a military rival and constitute a real danger. Therefore, sailing on to the Peloponnese without confronting the Greek fleet could not be the Persian strategy.

The Persians did not make haste after their successes at Thermopylae and Artemisium nor were the Greeks eager to rush into a risky adventure. This explains the lapse of three weeks between Artemisium and Salamis. Each fleet wanted to meet its opponent on a stretch of water of its own choice. The Greeks did everything they could to induce the Persians to join battle in the bay of Salamis. The Persians preferred a fight out at sea but could not wait too long. By this time it was the end of August and the storms

Figure 5.2 Battle at Salamis

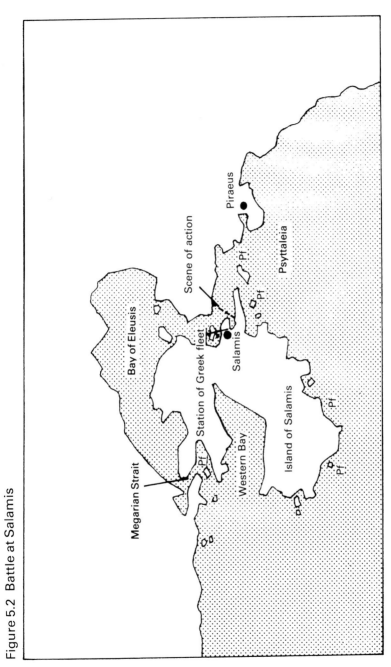

Pf= Persian fleet

that herald the month of September and occur much more frequently in autumn made an operation involving several hundred ships in the Aegean a perilous undertaking. The bay in which the Greeks had taken shelter was about 1600 m wide and could be defended by the available Greek ships (Fig. 5.2). According to Herodotus the Greeks had a total of 378 triremes and a small number of penteconters. Aeschylus speaks of 310 Greek and 1207 Persian triremes. Aeschylus probably under-estimated the numbers of the Greeks and exaggerated those of the Persians in order to enhance the merits of the Greek achievement. The Persian fleet in any case had fewer ships. If we start with an initial number of 600 to 800 triremes that set sail with the Persians (see p. 49) and then count the losses at Cape Sepias, Artemisium and Euboea, the Persian fleet cannot have been much greater than that of the Greeks.

From the day that the Persians had taken up position in Phalerum they had presented a certain threat. About their man-oeuvres our sources, in particular Herodotus, are rather vague. The Persian command possibly set up a blockade of both outlets of the bay, with the aim of starving out the Greek fleet and the many refugees in Salamis and forcing them to fight at sea. Against this it can be said that the Persians would not have dared to split their fleet in two against an enemy who was scarcely inferior numerically. It is also possible that the Persians rowed in for-mation from Phalerum to the eastern outlet of the bay in order to try and entice the Greeks to fight.[11]

The position of the Greeks was favourable because they were protected by the coast and could parry a Persian attack with only half the fleet. It is plausible that the rest of the fleet, even if it was not fully prepared for battle, was not beached but anchored in the bay. A surprise attack by the Persians was excluded. The distance from the Persian base at Phalerum to the Strait of Salamis is about 6.5 miles, so that any movements of the Persian warships would quickly be reported.

Whatever the original Persian plan may have been, it was changed by a message from Themistocles conveyed to Xerxes at night by the hands of Sicinnus, a faithful slave. In Herodotus' words it runs as follows:

> I am the bearer of a secret communication from the Athenian commander, who is a well-wisher to your king and hopes for a

Persian victory. He has told me to report to you that the Greeks have no confidence in themselves and are planning to save their skins by a hasty withdrawal. Only prevent them from slipping through your fingers, and you have at this moment an opportunity of unparalleled success. They are at daggers drawn with each other, and will offer no opposition — on the contrary, you will see the pro-Persians amongst them fighting the rest.

This information did not sound altogether unbelievable to a Persian king. It could not have escaped Xerxes that in the Greek ranks there was a dispute between the Athenians and the Peloponnesians who were convinced that they should abandon Salamis and take refuge in the Peloponnese. According to Aeschylus, the king understood from Sicinnus' words that the Greeks would secretly attempt to escape to their respective home cities.[12]

At any rate, Themistocles' ruse had worked. The Persians abandoned their original plan and set up a blockade of the entrances to the strait. Xerxes wanted to prevent at any price that a part of the fleet should escape and remain a potential danger. The Egyptians, who had distinguished themselves at Artemisium, were given the task of blocking the western entrance, which was so small that a few ships in line could defend it. A contingent of soldiers was disembarked on the island of Psyttaleia between Salamis and the mainland; they were to save their own men and finish off the enemy, once the naval battle had begun and shipwrecked men and damaged vessels would try to reach the shore. The rest of the fleet, far and away the greatest part, rowed in the night into the eastern side of the strait. The encirclement of the Greeks was a fact.

Around dawn Themistocles heard of all this both from his Athenian rival Aristides and from the crew of a trireme from the island of Tenos who defected to the Greeks. Immediately the Greeks took the offensive, to the surprise of the Persians who had expected to be facing a disorganised enemy. The Phoenicians, who had penetrated furthest into the bay, were confronted by over 180 Athenian ships. The Ionians in Persian service, who had been asked by Themistocles — without much success — to leave the scene of battle, found themselves facing the ships of the Lacedaemonians, of whom the Corinthians with 40 ships formed the greatest contingent. Stationed between the Phoenicians and the Ionians, the Cilicians faced a small Greek contingent from a number of islands. The first fighting contact was between an Athenian trireme and a Phoenician one. Before this there had been skirmishes, the significance of which has often been misinterpreted on the basis of Herodotus. When the Persians came close the Greeks rowed slowly backwards towards the coast, feigning retreat. There is a story that the ships only advanced again when a woman appeared on the beach, scolded them and shouted: 'You madmen, how long are you going to move backwards?' However attractive this emotional version of Herodotus may sound, it is not true. The retreat of the Greek triremes was intended to entice the Persian fleet into the bay, so that those units which would follow them inshore could be attacked before the rest of the ships could come to their aid. The more ships ventured into the bay, the less space there was, which was disastrous for the Persian triremes. When the Greeks felt that a sufficient number of Persian ships had entered the bay and the inshore wind drove the ships, which were so close together that they could scarcely use their oars, in their direction, they proceeded to attack. They took up position for the *diekplous*; they had rowed back not from fear but in order to choose the best position. Since the narrowness did not permit an attack by a number of ships in line abreast, they set out line ahead. The Athenians led their fleet in a *diekplous* against their direct opponents, the Phoenicians. Many of their ships were rammed and the formation in which they had entered the bay disintegrated. The openings allowed the Aeginetans, who were next to the Athenians, to sail through the Persian lines and to attack the ships from different sides. Because of the collapse of the Phoenician wing the Persian fleet tried to turn about and retreat. They were hindered by their own ships which were rowing up in order to come to the aid of the front-lines. Tremendous chaos and panic ensued; many Persian ships were rammed by the Greeks as well as by their own vessels. On the way back they were attacked and in part sunk by Greek ships who had made an outflanking movement. The Persian soldiers stationed on Psyttaleia were killed to the last man.

Immediately after the battle the Greeks prepared themselves for action once again. They expected the Persians to throw in the ships that had stayed out of battle at Salamis. Xerxes strengthened them in their belief by attempting to build a dam near Salamis. He had a number of Phoenician ships tied together to serve as a bridge and undertook other military measures as if he wanted to begin a second naval battle. This second Persian offensive was, however, prevented by the impaired morale of the sailors. In particular the defeat of the Phoenicians, who had also suffered the greatest losses in ships and men, had reduced enthusiasm to a minimum. The Phoenicians also got the blame for the defeat. They complained of the inadequate support of the Ionians during the battle, but Xerxes had unfortunately just witnessed a heroic exploit by the Ionians: the sinking of an enemy ship. Some of the Phoenician admirals were executed on account of their 'false' accusation. After the battle the Phoenicians sailed to Tyre under their own authority. Without them it was much too risky to attack the Greeks. The Phoenician ships were the fastest and most manoeuvrable and their shipbuilders and carpenters had been of great importance during the expedition. Xerxes could no longer count on the Ionians. Now that it was evident that the Greeks were a match for the Persians, their Greek origin took precedence over their fear.

After a short deliberation the Persian fleet left the Greek coast in the second night after the battle and made for Asia Minor with the intention of casting anchor in the Hellespont. The Greeks followed the demoralised fleet at a distance as far as the island of Andros but the proposal of Themistocles to extend the pursuit to the bridge over the Hellespont was rejected.[13]

The Persian army, for the most part dependent on the fleet for its provisioning, now found itself in a difficult situation. If it was decided that it should stay in Greece it could only fulfil a defensive role, for the Greek lines on the Isthmus of Corinth could not be dislodged without support from the fleet. The loss of face through the defeat of the Persian fleet was already so great that an eventual retreat of the army could not be tolerated since it would seriously undermine the Persian claim to be invincible. When diplomatic consultations with the Athenians had not been able to produce a settlement, they marched into Attica once again, under the command of Mardonius, and committed enormous ravages, above all in Athens, which was again set ablaze. A new confrontation was inevitable. This took place in Boeotia on the plain of the Asopus at some distance from the city of Plataea, where the Persians spent the winter. They hoped to find enough space for the cavalry to have free play. In the Greek ranks a certain optimism prevailed despite differences of opinion at the top. Ten years previously the

Persians had been beaten by the Athenians at Marathon, with a little support from the Plataeans. Why then should Greece be afraid, now that Athens and Sparta were marching together against the Persians, whose morale was undoubtedly affected by the unexpected loss of the fleet. Herodotus tells that the Greeks had stationed 110,000 men against about 300,000 Persians. Modern reconstructions have shown that there were about 45,000 combatants on the Persian and about 30,000 on the Greek side.

The most dangerous weapon of the Persians was the cavalry; the Greeks, above all the Spartans, relied on the infantry. The Persian cavalry took the offensive first. They penetrated the Greek lines and poisoned the Gargaphia-well on which the Greeks were dependent for their drinking water. The Greek commander, the Spartan Pausanias, was compelled to retreat. His opponent Mardonius, wrongly supposing that the Greeks were taking flight, ordered a massive attack. Chaos ensued because the soldiers thought they were only going to encounter Greeks seeking safety in flight. Pausanias, however, gave the signal for a counter-attack, which confused the Persians. A large number perished, including Mardonius.[14]

If the Greeks wanted to be spared further Persian aggression in the near future then the Persian fleet that had assembled in the spring of 479 BC at Samos had to be put out of action. The Persians did not expect the Greeks to cross the Aegean and attack the fleet before the coast of Asia Minor. They were, therefore, taken by surprise when 110 triremes under the command of the Spartan Leotychides arrived at about the same time as the battle of Plataea. The Persians were completely unprepared, all the more so because after the departure of the Phoenicians the Samians had, in the name of the Ionians, initiated negotiations with the Greeks about defection. Convinced that they had no chance at sea, they withdrew to Mons Mycale, the mainland promontory opposite Samos. On the approach of the Greek fleet they beached their ships, round which they constructed ramparts of stone and wood and round the ramparts, a palisade. The disappointment among the Greeks was great. Initially they considered returning home or going in the direction of the Hellespont to destroy the bridges. Finally they decided to sail along the shore hoping that the Persians would come out. When that did not happen they decided to land. The risk attached was great. The Persians had an army of nearly 10,000 men, whereas the Greeks could scarcely oppose them with more than 3300. When the Greeks approached the coast, the first thing they did was to tempt the Ionians to attack the Persians. A herald spoke to the Ionians in the Greek tongue as follows: 'Ionians listen well to what I have to say to you, for the Persians will not understand me. When we join battle, each of you must first think of freedom and of the watchword *Hebe*.' When the Persians, some of whom were undoubtedly proficient in the Greek tongue, heard this, they disarmed the Ionians exactly as the Greeks had hoped. Thereupon the Persians moved into the attack on the Greek army that had been brought into position. For a long time the fight was equal. Initially the Greek left flank ran into difficulties but when the centre and the right flank, which had encountered less resistance, came to their help, the Greeks began a massive attack. In an assault they broke through the lines of the Persians who sought refuge within their fortifications. The Greeks set about storming the rampart. The allies of the Persians fled and they themselves only lasted a short time but finally had to yield. The palisade and the ships were set on fire.[15]

The consequences of the battles of Marathon, Salamis, Plataea and Mycale were considerable. Persian prestige had suffered an enormous blow. Subject peoples became aware that the Persians were not invincible. The reputation of the Greeks, on the other hand, spread throughout the Mediterranean world. Yet, the problems for the Greeks continued to pile up. First there were the wishes of the Ionians. They were now freed from Persian domination but were afraid to be subjected again if the Greeks of the mainland could give them no support. Secondly, the Spartans, whose kings Eurybiades and Leotychides had been the commanders in the battles of Salamis and Mycale, had no fleet of their own so that their influence in Asia Minor was restricted. They proposed that the inhabitants of the Ionian cities should migrate to Greece and live in the cities which had made common cause with the Persians. It is not surprising that most of the cities and islands were not very enthusiastic about this plan. The Athenians were squarely opposed to the Spartan proposal. They were prepared to give guarantees to the Ionians and the islands before the coast based on their superiority at sea. The Athenians held that in the long run the Persians would be stronger on land but could be successfully opposed with a strong fleet. The Persians could no longer hope to count on the Ionians; the Egyptians saw an opportunity of freeing themselves from the Persians and the

Phoenicians were too demoralised to want a new confrontation with the Greeks.

Notes

1. HELLENIC LEAGUE: Hdt. 7.132; 7.145; 7.172.
2. STRENGTH OF THE PERSIAN ARMY: Hdt. 7.60.1; 7.184–5; the various points of view are discussed by Hignett, 1963, pp. 350–5.
3. STRENGTH OF THE PERSIAN FLEET: Aesch. *Pers.* 341–3; Hdt. 7.89–95; 7.184; cf. Hignett, 1963, pp. 345–50; Morrison and Williams, 1968, p. 136 suggest that the Persian fleet outnumbered the Greek fleet.
4. STRENGTH OF THE GREEK FLEET: Hdt. 8.1–2; 8.43–8; Aesch. *Pers.* 341–3; Thuc. 1.73–4. ATHENIAN SHIPBUILDING PROGRAMME: Hdt. 7.144; Thuc. 1.14.3; Arist. *Ath. Pol.* 22.7; cf. Lenardon, 1978, pp. 51–6.
5. PERSIAN CASUALTIES: Hdt. 7.188–92; Hignett, 1963, p. 174.
6. CAUSE OF THE SHIPWRECK: Hdt. 7.189; Paus. 10.19.1–2; cf. Frost, 1968, pp. 180–5. SNORKEL: Arist. *Hist. An.* 659[2] 8–12.
7. Hdt. 7.175–8.21 describes the battles of Thermopylae and Artemisium. GREEK STRATEGY: Evans, 1969, pp. 389–406. RECONSTRUCTION OF THE MOST IMPORTANT EVENTS: Hignett, 1963, pp. 105–92 and pp. 371–8; Burn, 1962, pp. 378–422; Green, 1970, pp. 109–46.
8. NAVAL TACTICS: Morrison and Williams, 1968, pp. 136–8; Evans, 1969, pp. 389–406.
9. ATHENIAN FLEET AT SALAMIS: Hdt. 8.40–2. THEMISTOCLES-DECREE: published in *SEG* 18, 1962, 153; Sealey, 1976, p. 229, note 6 gives a survey of the most important articles on the decree.
10. COUNCIL AT WAR: Hdt. 8.49–64.
11. PERSIAN STRATEGY: Both possibilities are treated by Hignett, 1963, pp. 215–27; Hammond, 1956, pp. 32–40 prefers the second possibility, Wallinga, 1969–70, pp. 136–7 the first.
12. MESSAGE OF THEMISTOCLES: Hdt. 8.74–5; Aesch. *Pers.* 355–83; see Hignett, 1963, pp. 403–11.
13. BATTLE AT SALAMIS: Hdt. 8.40–96 and Aesch. *Pers.* 350–471. Analyses are given by Hammond, 1956, pp. 32–54; Burn, 1962, pp. 423–75; Hignett, 1953, pp. 193–239; Morrison and Williams, 1968, pp. 139–43; Wallinga, 1969–70, pp. 127–48.
14. MARDONIUS' NEGOTIATIONS WITH ATHENS: Hdt. 8.136–44; 9.1–11. PLATAEA: Hdt. 9.12–89; Hignett, 1963, pp. 264–344.
15. MYCALE: Hdt. 8.131–2; 9.90–107; 9.114–21; Burn, 1962, pp. 547–54; Hignett, 1963, pp. 240–63.

Chapter Six

The Athenian Maritime Empire

The fifty years between the Persian Wars and the long-drawn (431–404 BC) Peloponnesian War between Athens and Sparta are generally regarded as the heyday of Athens. Merchants, sculptors, architects and craftsmen flocked to Athens, which became the cultural and commercial centre of the Greek world. In this chapter the two maritime pillars of the Athenian empire are discussed: the Delian League and international maritime trade.

The Delian League

Immediately after the Persian Wars the Athenians were faced with severe food shortages and the government was compelled to ask for help from the allies. Some gave food, either voluntarily out of gratitude for services rendered or forced to do so by the Athenian fleet; others refused. With a strong fleet at their disposal the Athenians readily resorted to tough methods; they had no qualms about using extortion and blackmail to encourage unwilling allies to make a financial 'contribution', ostensibly to the Athenian project of destroying the last enemy strongholds. Through these practices and through the renewed exploitation of the silvermines Athens' financial position improved, offering possibilities for investment. The construction of new warships was, indeed, a matter of dispute among the Athenian politicians, but after Salamis the proponents of an active fleet found more support than the opponents. As for the construction of merchantmen there was no difference of opinion. Now that even for its most basic needs Athens was dependent on foreign trade an increase in the number of merchant vessels was necessary in order to guarantee imports.

The investments in a merchant and war fleet had a favourable effect on the employment of the Athenian population. Most of the citizens were members of the lowest census-class, the thetes, who had little or no land of their own and earned their living in occasional jobs on large estates or in the ceramics industry. In the shipbuilding industry many of them found employment with better opportunities. The increasing activity on the wharves attracted people from outside Athens to the harbour districts. Thus, in a few years' time Piraeus turned into a bustling quarter with a most heterogeneous population. This development was not to the liking of some politicians, because the increase of maritime trade and commerce brought about social and political changes. Now, those Athenian citizens who were employed in manufacturing, commerce and trade began to acquire political power.[1]

Athens' military hegemony at sea had not been formalised in any treaty or agreement immediately after the Persian Wars. There was always the possibility of other states joining up and forming a competitive block against Athens or siding with Sparta, whose relations with Athens were rapidly cooling off. But this did not happen. In the Greek fleet which, under the command of the Spartan king Pausanias, besieged and conquered Byzantium, troubles arose because of Pausanias' authoritarian behaviour. The Ionians in particular and those recently freed from Persian domination complained about the admiral's attitude and turned to the Athenians for help, asking them to take over the command of the fleet. The Athenians agreed and, with the exception of a few Spartan contingents, the fleet of the Hellenic League was now entirely under Athenian authority.[2]

This leadership was formalised in the following year. In the summer of 477 BC envoys of the Greek cities met in Delos to discuss mutual relations in the immediate future. About 140 cities were represented at the conference. Its primary aim was to create an alliance strong enough to meet any possible Persian aggression. The best means to achieve this was to take the initiative and attack the property of the Persian kings. An invasion of the Persian mainland was out of the question, since for such a venture Greek military capability was insufficient; at sea, however, the possibilities were much greater. The conference agreed upon a naval treaty meant to guarantee Greek supremacy at sea, which could only be achieved by attacking the harbours of the Persians. The strategy of the Delian League, named after the place of assembly, was to be determined by joint decisions under the chairmanship of the Athenian deputy. Thucydides says the following about the agreement:

The Athenians assessed the various contributions to be made for the war against Persia, and decided which states should furnish money and which states should send ships. At this time the officials known as *hellenotamiai* [Hellenic treasurers] were first appointed by the Athenians. These officials received the *phoros*, which was the name given to the contributions in money. The original sum fixed for the tribute was 460 talents. The treasury of the League was at Delos, and representative meetings were held in the temple there.

On paper everything looked fine; a joint Greek fleet under the natural leadership of Athens. In practice Athens dominated every concern of the League. From the start Athens had a fleet that was far superior to that of any of the other member states. The superiority was emphasised even more when Athens began to demand money instead of ships. The member states offered no organised resistance. With the money thus raised triremes were built on the Athenian wharves and manned by Athenian oarsmen. Before the allies became fully aware of Athens' real intentions towards them, the Athenians ruled the Aegean. Attempts to leave the League were suppressed by force; faced with the fleet the revolting city either 'voluntarily' changed its mind or was forced to do so. The cities of Thasos, Aegina, Samos, Potidaea, Mytilene and Melos, which once had had considerable naval squadrons at their disposal, were in this way painfully reminded of their position.[3]

In spite of these internal problems the planned hostilities with the Persians were not forgotten. In 476–475 BC, Eion on the mouth of the Strymon was conquered and the inhabitants sold as slaves. The struggle against the Dolopians of the island of Scyros was more complicated. The Dolopians had not only sided with the Persians but they were also formidable pirates who with their small fast ships constituted a continuous threat for the heavily-laden Athenian merchantmen. Plutarch calls the battle that Cimon waged with them the *coup de grâce* for piracy although in his 'Life of Pericles' he says that the elimination of pirates from the Aegean was one of the points on the agenda of the Panhellenic congress organised by Pericles in 448 BC.

These fights could not have given the League much trouble but the battle at the river Eurymedon in Pamphylia in 465 BC certainly did. Themistocles, the founding father of the League, no longer had any influence on battle decisions. In 471 BC he was ostracised by the Athenian Assembly to end his life in exile at the Persian court. His political opponent Cimon was entrusted with the supreme command over the combined land and naval forces, which set out to attack the Persian bases in the east. A fleet consisting of 200 Athenian and 100 allied triremes sailed eastwards.[4]

Since Salamis the Athenian vessels had undergone a substantial alteration. Until then the triremes had been constructed for speed and manoeuvrability in order to ram enemy ships as effectively as possible or, if under attack, to be able to escape. They had a fairly small deck, which left the space along the quarters open. Cimon had the decks enlarged, thus giving the marines more space to fight the enemy. To what extent this change in construction contributed to the Greek victory is difficult to say. But in any case Cimon attacked the Persians in the narrow estuary of the Eurymedon using ships with this modified deck-construction. The Greek success in this battle, in which both the Persian navy — to which the Phoenicians had once again contributed a large contingent — and the land forces suffered heavy losses, did not only mean that the Aegean was now an entirely Greek sea, but also that Greek ships could now safely venture to the southerly shores of Asia Minor without being threatened by a hostile fleet.[5]

After the battle of Salamis Egyptian vessels and crews had been of little use to the Persians. The Egyptians had never got used to their subordinate position. A few years after the Persian catastrophe at the Eurymedon they rebelled. The Libyan Inarus conquered a great part of the Egyptian delta and with the support of the Egyptian population appealed to the Delian League for assistance. Pericles, leader in Athens for many years and the most important person in the League, got his way and sent the fleet to Egypt. In all likelihood Pericles was hoping to install important military bases in Egypt. The Ionians especially, seeing an opportunity to re-establish former trade relations, were very enthusiastic about the plan. The Greeks, perhaps a little reckless after the successes at Salamis, Mycale and the Eurymedon, set out with a great fleet. The expedition was a total failure. Of the 350 to 400 ships more than half were destroyed, not in a real naval battle, but through a clever stratagem of the Persian commander Megabazus. He cut off the Greek fleet at the Nile island Prosopitis and besieged them for 18 months. Finally, taking advantage of the low water-level of the Nile, he dug a canal to drain the water from the river-arm. As a result, the Greek triremes lay helpless on the dry river-bed. On receiving the news about this disaster a relief squadron of 50 ships was sent from Athens and other Greek cities. Before these triremes could come into action, they were surprised by Persian infantry and Phoenician triremes at Cape Mendes in the Nile delta.[6]

This defeat did not, however, lead to a restoration of the Persian influence in the Aegean. In 450 BC the Greeks defeated the Persian fleet at Salamis on Cyprus. We know that 200 Athenian vessels took part in this battle but there is no mention of allied contingents. This victory cleared the way for the accord reached in the following year between the Athenians and the Persians, which terminated hostilities and determined mutual relations. The Greek city-states in Asia Minor became free and autonomous and the Aegean was off limits for the Persian fleet. This peace is a turning point in Greek maritime history. The original function of the Delian League — protection from Persian aggression — had disappeared and the allies realised that they had ended up in Athenian hands. Sometimes the Athenians intervened in an allied city to modify its constitution and to impose a democratic form of government. Quite often Athens curtailed the judicial competence of its allies. Athens itself could indeed draw up a positive balance. The feeling of prestige had been given satisfaction in the leadership (*arche*) of the Delian League. Sparta, supported by the city-states of the Peloponnese, saw through the threat of the Athenian aspirations. Impotent through the lack of a good fleet, it could not take any measures when Athens set its sights on city-states that were well-disposed to Sparta.[7]

Did the supremacy of Athens at sea also have consequences for the average Athenians, the *zeugitae* and the thetes? As small farmers the *zeugitae* produced mainly for their own consumption, but when they had surpluses to offer to the market, they now had to compete with imports from overseas. On the other hand, if their farm did not yield enough, they could be selected as cleruchs (settlers): as citizens of Athens they were allotted land in the territory of rebellious allies, where they exercised a controlling function on possible unrest. This task was frequently done by thetes, whom the possession of land promoted to *zeugitae*. But they benefited from the supremacy at sea in other ways as well. The construction of triremes created job-opportunities in Athens. The import of timber from Macedonia and the construction of ships demanded many labourers. But that was not all. Many officials were paid either directly or indirectly from the proceeds of the Delian League. In the fourth century BC Aristotle wrote on the changes in Athens as a consequence of its predominance in the Delian League:

> Athens provided the common people with an abundance of income . . . More than 20,000 men were maintained out of the tribute and the taxes and the allies, for there were 7000 jurymen, 1600 archers, 1200 cavalry, 500 members of the Council, 500 guards of the arsenals, 50 guards of the Acropolis, about 700 other officials in the city and another 700 abroad. Besides, in wartime there were 12,500 hoplites, 20 coastguard vessels, ships collecting the tribute with crews of 2000 chosen by lot, the prytanes, war-orphans and jailers.[8]

Most of the League's income was spent on the fleet. The Athenian navy was a fully paid service. It is difficult to say how many oarsmen were involved, but certainly several thousand. The number was, of course, dependent on the number of ships that Athens put to sea, in war situations *c.* 200 ships. In less urgent circumstances Athens had at least 60 triremes at its disposal, equivalent at full complement to 60 × 170 (the number of oarsmen per trireme), that is, a total of 10,200 oarsmen, a number that could be raised to 30,000. Yet the levy remained restricted primarily to the citizens. Only when recruiting became difficult were resident aliens levied. There are no indications that the Athenians ever used slaves as rowers before 406 BC, when they were compelled to recruit slaves through lack of manpower. Any slaves on board were servants of the ship's officers or of the marines. Only when one of the rowers fell sick could they be consigned to the rowing benches. Many triremes could well have set out with a complement of less than 170 rowers, if recruiting was difficult.[9]

The rowers of the Athenian fleet had a high level of excellence. They were given a tough training which consisted of manoeuvring for ramming, rowing over long distances and changes in tempo. The co-ordination of the rowers was stressed, not only to raise the speed of the ship when required, but also to execute abrupt turns. Much attention was also given to reversing direction. After the ramming of an enemy ship the rowers had to withdraw as quickly as possible before another enemy ship came to its aid and made a counter-attack. The training periods were long. Pericles had a fleet of at least 60 ships at sea for a period of eight months every year. In his opinion only well-trained rowers were able to maintain Athens' supremacy at sea. Thus many rowers were out at sea from the beginning of spring (late February) to the time when the autumn gales came on (October). The rowers got an average of 3 obols (½ drachma) per day at the beginning of the fifth century BC, and 6 obols (1 drachma) at the time of the outbreak of the Peloponnesian war. With these wages the sailors had to support both themselves and their families in Athens. In many cases they could not make ends meet and during the months that they were not at sea had to look for alternative work in the harbour.[10]

The entire costs of the Delian League were paid from the treasury. At the time of Pericles Athens had 60 ships at sea and a fleet of 300 ships in the dockyards. The mere cost of the crews of the 60 triremes, 12,000 men at full complement, amounted during the service season to 240 (the number of days at sea) × 12,000 drachmae = 2,880,000 drachmae, which is equivalent to 480 talents (1 talent = 6000 drachmae). Considering that the total annual contribution of the member states came to between 400 and 600 talents, incidental payments and gifts of extra ships from the member states and from rich Athenians were very welcome. The craftsmen in the dockyards had to be paid too, as well as the 500 guards. Every year a number of ships had to be repaired and others had to be replaced. Some of the latter could be converted to troop- or horse-transports; others had to be taken out of service. Yearly 20 to 30 new ships were constructed at a cost of 30 to 50 talents. Finally, money was also required for the expansion and fortification of the harbours, specially of Piraeus.[11]

Whenever the sources mention the yearly allocation of the contributions, attention is always directed to the principal member of the League, Athens. The member states' share in the fleet is either disregarded or minimised. For the years directly following 480 BC this undervaluation is probably not correct. At that time League members other than Athens had ships at their disposal paid for and maintained out of the treasury. But later the members contributed ships without crew and, in the end, simply money, which the Athenians used to build, man and maintain ships. It may well be that some of the League members preferred to supply money instead of ships with crew, because they did not have enough men to row the ships. On the islands, for instance, which did not have

Figure 6.1 Plan and Reconstruction of the Boathouses at Zea

an unemployed urban proletariat, there was little enthusiasm to serve on the triremes.

Life on the narrow triremes was no unqualified pleasure. During the daytime the crew were on board, in war situations longer than during training voyages. Evenings and nights were passed on land. It was always a matter of concern to find a friendly region to pass the night, not so much to prevent the danger of nocturnal surprise attacks as to replenish food supplies. On the ships little room could be spared for the storage of foodstuffs. Only a day's ration of water was taken along in stone jars. The crew slept on the beach by the ships.[12]

In winter the ships were laid up in Piraeus, in boathouses specially constructed for the triremes and located in the two eastern inner harbours Zea and Munichia. The sheds were built in such a way that they could shelter four or eight triremes, separated by rows of pillars which supported a slanting roof. A boathouse consisted of a back wall and two side walls at right angles to it (Fig. 6.1). Close by there were warehouses constructed mainly of timber in which the rigging, oars and anchors were stored.[13]

The Athenian Market Economy

The western part of Piraeus served a rather different purpose. In this harbour, called Emporium, the Athenian merchant vessels loaded and unloaded their cargoes. As a result of the rapidly increasing growth of the Athenian population in the sixth and fifth centuries BC Athens was now heavily dependent on the import of certain products, in particular corn, which was supplied in great quantities along routes safeguarded by the navy. In addition to corn and timber, also marble, linen, exclusive wines, gold, horses and slaves were unloaded on the quays of Piraeus (Figure 6.2). The many imported goods were paid with the proceeds of the silvermines and the earnings of the export trade. Olive oil and wine became the most important articles of export when the rural regions had recovered from the Persian devastation. Besides, Attic ceramics and silver were in great demand in the Aegean area.[14]

The trade interests of Athens cannot be separated from its position in the Delian League. From the beginning the Athenian fleet patrolled areas which were unsafe because of pirates or the

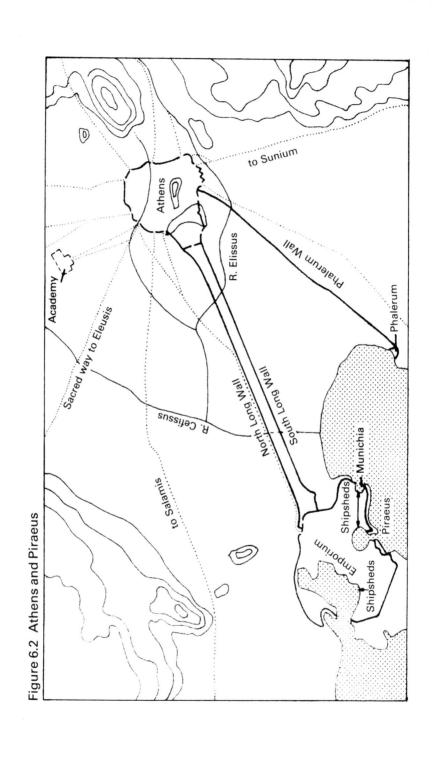

Figure 6.2 Athens and Piraeus

potential disloyalty of the inhabitants. Since in the first few years the crews of the triremes did not know whether they could touch at friendly harbours, they were often accompanied by freighters with supplies. The merchants bought food from the local inhabitants and sold it to the sailors, often with a significant profit. In turn, the oarsmen sold the booty taken from pirates or obtained in areas hostile to the merchants. In the long run permanent market-places sprang up from where the merchants not only provided the necessities of the fleet but also brought products to Athens.

As a result of the change in contribution (money instead of ships) the merchant fleet of the allies enjoyed much less protection than that of the Athenians. The Athenian war fleet protected first of all the Athenian ships and took little trouble to give the allies the feeling that at least their trade interests were being safeguarded. To what extent the commerce of the various cities was thus curtailed can only be guessed, because data are not available. But as the most important consuming centre Athens could certainly prevent political opponents from selling their goods. Athens also had the power to deny the use of certain sea lanes to the ships of unco-operative cities. On the other hand, captains of merchant vessels could also be forced to make for Athens and to exchange their goods there. In *c.* 445 BC the Athenians decreed that the allies were to use Athenian coins, weights and measures, so that the League contributions would have to be paid in Athenian minted silver. In order to comply with this rule, the allies would have to get hold of Athenian money, for instance by selling their products on the Athenian market.[15]

The merchant vessels were completely different from the triremes. They were shorter and broader and both prow and stern curved upward. The ancient historians are not very informative on the construction of the merchant vessels. Fortunately, during the past 25 years archaeologists have been able to shed some light by studying the remains of foundered merchantmen on the bottom of the sea. Though Greek cargo vessels have received much less attention than Roman ships, two wrecks of Greek freighters provide some information concerning this area of Greek shipbuilding: a fifth-century freighter sunk in the Strait of Messina near Porticello and a fourth-century one found off the north coast of Cyprus near Kyrenia, the construction of which closely resembles that of the fifth-century ship. The Porticello wreck could only be partially reconstructed so that the dimensions could not be estab-

Figure 6.3 The Kyrenia Shipwreck. (Courtesy M. Katzev)

a. The Small Visible Cargo

b. The Hull Lying *in situ* on the Sea-bed

c. Reconstruction Plan of the Vessel's Outer Hull

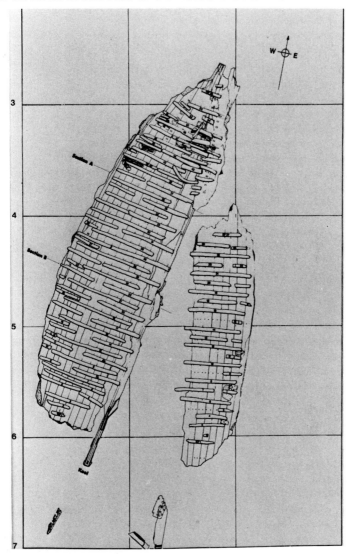

lished. The Kyrenia ship has a length of *c.* 15 m and a greatest breadth of 4–5 m, which seems to indicate a small ship (Fig. 6.3).[16]

The Greek shipbuilders constructed their ships on scaffoldings, a tradition continued by the Romans. They began by laying the keel (Fig. 6.4). Next the stem- and stern-posts were fastened to the

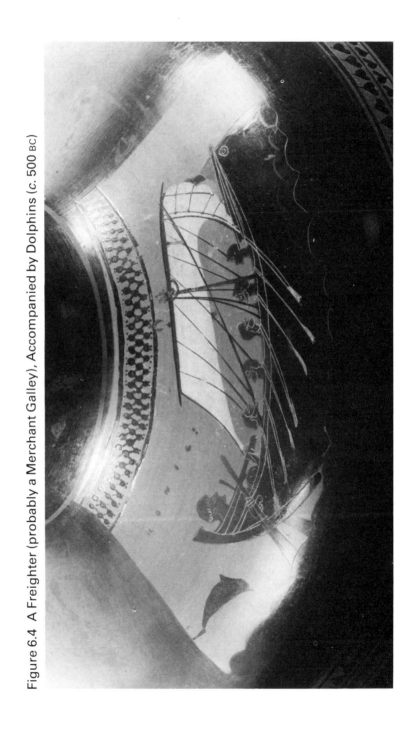

Figure 6.4 A Freighter (probably a Merchant Galley), Accompanied by Dolphins (c. 500 BC)

keel by bevelling. A number of temporary frames must have been used to represent the designed shape of the ship. The horizontal strakes were placed from the keel to the gunwales edge-joined to each other with close-set mortises, at a distance of 5 to 15 cm from each other. When the planking was completed the temporary transversal frames were removed and the definitive frames, ribs and strakes (longitudinal timbers) were shaped and fitted to the hull with treenails. Then the treenails were transfixed with bronze spikes. The frames were made of one piece of wood or of two pieces which were joined at the keel. The material from which keel, ribs and strakes were made was mostly pine, cedar and fir. In order to protect the hull against rough seas and rubbing, strakes known as wales were attached all around the hull. Sometimes they were fastened to the frames with long bolts. Caulking was only necessary if the joints were widely spaced. Then the seams of the entire hull were caulked with pitch or with a mixture of pitch and beeswax. Underwater many ships were covered with lead as a protection against marine borers. This was applied with copper nails on a layer of tarred fabric.

The deck ran over the entire length of the ship. The longer ships had a lower second deck. On the quarter-deck there was a deck-house, used by the proprietor of the ship and the captain with a few other crew members. The rest of the crew had to find a place to sleep among the cargo. Meals were prepared on a stove on the quarter-deck. If there was no deck-house cooking was done in the hold on a stone cooking-plate. On the quarter-deck there was sometimes a small altar. Here the sailors made offerings to ensure a favourable journey.[17]

During a normal voyage the hold and most of the decks were fully stowed with cargo, mostly packed in sacks (grain) or in amphoras (oil, wine). How much cargo the freighters could carry can only be estimated approximately. The Greeks and Romans had more than one universal unit. The size of grain ships was expressed in different grain measures. In Athens this was the *medimnos* (*c.* 40 kg), in Rome the *modius* (*c.* 7 kg). The tonnage of wine and oil ships was calculated according to the number of amphoras they could carry. Since jars of various sizes were used no accurate estimate of the tonnage can be given. Ships with mixed cargo were classified in talents (*c.* 26 kg). The tonnage must by no means be underestimated. From a fragment of the port regulations of Thasos dating from the second half of the third century BC it appears that the harbour was divided into two basins, one for ships with a capacity of 3000 to 5000 talents, which is equivalent to a tonnage of 78 to 130 tons; the other for ships with a capacity greater than 130 tons. Of the smaller ships, the merchant galleys, many varieties existed. As a rule, the smaller ships were rowed and the larger used sails. The oars were used only when approaching or leaving a harbour.[18]

Most merchant galleys sailed from island to island or along the coast, while the sailing ships set course straight out to open sea. The latter were probably used especially for the transport of grain from the Black Sea. Some vessels exceeded by far a capacity of 130 tons. Thucydides mentions a *muriophoros* (tenthousander) which, according to the units of measurement used (talents, *medimnoi*) amounts to a tonnage of anywhere between 260 and 400. Unfortunately we are in the dark about the extent of the sea trade. The sources do not permit a rational guess of the size of the Athenian merchant fleet.[19]

During the night the smaller merchant galleys were drawn on shore; the larger ones and the sailing ships either went on sailing through the night or cast anchor, preferably in sheltered bays. They all had various anchors on board, stored on the fore- and after-deck. Some still had trapezoidally shaped stone anchors, others used more sophisticated anchors consisting of a shank with two arms (Fig. 6.5). According to the historian Strabo, a Greek called Anacharsis who lived about 600 BC invented these anchors. The anchor itself was made of wood as were the two arms, which were fastened to the shank with a lead assembling-piece. This curved lead collar had three rectangular openings so that it could be slipped over the shank and the anchor-arms. At the top of the shank was the anchor-stock which ran parallel with the assembling-piece and consisted of two arms usually of equal length with a box-like opening in the middle to fit the shank. Since ropes, which were too light to weigh down the anchor, were used rather than chains, this heavy lead anchor-stock was fastened to the upper end of the anchor, in order to keep the anchor in the correct horizontal position on the bottom of the sea.[20]

The number of sailors depended on the type of ship. On merchant galleys propelled by oars there were 30 to 50 rowers, on the larger sailing ships no more than 20. They were commanded by the captain and a few steersmen, who were in charge of the equipment of the ship, the sailing list and all organisational

Figure 6.5 Wooden Anchor

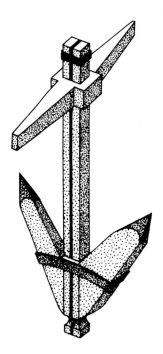

matters. The captain was accountable to the owner of the ship, who was sometimes on board but usually left navigation to the captain while he was represented by a commercial agent.

The social position of all these persons concerned in trade was widely divergent. The sailors' status was very low. They were thetes, but more often they were foreigners or slaves belonging to the merchant or the proprietor. In spite of his important function, the captain at best belonged to the class of *zeugitae*, if he was a citizen at all. Most merchants were not Athenian citizens, but immigrants from other city-states, Megara, Syracuse, Massilia and the cities on the shores of the Black Sea. They were respected by Athens in a special way; they were given the status of metics and had special rights in comparison with other foreigners, such as personal judicial protection and the right to take part in most cults and religious festivals. In return they had military and fiscal obligations. Full citizenship was reserved for Athenians and was only exceptionally conferred on others.[21]

The attitude of the Athenian citizens, especially the elite, must be judged with great care. Negative utterances by the Old Oligarch and Plato might create the impression that there was a rift in Athens between the citizens engaged in agriculture and the foreigners busy with shipping. But considering the tremendous grain imports from the Black Sea to Athens at that time, the immeasurable transport of other agrarian products and the amounts of timber and other materials brought from Macedonia, Asia Minor and the Levant, the absence of the elite in this branch is puzzling. It is highly unlikely that members of the elite were employed as *emporoi*, merchants who hired space in a vessel bound for a particular destination. It is even less probable that there were aristocrats among the *kapeloi*, small pedlars. But it can by no means be ruled out that members of the upper echelons of Athenian society were *naukleroi*, merchants who owned their own ship. They certainly acted as money lenders. Of the 69 money lenders attested in Athens in the fifth and fourth centuries BC 41 were Athenians, eleven metics, 16 foreigners, and one a slave. Most of the loans were not issued by bankers or professional money lenders but by family, friends and neighbours of the borrower. Most merchants depended on maritime credit. In order to pay for the cargo they borrowed money for the duration of the journey. The loan and interest were repaid from the proceeds of the sale of the cargo only on the condition that the ship safely reached its destination. If the ship and its cargo were lost through piracy or shipwreck, the borrower was relieved of the obligation to repay the loan and the loss was borne by the lender. Because this arrangement entailed high risks for the money suppliers the interest rates were high. Percentages of 12.5 to 30 per cent were not unusual. The amount lent varied from 1000 to 4500 drachmae. As a partial guarantee against fraud on the part of the borrower the ship itself could be pledged as security. As a further safeguard a written contract was drawn up, in which the terms and conditions of each loan were recorded in detail.[22]

Being the centre of trade in the Aegean, Athens earned enormous amounts of money in tolls and taxes. When a ship entered the harbour specially trained officials estimated the value of the cargo and levied a toll of 1 to 2 per cent. Dock dues had to be paid for mooring in Emporium. Upon leaving the shippers were once again obliged to pay 1 to 2 per cent of the value of the cargo carried. Even trans-shipment and transit were subject to taxation.

Many shippers tried to dodge these taxes by putting in at the 'thieves' harbour', a natural creek to the west of Piraeus. From there they tried to deliver their cargo to the customer by using all kinds of smuggling tricks.[23]

Most of the money earned by Athens from commercial taxes was invested in the improvement of harbour facilities. Piraeus was enlarged so that it put all other harbours in the shade. Aegina, Corinth, Megara and Chalcis, leading harbours before the Persian Wars, lost in importance and many merchants moved their business to Piraeus. This influx of foreigners turned the city into an international centre. The Athenian elite held themselves far from this melting-pot of nationalities. The bankers who invested their money in trade continued to live in Athens 8 km further inland, but had offices in Piraeus. The foreign merchants had houses built in Piraeus, preferably as close as possible to their warehouses and the market. The carpenters, masons and other craftsmen employed in the construction of jetties, quays, docks and boathouses also went to live in Piraeus just as the sailors of the navy and mercantile fleet. In the harbour district pubs and brothels sprang up which were also frequented by Athenians who had nothing to do with Piraeus. The underworld of Piraeus was notorious in all Greece. Gangs of cut-throats, longing to get rich in a short time, roamed the streets by night, looking for foreign merchants who had celebrated successful transactions in one of the numerous wine-houses.[24]

Run-up to the Peloponnesian War

Athens' dominating position in navigation was a thorn in the flesh for many. Sparta, in the Persian Wars still an ally of the Athenians, enviously watched the Athenian expansion in the Aegean and the fascination which Athens inspired in many Greeks. The Corinthians, all too used to a leading position in trade, grew jealous of the Athenians because they had succeeded in getting the better of their favourably situated harbour on the Isthmus. Athens' attempts to extend its trade in the direction of Sicily and southern Italy aggravated their misgivings, since they did not have the power to call a halt to the increasing influence of Athens' western base at Naupactus. It was they who tried to induce the Spartans to make war upon Athens, convinced that the

Athenians would not be able to stand up against the land forces of the Spartans combined with the Corinthian fleet. Sparta, the leader of the Peloponnesian League, did not yet share this optimism.

The resistance against the Athenian aspirations for power did not only come from outside. Within the Delian League the Athenian attitude met with growing opposition. Many of the allies wanted to break away but were restrained by the powerful Athenian fleet. Confident that in Athenian hands their interests were safe they had misjudged the real intentions of this city. Even when in 454 BC the Athenians transferred the Delian treasury to Athens, there had been no serious protests. After the peace with the Persians in 449 BC there had been proposals from the allied cities to lower the contributions to the League treasury, but in such cases a speech by Pericles was sufficient to torpedo the plan. For years the allies had contributed money to the enlargement of the Athenian fleet and to the embellishment of the city. They were left with only a few ships at their disposal and occasional uprisings by one of the League members were suppressed with increasing force. What the Athenians feared most was outside support for rebellious member states. When in 440 BC an Athenian squadron under the command of Pericles himself had defeated the fleet of rebellious Samos and blockaded the island, a Phoenician fleet was said to be approaching. Pericles took the report seriously and sailed southwards with 60 of the 100 ships that lay before Samos, thus giving the Samians the chance temporarily to break the blockade. No Phoenician fleet was, however, encountered and in the end the rebellion was crushed. There are indications that the Peloponnesian League also considered sending help, but finally decided not to. They wanted to comply with the stipulations of the so-called Thirty-years Peace of 446 BC, one of which was that the Delian and Peloponnesian Leagues acknowledged each other's allies and would refrain from intervention.[25]

Yet, a conflict in this divided Greek world was inevitable. As the power of Athens increased, so did Sparta's envy. The question remains whether the Peloponnesian War was deliberately planned by Sparta and its allies or was the unforeseen consequence of incidents which got out of hand. The island of Corcyra, strategically important on the route to Italy, had come into conflict with Corinth over the control of Epidamnus. In 435 BC the Corcyraeans won a naval battle against a Corinthian squadron.

When in the next year the Corinthians returned with a great fleet, Corcyra wanted to join the Delian League; the Thirty-years Peace, however, forbade the accession of new members. For this reason the Athenians only contracted a defensive alliance with Corcyra after the Corinthians had destroyed 70 of the 110 Corcyraean triremes in 433 BC in a naval battle near the Sybota Islands. The arrival of 30 Athenian triremes was sufficient to curb the aggressive intentions of the Corinthians. Although the Athenians had not violated the treaty of 446 BC, the enmity of the Corinthians now came into the open and they saw to it that the Spartans followed suit. The Corinthians did everything in their power to encourage Potidaea, situated on the peninsula Chalcidice and important for the supply of grain to Athens, to secede from the League. Although Potidaea was originally a Corinthian colony, the mother city had no right to disengage it from Athens. But that was what they did. Potidaea rebelled but was defeated and subsequently besieged. The treaty of 446 BC became a dead letter. At this moment Pericles, convinced that a war could not be avoided, forbade the inhabitants of Megara, who had recently joined the Peloponnesian League, access to the Athenian market and the harbours of the Delian League, thus making the outbreak of war inevitable.[26]

The period of peaceful prosperity in Athens was over. The commercial offices in Piraeus had to face bad times. The shippers were compelled to restrict themselves to the transport of grain and other primary necessities. The centre of maritime activity moved from the trade harbour of Emporium to the naval dockyards of Zea and Munichia. Old triremes were renovated and new ones built. All of Athens responded to the call of Pericles to prepare for the threatening war. Overlooking a sea which they dominated, they felt safe and strong behind their walls and expected a war to be of short duration. Too much trust was put in the loyalty of their allies and their own superiority at sea. They did not realise how much hatred they had aroused against themselves. When Sparta, itself not free from ambitious designs on cities in the Peloponnese who wanted to liberate themselves from her domination, raised banner with the motto 'freedom for all Hellenes', many were willing to give the Spartans the benefit of the doubt, as Thucydides pointedly remarks: 'So bitter was the general feeling against Athens, whether from those who wished to escape from her rule or from those who feared that they would come under it.'[27]

Notes

1. THEMISTOCLES' NAVAL POLICY: Hdt. 7.144.4; Thuc. 1.93.3; Plut. *Them.* 7; Nep. *Them.* 2.3; cf. Pl. *Leg.* 4.706 B–C; Plut. *Phil.* 14.2.
2. PAUSANIAS' COMMAND: Thuc. 1.94–5; 1.128–34; cf. Meiggs, 1972, pp. 71–3.
3. FOUNDATION OF THE DELIAN LEAGUE: Thuc. 1.96–7.1; Plut. *Arist.* 25.1. For literature see Meiggs, 1972, pp. 459–64; Sealey, 1976, pp. 264–5, note 3. ATHENIAN INTIMIDATION: Schuller, 1974.
4. CONQUEST OF EION: Thuc. 1.98; cf. Smart, 1967, pp. 136–8. CONQUEST OF SCYROS: Thuc. 1.98; Plut. *Cim.* 8; *Per.* 17 and 19; cf. Ormerod, 1924, pp. 108–9. GREEK SHIPS AT THE RIVER EURYMEDON: Plut. *Cim.* 12.2; Diod. 11.60.3–6; cf. Thuc. 1.104.2; 1.112.2.
5. CHANGES ON THE TRIREMES: Plut. *Cim.* 12.2; cf. Morrison and Williams, 1968, pp. 162–3; BATTLE AT THE EURYMEDON: Thuc. 1.100.1; Diod. 11.61; Plut. *Cim.* 12–13; Paus. 10.15.4.
6. EGYPTIAN ADVENTURE: Thuc. 1.104; 1.109–10; Diod. 11.71.3–6; 11.74–5; 11.76; cf. Meiggs, 1972, pp. 473–6.
7. BATTLE OF SALAMIS: Thuc. 1.112.2; Plut. *Cim.* 18.1. PEACE OF CALLIAS: Gomme, 1944, pp. 331–9; Meiggs, 1972, pp. 487–95.
8. CLERUCHS: Schuller, 1974, pp. 13–31. IMPORT OF TIMBER: Meiggs, 1982, pp. 125–6. CHANGES IN ATHENS: Arist. *Ath. Pol.* 24.3; cf. Finley, 1973, pp. 172–3.
9. NUMBER OF ROWERS ON THE TRIREMES: Wallinga, 1982, pp. 463–82; SLAVES ON THE TRIREMES: see Sargent, 1927, pp. 264–79; Amit, 1962, pp. 157–8; Amit, 1965, pp. 31–9; Jordan, 1975, pp. 260–6; Casson, 1966, 35–6; Casson, 1971, 322–3.
10. CAPABILITY OF THE ROWERS: Thuc. 2.83–92. TRAINING-PERIODS: Plut. *Per.* 11. PAYMENT OF THE ROWERS: Ar. *Vesp.* 684; Thuc. 3.17.4; 8.45.2; cf. Amit, 1965, pp. 51–2; Jordan, 1975, pp. 111–16 gives many references to ancient sources.
11. ATHENIAN FLEET: Plut. *Per.* 11; Thuc. 2.13.8. ANNUAL CONTRIBUTION: Finley, 1978, pp. 111–12. PAYMENT OF CRAFTSMEN AND GUARDS: Arist. *Ath. Pol.* 24.3. AGE OF THE TRIREMES: Casson, 1971, p. 90; cf. Amit, 1965, p. 27.
12. FOOD: Ar. *Ach.* 541–54. RATIONS AND SUPPLY: Thuc. 8.95.4; 8.100.2; 8.101.2; Xen. *Hell.* 2.1.25.
13. SHIP-SHEDS: Morrison and Williams, 1968, pp. 181–6.
14. IMPORT AND EXPORT: Gomme, 1937, pp. 42–6; Finley, 1973, pp. 132–4.
15. THREAT OF PIRATES: Ormerod, 1924, pp. 108–9. ATHENIAN TRADE POLICY: Meiggs, 1972, pp. 255–72, spec. pp. 265–6; Schuller, 1974, pp. 74–80. COINAGE DECREE: Meiggs, 1972, pp. 167–72.
16. PORTICELLO WRECK: Owen, 1971, pp. 118–29. KYRENIA WRECK: Swiny and Katzev, 1973, pp. 339–60.
17. CONSTRUCTION OF FREIGHTERS: see Casson, 1971, pp. 201–13; Gianfrotta and Pomey, 1981, pp. 230–59.
18. TONNAGE AND DIMENSIONS: Wallinga, 1964, pp. 1–40; Casson, 1971, pp. 170–3. PORT REGULATIONS OF THASOS: *SEG* 17, 1962, 417; cf. Casson, 1971, pp. 183–4.
19. MERCHANT GALLEYS/SAILING SHIPS: Thuc. 7.25.6; Casson, 1971, pp. 157–82. VOLUME OF TRADE: Casson, 1979, pp. 25–32.
20. Kapitän, 1973, pp. 383–4.
21. METICS: cf. Austin and Vidal Naquet, 1977, pp. 99–101; p. 110, note 11 (with further literature); pp. 267–84. SLAVES ON ANCIENT MERCHANTMEN: Dem. 33.8–10; 34.10.
22. APPRECIATION OF TRADE: Hasebroek, 1928, pp. 22–44 stresses the negative appreciation for the position of metics, *contra*: Gomme, 1937, pp. 42–6; Erxleben, 1974, pp. 460–520, spec. p. 502; Casson, 1979, pp. 25–32. INTEREST RATES: Dem. 34.23: 30 per cent; 35.10: 22.5 per cent.

23. TAXES: Meiggs, 1972, pp. 256–7. THIEVES' HARBOUR: Dem. 35.28.

24. LIFE IN PIRAEUS: Amit, 1965, pp. 73–88. STREETGANGS: Dem. 32.10.

25. ATHENIAN ATTITUDE TOWARDS THE MEMBERS OF THE DELIAN LEAGUE: Sealy, 1976, pp. 287–313. SAMIAN REVOLT: Thuc. 1.115–17; Meiggs, 1972, pp. 188–94.

26. BATTLE AT THE SYBOTA ISLANDS: Thuc. 1.49–55. ORIGINS OF THE PELOPONNESIAN WAR: De Ste Croix, 1972 and Kagan, 1971. The latter extensively discusses various other views on pp. 345–74.

27. Thuc. 2.8.4–5.

Chapter Seven

The Peloponnesian War

When under the command of King Archidamus the Spartans left the Peloponnese in the early spring of 431, advanced into Attica and commenced hostilities, they started a war the outcome of which was very difficult to predict. The powerful Athenian fleet was unequalled in the Greek world. The Spartans, on the other hand, had hardly any ships at their disposal and in naval matters largely depended on the know-how of the Corinthians; but they had an army which, though not great numerically, did not have its equal in Greece. The 6000–7000 men that the Spartans could bring into the field were, because of their intensive training, a match for many times that number of opponents.

The Spartans adopted the same tactics as the Persians in 480 BC. Plundering and setting fire they advanced through the vineyards and olive groves without encountering serious resistance. The effect of these destructive actions was, however, smaller than 50 years before. Though the olives and grapes were lost and many Attic farmers had to abandon their land and flee to the city, life in Athens itself, however, was not seriously influenced by the devastations in the countryside. Freighters sailed in from all directions with the necessary foodstuffs; the citizens felt safe behind the long walls built by Pericles following the plans of Themistocles. These walls linked Athens with the port of Piraeus and could be defended by small garrisons.

As long as the Athenians were masters of the seas, confinement behind the city walls did not disturb them, but enemy pressure on the Athenian bases rapidly increased. Corinth in particular was expected to take action, since it was the only city-state hostile to Athens that had a good fleet. The trade routes from Athens to the west, where Naupactus, Corcyra and to a lesser extent Messina were the principal bases, could be badly affected by attacks from Corinth and its daughter city and ally Syracuse. To go west Athenian ships had to sail round the hostile Peloponnese. Fully aware of this, Pericles personally led an expedition with the objective of looking for possible bases in the Peloponnese.[1]

In 430 BC the Athenians had to endure a terrible blow. In the overcrowded harbour quarter of Piraeus a pestilence broke out which soon spread to Athens and claimed more than 5000 victims including Pericles. Panic seized the masses and allowed more radical figures, who thought that pushfulness could quickly restore Athens to its old glory, to take charge. Yet, the Spartans were still in Attica and threatened the silvermines, so vital for Athens' economy. Moreover, many of the allies were eagerly waiting for a chance to free themselves from the Athenian yoke.[2]

Since the Athenians put less and less trust in others, they had to conduct war and patrol in many places at the same time. In the Aegean their main objective was to stay in control of the sea lanes. The movements of unwilling allies were closely watched. The fleet units patrolling the west of Greece were smaller; the Athenian interests in the region were less important and Athenian triremes mainly operated close to their base, the harbour of Naupactus. Sometimes, however, they were forced into action, as in 429 BC when an Athenian squadron of 20 ships under the command of an admiral named Phormio was confronted by a superior force of 47 Corinthian ships. These were heavier than the Athenian ones and consequently less manoeuvrable and less fitted for tactical purposes. The crews too were of unequal quality. The Athenian rowers were experienced and well-trained. The Corinthians, on the other hand, had added few war exploits to their record in the recent past. Afraid that the swift Athenian triremes should perform a breakthrough, the Corinthians arranged their ships in as great a circle as possible with the prows facing outward and the sterns facing inward, so close together that the Athenians could not possibly sail through. Possibly they adopted this strategy because of the success Themistocles had had with it at Artemisium (see p. 52).

Phormio's reaction was as daring as it was genial. He ordered the Athenian captains to sail in line ahead and to encircle the enemy without attacking them. They were to sail continuously closer to the enemy circle, thus giving the impression that an attack was imminent. Phormio based this strategy on the assumption that the wind, though weak at that moment, as on most mornings, would freshen in the course of the day and create problems for the close formation of the Corinthian ships. This did, indeed, happen. The ships collided, the oarsmen shouted all sorts of insults to each other and panic broke out. Commands were lost in the hubbub and the rowers' lack of experience showed itself in the resulting confusion. They rowed without rhythm and the steersmen lost control of the ships. This was what Phormio had been waiting for. His ships went from line ahead to line abreast and attacked the enemy whose circle defence was hopelessly upset. The first ship that the Athenians captured was one of the admiralty ships. Subsequently they overpowered every ship they came across. In total they captured twelve ships and took the crews prisoner.[3]

This defeat was a blow for the Peloponnesians. The superiority of the Athenian fleet over the Corinthian was accepted, albeit reluctantly, but that a small Athenian squadron was able to make a laughing-stock of a much larger unit of Corinthian ships was an unexpected disappointment. The Corinthians did not acquiesce in this situation but started preparations for a new sea-fight to wipe out their shame. Many cities of the Peloponnese had to contribute the few ships they possessed. Within a short time the new fleet consisted of 77 ships, whereas Phormio still only had the 20 ships that had brought him his victory. Yet the Corinthians were by no means confident about a successful outcome, nor were, however, the Athenian oarsmen. Although they felt stronger than their opponents, they feared that a ratio of 4:1 might be too much even for them. In a glowing speech designed to restore calm, Phormio impressed on his men that little was to be feared from the enemy fleet which was, he said, as inferior in morale as it was superior in numbers.

The Corinthians had learned from Phormio that a sea-battle could not be won with a great fleet propelled by enthusiastic but untrained crews. They now set to work more warily. They knew that, since their ships were more sluggish than the Athenian ones, they had to avoid fighting the Athenians in open sea. Everything had to be done to entice the Athenian ships into the entrance of the Gulf of Corinth. For six long days the two fleets confronted one another without anything happening. At sunrise on the seventh day, the Peloponnesians set out in a formation of four lines of 19 ships, keeping close to their own coastline. With the 20 swiftest ships on the right wing they entered the bay, pretending that they were going to attack Naupactus. The Athenians, concerned about their western base, followed line ahead along the coast in the direction of the threatened place, under the cover of a small land force of Messenians. Suddenly the Peloponnesians turned around and rowed at the Athenians at a very high speed hoping to cut off their return to the open sea. Eleven ships escaped the Peloponnesian attack, but the other nine were pursued to the coast and destroyed. Many of the crews were killed. The Corinthians also suffered losses because the Messenians ran into the water with full equipment, clambered on board and joined the fight.

The remaining Athenian ships fled to Naupactus. There they cast anchor before the entrance of the harbour with their prows directed at the enemy, waiting for the final attack. By chance they avoided a defeat. In deep water outside the entrance a freighter was at anchor. An Athenian captain, chased by the Peloponnesians, thought of a desperate manoeuvre: he made directly for the freighter, suddenly swerved around it and came into a perfect position to ram the pursuing enemy ship, which sank instantly. The frustration of the Peloponnesian crews was great and the Athenians immediately launched a counter-attack, captured six Spartan ships and re-captured their own.[4]

These first confrontations at sea showed that the Athenians were still tactically superior but it had to be acknowledged that their opponents were going to be a serious threat at sea. And when the Peloponnesian fleet, unsuccessfully, attempted to take Piraeus by surprise, uneasiness took hold of the Athenians as they realised that they had to watch the east coast as well. From then on they took care to guard the harbours, in particular Piraeus. Yet in the first years of the war the Athenians had some successes. The revolt of Mytilene on Lesbos was crushed, which deterred some other rebellious League members. Trade in the Aegean was untouched and on Sicily Athens obtained a foothold when the city of Messina, strategically situated on the passage between Sicily and Italy, fell into Athenian hands.[5]

Indirectly Messina caused a new confrontation. In 426 BC an Athenian naval squadron was sent to this city, to the great dislike of the inhabitants, who interpreted this as the beginning of further troop concentrations. Caught in a violent storm the 40 Athenian triremes had to take refuge in the harbour of Pylos on the west coast of the Peloponnese. Because the storm continued for several days, the crews, urged by the admiral Demosthenes, proceeded to strengthen the harbour and to build a rampart. When the storm had abated, Demosthenes stayed behind with five triremes in order to set up a new base. The Spartans assumed that they could easily raze to the ground what had been built in haste. Afraid of the Athenian fleet, they blocked the entrances to the harbour, among other things by occupying the island of Sphacteria, separated from Pylos by a narrow channel. Here they stationed c. 420 hoplites. The plan was to launch an attack from the north-east with a land force and from the south-west by sea. Aided by the natural formation of the terrain, which through its inhospitable character was to the advantage of the defenders, the Athenians succeeded in beating off the attack on both sides. The arrival of a large fleet did much to raise their spirits. The Spartans, on the other hand, became despondent.

Once again an action unexpected by the Spartans settled the matter. After the successful tactical manoeuvres in the first battle in the Gulf of Corinth and the stroke of luck in the second battle, this time it was the element of surprise that brought victory to the Athenians. While, on the second day after the arrival of the Athenian reinforcements, the Spartans were still organising their defence, the Athenians suddenly attacked through both channels, captured five Spartan triremes and cut off the garrison on Sphacteria from the main body of the Spartan army. Faced with the possible loss of 420 men the Spartans proposed an armistice as the basis of a peace agreement. As evidence of their good will they gave all the 60 warships at their disposal to the Athenians, on condition that they would get them back if no definitive peace came about. The decision was up to the Athenian Assembly and following a motion of the radical Cleon the citizens rejected the proposals. Cleon even refused to give back the 60 Spartan warships offered as security. Sparta's fleet, built up with so much effort, was lost without striking a blow, so that the Peloponnesians became completely dependent on the Corinthian fleet. Under the command of Cleon and Demosthenes the Spartan garrison on Sphacteria was finally overpowered and taken prisoner.[6]

Yet, in Athens, too, a desire for peace existed, as became evident a few years later. The negative results of the hoplites at Delium in Boeotia and the capture of the Athenian colony of Amphipolis in Thrace by the Spartans had a bearing on this desire. It was the loss of Amphipolis, a port of call on the long corn supply route from the Black Sea, that particularly hit the Athenians. They did everything they could to regain possession but failed. Cleon, who was personally in charge of the attacking forces, lost his life as did his Spartan opponent Brasidas. The death of the two protagonists of the war cleared the way for a peace concluded in 421 BC. It was agreed that conquered territories would be given back.

Looking back upon ten years of warfare it may be concluded that the balance of power had not been changed very much. On land Sparta was clearly superior, but as long as the Athenians and their allies could compensate by naval supremacy, this had few negative consequences. The Athenian trade in the Aegean was unaffected and in the western trade area it had been possible to check the interests of the Corinthians. Athens had, however, become much more dependent on trade than before the Peloponnesian War because the landed estates in Attica had been devastated by the repeated Spartan invasions to such an extent that they remained unfit for cultivation for a long time. Because Sparta, against the terms of the peace, refused to withdraw from Amphipolis which was so important for the Athenian imports of grain, a fresh outbreak of hostilities never seemed far away, all the more so since the increasing Athenian population demanded more grain. To satisfy at least part of this demand hopes were set on Sicily.

In Sicily a situation had arisen which resembled that in Greece itself. The Dorian and the Ionian cities were continuously at odds with one another. Led by Syracuse, the former were much stronger. The Ionian part of the population repeatedly tried to get support from their kinsmen in Greece but so far their assistance had been confined to sending small squadrons of 20 to 30 triremes, which did not alarm Syracuse. Some cities who had at first built their hopes on Athens had gone over to Syracuse. Initially, Athens had not taken all this too seriously because full attention was needed on other fronts. But after 421 BC Athens began attempts to increase its influence in the west both for economic and strategic reasons. While the Sicilian grain would be a welcome addition to the supplies from the Black Sea, the growing power of Syracuse was a cause of serious concern for the Athenians. In 474 BC Syracuse had defeated the Etruscans, up to then masters of the Tyrrhenian Sea, and had built up a maritime empire which brought great prosperity. Like Athens, Syracuse repeatedly tried to ally itself with other cities, if need be by force.[7]

One of the cities rebelling against the interference of Syracuse was Segesta, involved in a conflict with Selinus, which received help from Syracuse. When the Segestan request for aid from

Athens was granted a conflict began that was to bring about drastic changes in the Greek world. The honeyed words of the Segestan emissaries persuaded the Athenians into a war the consequences of which they could not foresee. In the first instance the Assembly decided to despatch 60 triremes under the command of Lamachus, Nicias and Alcibiades. Between the latter two, who each had a considerable body of supporters, a heated discussion broke out over the use of an expedition of this kind, which was unprecedented in Greek history. Nicias went out of his way to withhold the Athenians from this risky adventure, but his words: 'I say that by sailing to Sicily you will not only leave many enemies behind, but will also attract new ones', found little sympathy. His opponent Alcibiades, a man of doubtful reputation in view of his extravagant manner of living but very popular on account of his clear tongue, was more successful. Prompted by a limitless confidence in the Athenian naval superiority, his words roused the people's enthusiasm. Like Alcibiades most Athenians were convinced of their ability to extend their influence, not only in Sicily but all over the Greek world, because their opponents would be filled with fear at the sight of their power. Therefore, Nicias' attempt to deter the Athenians by pointing out the massive preparations necessary for such an expedition had just the opposite effect. Everything was done in order to organise an expedition on the grandest scale.

In June 415 BC, waved farewell by the crowds jamming the quays of Piraeus, a fleet set sail to join the allies at Corcyra; it consisted of two penteconters and 134 triremes, 60 of which were slimmer and faster than the others, accompanied by 131 transport ships carrying 5100 hoplites, 480 peltasts, 700 slingers and 120 mercenaries from Megara as well as immense quantities of provisions.

It was clear that the aim of the mission, support for Segesta, hardly justified a fleet of this size. In Syracuse the real intentions of Athens were well understood, but in spite of the exhortations of their most experienced leader Hermocrates, its inhabitants were not too concerned about the threatening invasion. Up to a point they were right in not being too anxious because the irresolution of the Athenian command was considerable. Nicias proposed to attack Selinus — since this was the pretext under which they had set out — and having captured the city, to sail along the coasts of Sicily to show their power and then to return home. Under the

Figure 7.1 Siege of Syracuse

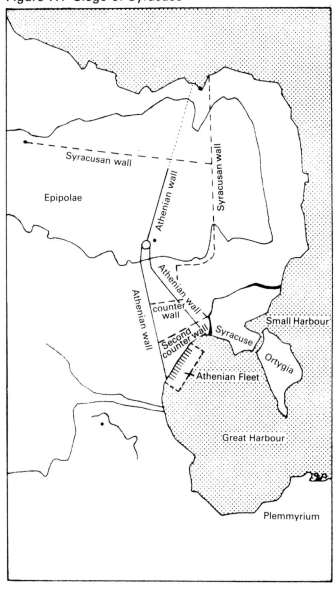

—————— Athenian walls

– – – – – – Syracusan walls

circumstances Lamachus had by far the best plan. He wanted to attack Syracuse, the real aim of the expedition, without delay. His standing was, however, not high and he found no support. Alcibiades' plan met with approval: he proposed to incite the cities of Sicily to defect from Syracuse and to set up Messina as a base. Alcibiades himself would not be there any more to take part in this. He was recalled to Athens on a charge of having intentionally damaged the heads of the Hermes statues in Athens the night before the departure of the fleet. But during the return journey he managed to shake off the *Salaminia*, the ship that was escorting him back to Athens, and fled to Sparta.

This is not the place to give a complete account of the experiences of the Athenian army, which in the beginning of the 'Sicilian Adventure' saw far more action than the fleet. The oarsmen passed their days in idleness. Even training was neglected, convinced as the Athenians were of an easy victory when it should come to a sea-battle. Only occasionally did they undertake a surprise attack on merchant ships of the Sicilian cities. In the spring of 414 BC the Athenian hoplites attacked Syracuse, occupied the heights of Epipolae which overlooked the city, and expected, not without reason, to be able to win the war of attrition that was bound to follow. They tried to cut Syracuse off from the rest of Sicily by constructing a wall in a north-south direction, which the Syracusans in their turn hoped to break through by building another wall perpendicular to it. The fleet sailed into the 'Great Harbour' of Syracuse and a link between the two units merely seemed a question of time (Fig. 7.1).

In the meantime in Greece tension was mounting. Now that the fleet had been away for a year already, the Athenians felt increasingly uncertain, particularly when a letter from Nicias reported that the opposition was stronger than expected and recommended that either new ships and men be sent or that the expedition be ended, which was scarcely possible without loss of face. In this matter the interference of the Peloponnesian cities was not without significance. Corinth, the mother city of Syracuse, had sympathetically received a delegation from the beleaguered colony and had had little difficulty in persuading the Spartans to intervene in the Sicilian conflict. Alcibiades had a considerable influence on the Spartan strategy. He had advised the Spartans to transfer the war once again to Attica by occupying the deme of Decelea from which they could control the silver mines of

Laurium. So Athens found itself in great need now that it had to divide its attention over two fronts. The siege of Syracuse stagnated with the arrival of the Spartan Gylippus, who had a stimulating influence on the Sicilian cities. He entered Syracuse without the Athenians being able to do much to stop him and boosted morale. The departure in the spring of 413 BC from Piraeus of 60 Athenian warships under the command of Demosthenes, accompanied by an unknown number of transport ships with *c*. 1200 heavily armed soldiers, was much less exultant than that two years earlier when thousands of Athenians had gathered on the harbour front.[8]

Gylippus' energetic action began to yield success immediately. He completed the wall perpendicularly to that constructed by the Athenians; thus the continuity of the Athenian attack line was broken. Thereupon the Athenians shifted their camp from Epipolae to Plemmyrium, the hilly country to the south of the harbour, in order to guarantee co-operation between army and fleet. From there, however, a direct siege of Syracuse was no longer possible; water had to be fetched from a long distance and other foraging in the hinterland of Sicily ran into difficulties through the activities of the Syracusan cavalry.

Gylippus' decision to transfer the war to the harbour somewhat surprised the Syracusans, even when he gave a detailed explanation: The Athenians, he said, were no experienced seafarers by origin; they were really landlubbers, even more so than the Syracusans, and had been compelled by the Persians to become a sea-power. By unexpectedly standing up to the Athenian fleet the Syracusans would score a moral victory. At that time, the fleet of the Syracusans consisted of 80 triremes, 35 on the north bank of the 'Great Harbour' and 45 in the 'Small Harbour'. Since the docks and ships' warehouses were also situated here it looked like a naval base much more than the 'Great Harbour', where the ships were only protected by emergency facilities. At *c*. 40 m from the shore, a little more than the length of a trireme, rows of stakes ensured a safe mooring place for the ships and served as protection for the provisional wharves.

Since the Syracusans were taking the initiative they had to seek out the Athenians in the 'Great Harbour'. Before their fleet was properly assembled, the Athenians had manned 60 triremes, 35 of which intercepted the Syracusan squadron from the 'Small Harbour' at the entrance of the 'Great Harbour'; the remaining 25 triremes attacked the enemy ships on the north bank of the 'Great Harbour'. There was no question of tactical manoeuvres. The Syracusan ships doing battle before the harbour entrance forced back the Athenians and sailed into the harbour. But due to a serious lack of order they got in each other's way and were finally driven back to their base by the Athenians. Thereupon the Athenian ships turned *en masse* against the enemy in the 'Great Harbour'. They drove them into a corner by the hastily constructed wooden palisade and sank eleven enemy ships, losing three themselves. Convinced that behind the palisade even more ships could be captured, the Athenians attempted in various ways to destroy the wooden wall. A ship of more than 250 tons, equipped with wooden towers and parapets, pulled out the stakes with windlasses or broke them off. Divers sawed off the stakes under water. The effect of all these activities was small, because the Syracusans set up a new palisade directly behind the stakes destroyed by the Athenians.[9]

In spite of the Syracusans' lack of success in this first sea-battle, their morale had remained high, for when the attention of the Athenian hoplites was fixed on the fight in the harbour, the land forces had made a successful raid on the Athenian forts of Plemmyrium. They killed many Athenians and captured large amounts of material including sails and oars. This was a heavy blow to the Athenian army: convoys of transport vessels carrying essential supplies of food now had to sail along enemy territory.

The Athenian fleet had, it is true, beaten off the first attack on its position but the Syracusans became more and more dangerous, particularly when a Syracusan squadron of twelve ships had intercepted and destroyed a convoy of Athenian freighters laden with timber for the Athenian warships. The Syracusans had decided to take the offensive again after reports of an otherwise trivial confrontation in the Gulf of Corinth had reached them. In the same narrow bay where 16 years previously Phormio had won a dazzling victory, 25 Corinthian and 33 Athenian triremes came to grips with each other. The Corinthians had in the meantime introduced a modification in the construction of their vessels. They had reinforced their ships with extra beams, so that they could ram their opponents with greater force while incurring less damage due to blows inflicted on them. Because the projecting beams were located at different heights, the outrigger constructions could also be pierced. The Corinthians destroyed seven Athenian vessels, while they themselves lost only three.

Gylippus tried to re-create this situation. Everything had to be done to prevent the Athenian rowers from carrying out their open sea tactics and proceeding to the *diekplous* or the *periplous*. The smaller the space in which the fighting was to take place, the more likely the Syracusans would be to win. They wanted a fight between ship and ship, prow and prow, a tactic which in Athenian circles was interpreted as lack of skill. But the Syracusans were convinced that this tactic would bring them success, particularly since the Athenians, if they should be driven back, could go nowhere else except to the shore and then only a short distance to their own camp; the rest of the harbour was in the hands of the Syracusans, who were expecting the Athenian ships to get in each other's way due to the lack of room. The outlet of the harbour was also controlled by the Syracusans and was partly blocked by sunken merchantmen.

Whether the Athenians liked it or not, they had to go into battle under unfavourable circumstances. But for a while they held their position without appreciable losses, due to lack of co-ordination on the part of the Syracusans rather than to the strategy of the Athenian admiral Nicias, who with his 80 fighting-fit triremes did not dare to engage in an open fight with the 75 Syracusan vessels. Nicias' indecisiveness did not further the Athenian cause, as soon became clear. The Syracusans, who had good connections with the hinterland and could replace exhausted crews, exploited the weariness of the Athenian oarsmen. After an insignificant skirmish the Syracusan oarsmen made off as if they were returning to their base. The Athenians, delighted because they had so easily shaken them off, disembarked and started to eat, believing that there would be no more fighting that day. Suddenly, however, the Syracusan vessels appeared once more. Cursing and grumbling the Athenians reluctantly confronted the enemy. Exhausted as they were, they wanted, against the will of Nicias, to force a decision and took the offensive. According to their plan, the Syracusans attacked the Athenians frontally. The battering beams on the Syracusan ships tore open the bows of the Athenian triremes and caused heavy damage to the outrigger constructions. The Athenians panicked. Moreover, Syracusans sailed in small vessels between the Athenian ships and hurled spears at the rowers. The Athenians turned about and sought refuge under the protection of freighters hastily moored before the palisade. The freighters, fitted with grappling-irons, prevented further Syracusan attacks.

But this did not affect the joy of the Syracusans. They had destroyed seven Athenian ships and damaged the outrigger constructions of many others to such a degree that repairs were scarcely possible, particularly due to lack of timber.[10]

The arrival of the reinforcements under the command of Demosthenes gave the Athenians new courage. Particularly the 73 new triremes, 22 of which were supplied by allies, were a welcome addition to the battered Athenian fleet. Demosthenes straightaway took the offensive; with the 5000 hoplites he had brought with him, he launched an attack on the Syracusan wall, but after some initial successes he had to give up. Demoralised by this failure he wanted to break off hostilities altogether, go back to Athens by sea as long as it was still possible and continue the struggle from there. But Nicias, terrified to be held personally responsible for the failure of the expedition, persuaded him to stay. Valuable time was wasted. In the end the Athenians had no choice but to depart, but then an eclipse of the moon occurred and the soothsayers advised a waiting period of three times nine days, which created another delay and an almost hopeless situation.

As soon as the Syracusans got wind of the Athenian plans to evacuate, they did not give them another moment's peace. The Athenian fleet became their main target. In the harbour, which was slowly beginning to resemble a ships' cemetery, 76 Syracusan triremes advanced on the Athenians, who confronted them with 86 vessels. One of the Athenian admirals, Eurymedon, stayed on the right wing, far from the battle area in the centre where fighting had started instantly, with the intention of executing a *periplous*. But there were no signs of the co-ordination which had characterised Athenian manoeuvres in the past. The exhausted oarsmen in the centre were no more than a shadow of the proud crews who only a few years before had conceitedly looked down on their opponents. Now they were beaten in a very short time. Next the Syracusans turned against Eurymedon, who was isolated from the rest of the badly battered fleet, killed him and many of his rowers and destroyed his ships. The left wing of the Athenian fleet had not yet been involved in the fight but fled off along the coast in despair hotly pursued by the Syracusans. If the auxiliary troops from Etruria had not performed a magnificent feat of arms, Athenian losses would have been far greater than the 18 vessels which they already had lost.

Although the Athenian land forces had not yet suffered any

such disastrous defeats, their morale had dropped below zero. The fleet, once consisting of two powerful armadas, was apparently unable to beat the Syracusans; worse still, the Syracusans were preparing to defeat the Athenian fleet once and for all. For the Athenians there was only one way out: the open sea and then back to Athens. The Syracusans did not even grant them that. Fully confident as a result of the successful events of the last few weeks, they wished to set an example for the whole Greek world.

Thucydides, who appraises the situation with great precision, describes the preparations on both sides. Both parties were convinced that the coming engagement would be decisive. The Athenians, weakened by losses, tried at all cost to evade a fight and to get away. But this was precisely what the Syracusans wanted to prevent. The Athenian fleet, which for a long time had ruthlessly attacked its opponents, was now in its turn threatened by an enemy who was not prepared to compromise. The Syracusans wanted to acquire fame and honour for now and for later; future epics were to tell the story of the Syracusans who defied and defeated the Athenians and their allies, while jeopardising their own city.

The preparations of the mightiest city in Sicily aimed at the total destruction of the Athenian fleet. The harbour mouth, 1600 m wide, was closed off by triremes, merchant ships and small boats. The Athenians, on the other hand, took countermeasures which clearly betrayed their panic. All the tactical skills acquired in the course of half a century of naval hegemony were neglected. Instead they reverted to the strategy with which they had beaten the Persians in the bay of Salamis in 480 BC. They felt compelled once again to conduct a land battle at sea. It was, they believed, the only method to stand a chance against the massive battering beams that had created so much damage in the previous fights. They constructed grappling-irons intended to prevent enemy ships from withdrawing after dealing a blow. The most difficult task was given to the hoplites. In great numbers — the exact number per trireme is not known — they were posted on the deck with the express command not to detach the irons from the enemy ship until its deck had been cleared of all soldiers. About 110 ships were thus equipped and manned. In the meantime, the Syracusans had got wind of the new Athenian weapon. To protect themselves against it they covered the prows and large parts of the decks of their ships with leather. They reckoned that the grappling-irons would slide off or merely tear the leather.

All preparations having been made, the commanders delivered their last speeches. Without trying to conceal the wretchedness of the situation, Nicias impressed upon the Athenians that only victory would let them see their city again. Gylippus, who could tell a much happier story, duly emphasised the changed method of combat of the Athenians. In his opinion the Athenians, so experienced in naval battles, betrayed their present impotence by putting on board the vessels heavy infantry and spear-throwers. That the Syracusans had only 75 triremes to oppose the 110 of the Athenians, they regarded as an advantage; in the harbour 110 ships could not all manoeuvre at the same time without getting in each other's way.

The Syracusans were the first to set out. A part of their fleet rowed to the blockade which sealed the harbour in order to defend it. The remaining ships formed a large circle to be able to surround the Athenians from all sides if they attacked the obstructions. After weighing anchor the Athenians went straight to the harbour mouth, encouraged by the land forces.

How precisely the battle proceeded, what tactics the various admirals and captains used, we do not know. It may well be that the Athenians merely wanted to break the blockade and wore themselves out by attacking the massive prows of the Syracusan ships. We do know that there had never been such a bitter fight in Greek naval history. In all its simplicity Thucydides' account offers an outstanding description of the atmosphere of the battle:

When the Athenians on their side came up to the barrier with the impetus of their first charge, they overpowered the ships stationed in front of it and tried to break down the obstructions. After this the Syracusans and their allies bore down on them from all sides, and soon the fighting was not only in front of the barrier but all over the harbour. And hard fighting it was — more so than in any of the previous battles. There was no hanging back among the rowers on either side in bringing their ships into action whenever they were ordered, and among the steersmen there were great battles of skill and great rivalry between each other. And when ship met ship, the soldiers on board did their best to see that what was done on deck was up to the standard shown elsewhere; every one, in fact, each in his own job, strove to appear the best. Many ships crowded in upon each other in a small area (indeed, never before had so many ships fought together in so narrow a space. There were almost 200 of them on the two sides); consequently there were not many attacks made with the ram amidships, since there was no backing water and no chance of breaking through the turning about; collisions were much more frequent, ship crashing into ship in their efforts to escape from or to attack some other vessel. All the time that one ship was bearing down upon another, javelins, arrows, and stones were shot or hurled on to it without cessation by the men on the decks; and once the ships met, the soldiers fought hand to hand, each trying to board the enemy. Because of the narrowness of the space, it often happened that a ship was ramming and being rammed at the same time, and that two, or sometimes more, ships found themselves jammed against one, so that the steersmen had to think of defence on one side and attack on the other and, instead of being able to give their attention to one point at a time, had to deal with many different things in all directions; and the great din of all these ships crashing together was not only frightening in itself, but also made it impossible to hear the orders given by the boatswains. And indeed, in the ordinary course of duty and in the present excitement of battle, plenty of instructions were given and plenty of shouting was done by the boatswains on either side. To the Athenians they cried out, urging them to force the passage and now, if ever, to seize resolutely upon the chance of a safe return to their country; and to the Syracusans and their allies the cry was that it would be a glorious thing to prevent the enemy from escaping and for each man to bring honour to his own country by winning the victory. Then, too, the generals on each side, if they saw anyone at all backing away without good reason, would shout out to the captain by name and ask, in the case of Athenians, whether they were retreating because they thought they would feel more at home on land where their enemies were supreme than on the sea, which, with so much labour, they had made their own, and, in the case of the Syracusans, whether they were running from an enemy who was himself in flight, since they knew well enough that the Athenians, for their part, were longing to get away as best they could.

Finally, after the battle had lasted for a long time, the Syracusans and their allies broke the Athenian resistance, followed them up with great shouting and cheering, and chased them back, clearly and decisively, to the land. And now the whole fleet, apart from the ships which were captured afloat, ran on shore, some going one way, some another, and the men fled from their ships towards the camp. As for the army on land, the period of uncertainty was over, now one impulse overpowered them all as they cried aloud and groaned in pain for what had happened, some going down to give help to the ships, some to guard what was left of their wall, while others (and these were now in the majority) began to think of themselves and how they could get away safe. Indeed, the panic of this moment was something greater than anything they had ever known.

So much for Thucydides' account. The Syracusans scored a dazzling victory, put the wrecks in tow, the dead on board and returned to the city for an enormous celebration. Yet the Athenians still had 60 more or less usable vessels left. When Nicias proposed to try a breakthrough once again, the oarsmen refused, completely demoralised by the defeat. The next decision of Nicias and Demosthenes was the most degrading in Athenian naval history. They ordered the oarsmen to set fire to their own triremes to prevent them from falling into Syracusan hands. But even this task was only partly carried out. The Syracusans captured most of the ships. The defeated Athenians fled overland in the hope of reaching a friendly city. Catana was mentioned as a place of refuge. They never got that far. Retreating in disorder, they were pursued by Gylippus and repeatedly forced to give battle. The Athenians held out for a few days only and then they were defeated. The remnants of the army surrendered to Gylippus. The Athenian commanders Nicias and Demosthenes were put to death; the rest were thrown into the stone-quarries of Achradina and died miserably or were released to become slaves. Only a few escaped the vengeance of the Syracusans and reached hearth and home.[11]

When these events were first reported in Athens, they were scarcely believed. When, six months later, the gravity of the situation sank in, the Athenian citizens thought that the end of their city was at hand. People generally expressed the fear that the Syracusans would take advantage of Athens' shortage of ships and crews and would sail to Attica to help the Spartans, who still held Decelea, in the siege of Athens.

When after some time the emotions had died down and the Athenians had got a clearer view of the situation, they directed their attention wholly to the Aegean area, where they were still lords and masters. Although the Sicilian defeat had no immediate consequences for Athens' sovereignty in the Aegean, their image of invincibility had suffered considerably. Member cities who had stayed in the Delian League out of fear of the mighty fleet of Athens now saw the chance to get out. The Spartans showed themselves more frequently in the Aegean. Instructed by the Corinthians they had mastered the art of naval warfare. The member cities, not unaware of this, turned to Sparta for help in their defection from Athens. Lesbos and Chios were the first to change sides.

To Athens it was a matter of vital interest to maintain their supremacy at sea. All grain came in by sea. A blockage of the supply route could have disastrous consequences. It was, therefore, essential to keep open the supply routes from the Hellespont and the harbours where the heavily laden corn-ships could shelter for the night outside the enemy's sphere of influence. Most important for the balance of power in Greece was the renewed interference of Persia in Greek affairs. Since the peace of Callias in 449 BC the Persians had not shown themselves in the Aegean. The satraps in Asia Minor, Pharnabazus and Tissaphernes, were instructed by King Darius II to bring about the defection of the small cities in that region. Pharnabazus directed his attention first and foremost to the Hellespont; Tissaphernes was active in Ionia. Both had hopes of putting the cities' tribute to Athens into their own pockets in order to be able to pay the taxes to the king in Susa. Since they had not got a good fleet at their disposal, they approached the Peloponnesian League and promised support in the fight against Athens.

Despite this hostile coalition, the year 412 BC, which they had viewed with so much concern, was not unfavourable to the Athenians. They used all the money and timber they could lay their hands on to build new ships and train new crews. Various bases were set up in order to check hostile forces. The greatest part of the fleet cast anchor in the harbour of Samos in order to keep a close watch on the Peloponnesian fleet.

The following year, 411 BC, brought new, unforeseen difficulties for Athens. The oligarchic party, a faction of little significance during the time of Athens' prosperity, saw its opportunity, overthrew democracy and limited citizenship to 5000 men. If their plans had been carried out, the crews of the fleet would no longer have been Athenian citizens. But it did not get as far as that. The crews of the fleet at Samos opposed the new rulers with might and main and enlisted a man who was feared by the leading Athenians, Alcibiades. He had lost the confidence of the Spartan king Agis for several reasons including the seduction of the queen. When he was on the point of being arrested he fled to Ionia and advised the Persian satrap Tissaphernes not to ally himself with the Spartans against the Athenians. He would do better to stay out of the conflict while ensuring that the balance between Sparta and Athens remained even. Tissaphernes followed the advice of Alcibiades, reduced the subsidy to the Spartan fleet and abandoned his plan to introduce the Phoenician fleet once again in the Aegean. When the oligarchs did not recall Alcibiades to Athens as a reward for his diplomacy he took the side of the crews of the fleet and was appointed commander. Within a short time the Athenian democracy was restored.[12]

As long as hostilities, consisting of threats from the Peloponnesian fleet and Athenian counteractions, were limited to the coast of Ionia, they were not taken too seriously in Athens. The fleet of the Spartans and Corinthians, reinforced by 20 Syracusan ships, lay in the harbour of Miletus but was kept in check by the Athenian fleet based on Samos. Trade in the Aegean was not hampered by the small scuffles which took place from time to time. Things got more difficult for the Athenians when the Peloponnesian fleet transferred its activities to the Hellespont and threatened to endanger the Athenian trade routes from the Black Sea. The chances of success were not negligible because the Spartans could count on an increasing number of defectors from the Delian League and on the Persian satrap Pharnabazus, who, unlike Tissaphernes, willingly provided extensive financial and military support.

When in the summer of 411 BC the Spartans left the harbour of Miletus, the Athenians weighed anchor and likewise made for the Hellespont. Keeping a close eye on each other and denying their opponent the position and opportunity for a surprise *diekplous* or *periplous*, they took the risk of fighting in the Hellespont itself. The Athenians, bearing in mind the shattering defeat in the harbour of Syracuse, were rather nervous to take action, all the more so since the Spartans had got the better strategic position.

The Spartans had sailed deep into the Hellespont as far as Abydus and Lampsacus and now advanced from the north with 87 ships in line ahead following the current. The Athenians, who had to row against the current, had 76 ships at their disposal, mostly of poorer quality than the Spartan ships — after the losses in Sicily the new ships had been built in great haste — but with crews trained in the Athenian tradition. The Spartan oarsmen had had little practice since they had been trained by Corinthian and Syracusan instructors, who emphasised boarding rather than ramming tactics.

After the Athenian left wing, sailing in line ahead, had passed the prominent mountain range of Cynossema so that the other ships could no longer see them, the Peloponnesians moved in. The Athenians turned their right wing away from the coast. The Spartans attacked the weakened centre and drove many ships on to the shore. Discipline, however, was lacking: made careless by their success they pursued the enemy with a great number of ships, but in breaking their formation they fell into disarray. The distance between individual ships carried away by the current grew greater and greater, but they paid no attention, busy as they were driving away the Athenians. When the right wing of the Athenians unexpectedly turned up again, the Spartans fled. Spread over the Hellespont they were an ideal target for the Athenians, who took full advantage of the situation, especially when the left wing which had stayed in the vicinity of Cynossema joined in. As if losing 21 ships was not yet enough the Spartans were also thwarted by the elements. Reinforcements summoned from Euboea were wrecked near Mount Athos. About 50 ships were lost. Once again this mountain had helped the Athenians.

The Athenian victory at Cynossema was not due to any carefully worked out strategy but to the rashness of the enemy and the skill of the Athenian helmsmen. Though insignificant in the total power struggle, this victory was important in that it clearly demonstrated that the defeat at Syracuse had not ushered in the complete end of Athens. On the other hand, the Athenians overlooked the fact that this confrontation was by no means comparable to the major trial of strength at Syracuse.

Fortune continued to smile upon Athens. In the late autumn of the same year a battle was fought near Abydus against the Peloponnesians, who were aided by Pharnabazus' cavalry and infantry. In this confrontation, partly at sea and partly on land, the Athenians, commanded by Alcibiades, captured 30 empty triremes.

In spite of these Athenian successes, the situation was by no means secure. In contrast to the Spartans, who received money from Pharnabazus to build ships and to pay the crews, the Athenians had to scrape together money from wherever they could. With every passing day this became more difficult because their allies either had run out of money or were unwilling to pay. When Byzantium defected and started to impede the transit of merchant ships from the Black Sea, the Athenians, in the spring of 410 BC, were compelled to send a war fleet through the Hellespont to the Propontis (Sea of Marmora). The Spartans too sent a strong fleet, which cast anchor in the vicinity of Cyzicus and captured the town after a short siege. The Athenian reaction, however, was quick and effective. Hidden from the Spartans by mist and rain the Athenians sailed in the direction of Cyzicus. When the Spartans realised what was happening, it was too late: the 83 Athenian ships had sailed between their own 60 ships and the harbour of Cyzicus. This was too much for the Spartans. They had always considered themselves inferior to the Athenian sailors, a feeling that was now strongly reinforced by the Athenian numerical superiority. They withdrew to the nearest coast. With 63 ships Alcibiades, eager to muzzle the sceptics in Athens by winning a big success, moved in on the Spartan ships which were moored very closely together. The remaining 20 ships landed at a distance, so that the crews, equipped with bows, slings and short swords, could attack the Spartans from the rear. In this bitter fight the Athenians scored a brilliant victory. Only the intervention of the Persian cavalry prevented a massacre. But the Spartans lost all their ships, some of which fell into Athenian hands completely undamaged.[13]

As a consequence of these events the Athenians were once again masters of the Hellespont and the Propontis. To compensate for the defection of Byzantium a garrison was stationed on the other side of the Bosporus, in Chrysopolis. In the following year Byzantium was brought back under Athenian control. For the time being the Black Sea trade was safe. Athens went on as though nothing had happened. They rejected peace proposals and even when Sparta started to build a new fleet, once again with Persian money, the Athenians continued to follow their old policies. Ships sailed into and out of Piraeus over a sea which, the Athenians thought, was and would remain theirs.

Since the beginning of the Peloponnesian war naval battles had lost much of their glamour. The modification of the triremes invented by the Corinthians and adopted with great success by the Syracusans had exposed their weakness. It seemed as though, with the introduction of battering beams at stern and prow, naval tactics had become of secondary importance. The advent of the Spartans at sea may have contributed to this. They felt more at ease in a fight at close quarters than in an exercise of tactics, which demanded a high degree of seamanship. Even the Athenians, having lost their best crews and their fastest galleys at Syracuse, were no longer averse to a 'straightforward' fight.

As a consequence of these developments the hegemony at sea was no longer disputed in highly tactical battles but in a war of attrition. Sufficient money and manpower became the deciding factors. In this respect the Spartans got the better of the Athenians. The new Spartan king Lysander won the sympathy of the Persian prince Cyrus, who promised him financial support, whereas Athens was still dependent on the contributions of the member cities of the Delian League, who were reluctant to pay.

In 407 BC — 409 and 408 BC had passed relatively peacefully, apart from a few skirmishes — the Ionian coast once again became the scene of hostilities. In Ephesus the Spartans assembled 90 ships. The Athenians, who had forgiven Alcibiades his role in the Sicilian adventure and had completely rehabilitated him, based 100 triremes at Notium, at a short distance from Ephesus. During a brief absence of Alcibiades, who was seeking contact with other units of the fleet, one of his subordinates disobeyed orders, engaged in a fight with the Spartans and lost, at the expense of 15 to 20 ships. The blame was laid on Alcibiades, who made off to his private estate in Thrace before he could be summoned to account to the Athenian Assembly.[14]

This small naval success gave the Spartans new courage. With the aid of Persian money they expanded their fleet to a total of 170 ships. In the following year they dared to take the initiative once again. Their admiral Callicratidas, Lysander's successor, sailed northwards and captured the city of Methymna on the island of Lesbos. Under the command of Conon the Athenian ships followed the Spartan fleet closely but were taken by surprise. The Spartans intercepted the Athenian ships in the narrows between Lesbos and the mainland. They forced the Athenians into action and again proved successful in a fight at close quarters. The Athenians lost 30 ships and a greater loss was only prevented by a chaotic flight into the harbour of Mytilene, which was promptly blockaded by the Spartans. A daring rescue attempt by an Athenian squadron was not only unsuccessful but also caused an extra ten ships to be lost. After a blockade of five days two swift galleys managed to take advantage of the decreased watchfulness of the besiegers and got away. One of the ships was captured later in the day; the other kept ahead and reached Athens.

The Athenian citizens instantly recognised the seriousness of the situation. The expenses of the war over the last few years had exhausted the treasury and the allies felt strong enough to refuse contributions to the League funds. Despite these reverses, the Athenians did not sit down in despair, but immediately took action. The gold and silver in the numerous temples were melted down to finance the construction of new ships and the repair of the old ones. Within 30 days the Athenians launched a fleet of 110 triremes manned by *c.* 20,000 men. How critical the situation was, is perhaps best illustrated by the recruitment of slaves for the fleet — so great had been the decline in the number of citizens able to serve as rowers. Metics, too, were called up in large numbers. These hastily recruited rowers could, of course, not hold a candle to the well-trained crews who only ten years previously had ruled the waves.

The allies' contribution to the fleet was also incomparable to that of former days. Only 40 ships joined the Athenian fleet in the vicinity of the Arginusae, small islands to the south of Lesbos, bringing the total up to 150 ships. The Peloponnesians opposed them with 120 vessels — they left 50 behind to guard the harbour of Mytilene — presumably of better quality, manned with crews who had a high morale due to their recent successes.

With great care the Athenians chose the site for this naval battle, described rather exaggeratedly by the writer Diodorus as 'the battle of the century'. They picked one of the islands for rear protection and in front of this they divided the fleet into two lines. The reason for choosing this formation presumably was that the Athenian admirals were well aware of the inferiority of their ships. The first line consisted of 60 ships, the second line of 70 ships. The centre, covered by the island, consisted of only 20 ships in the first line and 10 in the second line, but covered a vast area. The wings, both consisting of 60 ships divided over two lines, were much more compact. The Peloponnesian fleet approached in one broad line. Breaking through the Athenian lines was excluded by the double formation, but even an encircling movement was difficult to carry out because of the island. Therefore, the Spartan admirals decided to split up the fleet and to attack the flanks of the Athenian formation; they expected the Athenian ships, lying so closely together, to get in each other's way. When the two Athenian wings were each attacked by 60 ships, the centre supported them. The right wing of the Spartans was put to flight by the bitterly fighting Athenian crews. On the left the Peloponnesians held out longer. When, however, their commander Callicratidas had been killed and panic had spread through the rank and file, these ships, too, took to flight, leaving victory to the Athenians. The Spartans lost 70 ships and the Athenians 25.

The Athenian victory was, however, overshadowed by later events due to which Athens lost its successful commanders. Immediately after the battle it was decided that 75 triremes should attack the 50 Peloponnesian ships blockading Mytilene in order to free the fleet bottled up in the harbour. The Spartans, however, were warned by the crew of a fast sailing cutter, lifted the blockade and left the threatened area. The remaining 47 Athenian triremes had been given orders to search the sea for wounded, dead and wreckage, but an oncoming storm prevented the search. Xenophon calls this 'storm' only 'a strong wind' and may have been right, since the Spartan ship defied the 'storm' in order to warn the fleet at Mytilene of a possible Athenian attack. However that may be, the commanders were blamed for not carrying out the salvage operation; they were prosecuted in an illegal trial and sentenced to death by the Assembly.[15]

The delusion which apparently held the Athenians in its grip also affected their foreign policy. A Spartan proposal in which they offered to return the Athenian deme of Decelea was contemptuously rejected. Then the Spartans concluded a new treaty with the Persian king Cyrus, who generously subsidised the construction of a new, first-class Spartan fleet. The Athenians had to make do with the ships which had fought at the Arginusae.

Embittered by the rejection of their peace offer, the Spartans now wanted to crush the Athenians once and for all. The occupation of Decelea was extended and the transit route through the Hellespont, so vital for Athenian food supplies, was blocked; Lampsacus, a strategically important harbour, was set up as a base. Athens had to equip its fleet again to dispatch it to the north. Morale was, however, low and desertions took place on a large scale. Everybody was painfully aware that despite the victory at the Arginusae the opposition had become stronger.

The last battle took place in the Hellespont in 405 BC. An Athenian victory would for a short time free the city from the Spartan competition in the north and grain supplies would not be interrupted. An Athenian defeat would be disastrous because the cut in food supply would bring about acute starvation and lack of money excluded the construction of a new fleet.

The Spartans chose their position in Lampsacus where ships lying in the sheltered harbour were protected from surprise attacks. The Athenians had to content themselves with the unsheltered shore of Aegospotami at the mouth of the 'Goat's Rivers'. Foraging would have to take place in Sestus, 20 km away. The Athenians wanted to give battle as quickly as possible, the Spartans did not, since any delay would be to their advantage. Accordingly they did not react to the threats of the Athenian fleet. Every morning the Athenians sailed out to entice the Spartans to fight, but the latter were not at all eager to take on 180 Athenian ships. They had other plans. Gambling on the increasing weariness and hunger of the Athenians, the Spartans worked out a tactical stratagem by which they would capture the enemy fleet without striking a blow. Every time the Athenians executed threatening manoeuvres, the Spartan admirals sent out scouts to watch what the Athenians did afterwards. Every day the same routine appeared to be followed: the ships were beached, meals were prepared and the troops rested; the Spartans knew enough. On the fifth day the Athenians carried out their 'attack' and as usual sailed back to the beach of Aegospotami. Scouts informed the Spartans by means of light signals (the reflections of sunlight on uplifted shields) that the enemy had disembarked; they sailed out with the entire fleet. Before the Athenians had recovered from the surprise and could get back on board, their whole fleet, with the exception of nine ships, was destroyed. Conon, the commander of these nine ships, accomplished a *tour de force* that, however unimportant in the light of the battle as a whole, cannot be passed over. Driven by a strong north-easterly wind he crossed the Hellespont and picked up the sails left behind at the Spartan base (the sails were always left ashore during a battle). Then he escaped safely to the Aegean.[16]

Thus Athenian supremacy at sea came to an end. The fleet was crushingly defeated in a battle which did not really deserve to be called one. The consequences for Athens were disastrous. Of the allies only Samos remained loyal; the rest either deserted Athens of their own free will or were induced to do so by the Spartans.

The food supply was endangered because grain transport from the north came to a standstill. The Athenian grain ships that still ventured a voyage to the Black Sea ran the risk of not reaching the ports at all or of being intercepted on the return journey. Athens, more crowded than ever because the colonists who had been sent out to check possible unrest in the member cities returned, was struck by starvation. From Decelea and from the sea, the enemy's grip on Athens became steadily stronger. Yet the Athenians refused to surrender, frightened by the hard conditions and doggedly hoping for help from outside. Finally, forced by hunger and exhaustion, they had to accept that the harbour and the long walls of Piraeus should be destroyed. Athens escaped complete destruction but its political role was finished. The Delian League was dissolved and the Athenian fleet was limited to twelve triremes.

Notes

1. DESTRUCTION OF ATTICA: Thuc. 2.20–1; Kagan, 1974, pp. 48–53. ATHENIAN NAVAL POLICY IN 431–430 BC: Thuc. 2.23–4.
2. PLAGUE: Thuc. 2.47–54; 2.59; 3.87.
3. FIRST CONFRONTATION BETWEEN THE ATHENIAN FLEET AND THE PELOPONNESIAN FLEET: Thuc. 2.83–4; cf. Rodgers, 1937, pp. 131–3.
4. SECOND CONFRONTATION: Thuc. 2.85.5; 2.92; cf. Morrison and Williams, 1968, pp. 315–17; Morrison, 1974, p. 21.
5. PLANS TO ATTACK PIRAEUS: Thuc. 2.93–4. REVOLT IN MYTILENE: Thuc. 3.2–6; 3.8–18; 3.25–50. AFFAIRS OF SICILY: Thuc. 2.7.2; 3.86; 3.88; 3.90; 3.103; 3.115–16.
6. SPHACTERIA: Thuc. 4.8–23; 4.27–41; cf. Kagan, 1974, pp. 218–48.
7. RIVALRY ON SICILY: Finley, 1968, pp. 58–68.
8. SICILIAN EXPEDITION: Thuc. book 5 and book 6; the various aspects are analysed by Kagan, 1981, pp. 157–353 and Green, 1971. STRENGTH OF THE ATHENIAN FLEET: Thuc. 6.43–44.1; Diod. 13.2.5. SACRILEGE OF ALCIBIADES: Thuc. 6.27–9; Diod. 13.2; Plut. *Alc.* 18. FIRST ATTACK ON SYRACUSE: Thuc. 6.96–103; cf. Kagan, 1981, pp. 228–87. AUXILIARY FLEET UNDER DEMOSTHENES: Thuc. 7.20.
9. GYLIPPUS' ROLE: Kagan, 1981, pp. 270–7. FIRST CONFRONTATIONS IN THE HARBOUR OF SYRACUSE: Thuc. 7.22–5.
10. CONFRONTATION IN THE GULF OF CORINTH: Thuc. 7.34. ACTIONS IN THE HARBOUR OF SYRACUSE: Thuc. 7.36–41; cf. Morrison and Williams, 1968, pp. 318–20.
11. AGGRESSION OF DEMOSTHENES: Thuc. 7.42–5. BATTLE IN THE HARBOUR OF SYRACUSE: Thuc. 7.51–4. PREPARATIONS FOR DECISIVE CONFRONTATION: Thuc. 7.55–6; cf. Kagan, 1981, pp. 329–31. LAST NAVAL BATTLE: Thuc. 7.59–71. RETREAT AND DESTRUCTION: Thuc. 7.72–85; cf. Green, 1971, pp. 315–56 and Kagan, 1981, pp. 329–53.
12. PANIC IN ATHENS: Thuc. 8.1–2. ATHENS AND THE AEGEAN UNTIL 412 BC: Meiggs, 1972, pp. 351–70; Sealey, 1976, pp. 355–8. REVOLUTION IN 411 BC: Thuc. 8.47–98; Lintott, 1982, pp. 135–55.
13. BATTLE AT CYNOSSEMA: Thuc. 8.104–6. BATTLE AT CYZICUS: Xen. *Hell.* 1.1.16–18; Diod. 13.50–1; Plut. *Alc.* 28.

14. EVENTS OF 408 AND 407 BC: Robertson, 1980, pp. 284–99. BATTLE AT NOTIUM: Xen. *Hell.* 1.5.11–14; *Hell. Oxy.* 4; Diod. 13.71.2–4; Plut. *Alc.* 35.4–6; *Lys.* 5.1–2; cf. Breitenbach, 1971, pp. 152–71.

15. BATTLE AT ARGINUSAE: Xen. *Hell.* 1.6.26–33. NAVAL TACTICS: Rodgers, 1937, pp. 185–90; Morrison, 1974, pp. 23–5. USE OF SLAVES: Xen. *Hell.* 1.6.24.

16. BATTLE AT AEGOSPOTAMI: Xen. *Hell.* 2.1.17–28; Plut. *Alc.* 37; Diod. 13.105–6.

17. TERMS OF PEACE: Xen. *Hell.* 2.2.20–3; Plut. *Lys.* 14; Diod. 13.107.

Chapter Eight

The Fourth Century: The Invention of the Polyremes

The collapse of Athenian naval supremacy ended a period of relative safety at sea. The pirates, who had been kept out of the Aegean since the middle of the fifth century BC, reappeared and penetrated as far as Athens. This was particularly easy in the year following the end of the Peloponnesian War. Athens no longer had a war fleet and the oligarchic party, put into power with the support of Sparta, opposed the restoration of the former naval forces. The 30 tyrants who governed Athens for a short time went so far as to try to separate Piraeus — in their eyes the bulwark of popular rule — from the city.

The destruction of the walls between Athens and Piraeus was only part of their policy to remove all traces of Athens' supremacy at sea. The boathouses at Zea and Munichia, where the triremes were kept, were demolished and the remnants sold for three talents; the costs of construction had amounted to c. 1000 talents.

The harbour district became the centre of all those who wanted to restore democracy. During a short transitional period the 30 tyrants were replaced by ten moderates, and in 403 BC democracy was reintroduced as the form of government. In the following years every effort was made to make Athens once more the centre of the Greek world. As before, emphasis was laid on Athens' role at sea. First the boathouses were rebuilt, but this renovation cannot have been very extensive, for in 395 BC, c. nine years after the tyrants were deposed, most of the boathouses were still in a bad state. It is not surprising that the restoration took some time. In the fifth century BC the contributions of the member cities of the Delian League had been Athens' chief source of income. Now appeals had to be made to private individuals, wealthy citizens and metics, to finance the reconstruction of the harbour and the fleet; they were for the greater part not unwilling to do so. Within a short time Athens once again had several dozen triremes to protect the grain imports. Help came from another, unexpected, source as well. Conon, who after his flight from the Hellespont had been hospitably received by the Cyprian king Evagoras, convinced the Persian satrap Pharnabazus that Spartan supremacy in Greece was not in the interests of Persia. With Persian money the Athenians built 90 triremes and defeated the Spartan fleet of 85 triremes near Cnidus. Spartan garrisons disappeared from the eastern part of the Aegean and from the islands. Pharnabazus allowed Conon to return to Athens and in addition subsidised the rebuilding of the walls.

Conon's triumphant arrival in Piraeus was the beginning of a revival of Athenian military and economic power. The long walls were rebuilt. Athenian ships, financed by Persian capital, patrolled the Aegean once again and Athens became once more a centre of trade. Athenian influence was felt as far as the coasts of Asia Minor and the Black Sea. Even in Sicily Athenian ships were seen again.[1]

In the fourth century BC Athens no longer dominated trade and commerce. Cities which had earlier been important markets for Athenian merchants now followed their own initiative. Even when in 378–377 BC, after the collaboration with Persia had come to an end, Athens set up a new confederacy directed against Sparta, it wielded no predominating influence. Commerce acquired a more international character; Greek cities in the Black Sea area, Thrace and Illyria became important trade centres and opened agencies in many places. Trade had become more sophisticated and better organised than before; Sicilian merchants were usually well-informed about grain prices in the Black Sea cities. As a result, a poor harvest in a certain area caused prices in other grain-producing areas to rise. But more co-ordination in trade did not mean that financial matters were controlled by the Greek cities. In the fourth century BC banks for the most part remained in private, mostly foreign, hands. In the first decades of the fourth century BC Athens had eight private banks, which made large profits. There is the well-known story of Pasioon. He started as a slave in the service of Antisthenes and Archestratus, who had a bank in Athens. Pasioon worked his way up and when the two proprietors retired he took over the office. In the following year he extended the services of his bank. Merchants from anywhere could deposit money and make payments to other account holders, thus avoiding the risk of transporting money. The most important service of Pasioon was the establishment of banks in other trade centres. Merchants no longer needed to bring money with them on their voyages, but could, if they had an account with Pasioon, withdraw money anywhere in order to make their payments.

However much prosperity and employment the rise in trade and commerce brought to Athens, the standard of living of the fifth century BC could no longer be reached. The return of the colonists (cleruchs) to Athens had created a large proletariat only part of which could be employed in the city and in the harbour. Many could scarcely afford to buy grain, although, to keep prices down, the government sometimes intervened either by buying up grain or by having the freighters escorted by warships. Many thetes lived on the verge of minimum subsistence. All the same, they were not keen on serving on Athenian warships. The wages earned on the rowing benches were low and compared very unfavourably with the sums paid by foreign governments. Many Athenians, therefore, left their mother city to become mercenaries or to serve in competing fleets. The one who offered the highest pay acquired the best fleet. The best rowers were to be found where Persian money was available. When in 377 BC Athens set up a new naval alliance against Sparta, its political influence in the Aegean and Ionian Seas increased; yet, there was a continuous threat from fleets financed with Persian gold. The Persian king was very eager to maintain the balance of power in Greece.[2]

In the first half of the fourth century BC the struggle for power in Greece had been fought with the same types of ships as in the fifth century BC. Elsewhere, alterations in the designs of warships attracted attention. In the cities of Phoenicia shipbuilders were designing new types to replace the old ones. That such experiments took place on the Phoenician dockyards is not surprising: the Phoenicians had always played a leading role in the invention of ships. In Sicily the rivalry between Greeks and Carthaginians stimulated developments in ship construction.

The search for new types of vessels was stimulated by the shortage of skilled, well-trained rowers. Both the Carthaginian and the Syracusan army consisted mainly of mercenaries who were attracted from the 'old world' with large sums of money; their ability varied. Some had served in the armies of Sparta and Athens and were quite experienced. Others, in particular the hired rowers — a heavy, unpopular job — were of poorer quality. Dionysius, since 406 BC tyrant of Syracuse, wanted to build a fleet of several hundred ships. He quickly saw that he could not recruit enough skilled oarsmen. Every trireme required 170 oarsmen, each with his own oar. Only good oarsmen could make the trireme into a dangerous ship. For that reason experiments were done on the wharves of Syracuse in order to design ships that depended less on the skill of individual oarsmen than on mass muscle power. According to the historian Diodorus, in 399 BC the Syracusan shipbuilders introduced on a limited scale ships that would become known as quadriremes (Greek: *tetreres*, 'four') and quinqueremes (Greek: *penteres*, 'five'). Pliny, the Roman encyclopaedist, credits the Carthaginians, and not the Syracusans, with the invention of the quadriremes, a view supported by Clement of Alexandria (see p. 121).[3]

The oarage of these new ships is as much disputed as that of the triremes. The theories put forward can be divided into three main schools of thought. Initially it was assumed that the oarsmen were placed as in the triremes: four or five rowers above each other, each rower with his own oar. Since ships of such height cannot have been seaworthy to any degree, this point of view is very improbable. Moreover, one of the reasons why the new types of vessels were designed, the lack of experienced oarsmen, is not dealt with by this theory. Rowing at four or five different levels would still require a high degree of experience and training.

The second theory assumes that four or five oarsmen sat on one bench, using the same oar. This hypothesis is attractive in that only one experienced oarsman is required to lead the tempo of the others. The main objection against it is that the rowers would be placed at the same height. Previous centuries had seen the development from the penteconter, rowed at one level, via the bireme to the trireme. To brush aside the evolution of two centuries would be a big step backwards. It is, however, not impossible that quadriremes and quinqueremes existed which were rowed at one level, particularly in fleets where the number of trained rowers was limited.

Proceeding from the idea that several oarsmen sat at a single oar but that the system of benches placed above each other cannot be ignored for quadriremes and quinqueremes, R. Anderson has probably found the solution. Besides the quadrireme and the quinquereme he includes in his theory the sexireme (Greek: *hexeres*, 'six'). He wisely takes the trireme as his starting point, since that type of vessel was constructed on every wharf of the

Mediterranean world. Anderson assumes a direct development from the trireme to the sexireme, by means of the system of double benches. In this way the arrangement of the thalamites, zugites and thranites in the trireme was maintained; now, however, there were two men to a single oar (Fig. 8.1). The oars were longer, but did not differ from each other in length. In the case of the quinquereme, which according to Anderson was rowed by two thranites from an outrigger, two zugites on the deck and one thalamite on a level with the waterline, the oars of the thalamites were shorter than those of their more highly seated colleagues (Fig. 8.2). The quadrireme, on the other hand, had two rows of oarsmen with oars of equal length (Fig. 8.3).[4]

Figure 8.1 Oarage of a Sexireme

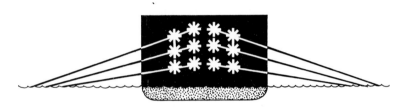

Figure 8.2 Oarage of a Quinquereme

Little can be said about the dimensions of these new galleys. Reports by authors from the fourth century BC are lacking; our only source is the information provided by Polybius more than two centuries later. He relates that in the naval battle between the Romans and the Carthaginians at Ecnomus in 256 BC the quinqueremes carried 300 oarsmen, 120 marines and *c.* 50 officers and

Figure 8.3 Oarage of a Quadrireme (Three Variations)

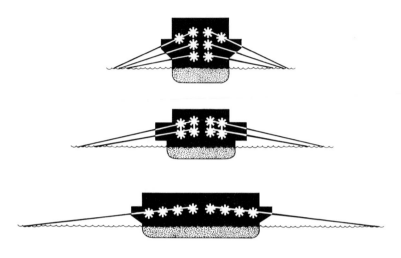

non-military personnel. Assuming that there were, in fact, three files of rowers, a division of 2 × 29 thalamites, 2 × 29 zugites and 1 × 34 thranites on each side seems a reasonable estimate, given the disparity between the files. The vessels must have been longer than the triremes operating with 170 rowers, which were about 35 m long.

Ships of this new type were doubtless more robust and stronger than the triremes. In the battles in the harbour of Syracuse in 413 BC it had become evident that in a fight at close quarters the highest file of rowers was too vulnerable. The deck of the quinquereme was accordingly broadened and lengthened. All rowers now sat below deck. The reinforced deck led to an improved construction of the hull. Moreover, the deck had to be redesigned in order to accommodate the increasing number of soldiers taken on board, a change to which Dionysius himself devoted great attention. This is not surprising, since he is also credited with the introduction on these ships of ballistic machines which, based on the principle of the bow or perhaps already on that of the catapult, required a lot of space to project missiles at the enemy over a large distance. At the same time the deck accommodated many archers, slingers and spear-throwers who could increase the pressure on the enemy, thus facilitating the actual attack, ending with ramming or boarding.

How the Syracusans manoeuvred these prototypes is not known. It was not until the Hellenistic period that specific tactics for these ships were properly standardised. All we know is that in 397 BC Leptines, the brother of Dionysius, was defeated near Catana with 30 vessels including an unknown number of quinqueremes. A possible explanation for this defeat may be that the heavy quinqueremes, less manoeuvrable than the light triremes, were not placed in the centre among the triremes, and could, therefore, be rendered ineffective by enemy triremes.[5]

In the Aegean world there was great scepticism about these ships. They were only gradually incorporated in the existing fleets during the fourth century BC. In particular the Athenians were, for a long time, reluctant to adopt the new designs. The oldest mention of quadriremes in Athens dates from 330–329 BC; the naval lists mention 18 quadriremes. They are listed after the 492 triremes and the penteconters. Five years later 50 quadriremes and seven quinqueremes are listed. On the coasts of Palestine the new ships were received more enthusiastically: according to the historian Diodorus in 351 BC the Phoenician cities had many quinqueremes at their disposal. It has been said that the late introduction of the new galleys in the Aegean indicates that they were invented in Phoenicia. If Syracuse had supplied the first types, Corinth, its mother city, would have known and Athens would certainly not have remained unaware of them. Athenian objections against the new vessels would not have prevented tests on a limited scale. The conclusion of the proponents of this theory is that the quinqueremes were designed on the wharves of Phoenicia and Cyprus, a view which is corroborated by the fact that the further developments of these galleys took shape mainly in Phoenicia and Cyprus.[6]

Against this theory there are many objections. Athens had, in fact, had ample opportunities to introduce quadriremes and quinqueremes at an early stage. In 371 BC Dionysius, who only two years previously had given aid to the Spartans by sending ten ships (no quadriremes or quinqueremes), concluded a naval treaty with Athens. This would have been the outstanding opportunity for Athens to introduce a novelty in naval warfare just as the Thebans did in the same year in the war on land by adopting a new hoplite phalanx. If the negotiations with Dionysius led to no such result, the reason was that the Athenians were not interested in these innovations. In the seventies the Athenian trireme fleet had gained some spectacular victories. In 376 BC Chabrias, a capable Athenian admiral, had defeated a Peloponnesian fleet at Naxos. In the following year, the same admiral successfully operated along the Thracian coast while Timotheus, son of the former admiral Conon, defeated the Spartans in the vicinity of Acarnania. When, following these events, in 371 BC a peace treaty was concluded the Spartans were given supremacy on land — which was a few months later harshly brought to an end by the Thebans at Leuctra — and the Athenians supremacy at sea. Consequently, the Athenians seemed to have no reason to adopt new ships whose efficiency had still to be proved.

Even when the Thebans, who had taken little interest in seafaring until then, constructed a fleet of 100 triremes, obtained financial support from Persia and threatened the Athenian supply routes in the north, the Athenians did not decide to replace the triremes. On the contrary, their confidence in these tried and trusted vessels remained so high that in the sixties many new triremes were built as can be seen from the ships' lists of the Athenian fleet. These lists also contain information about the careful maintenance of the Athenian triremes and confirm the remarks of the orator Demosthenes, who informs us that there were three categories of triremes. Unfortunately, neither source explains the difference between these categories, but one might assume that the division was based on age and state of seaworthiness.

International pressure forced Athens to unremittingly keep up the level of its naval strength. A defeat of the fleet would result in an increasing activity of other cities along the Aegean. An alliance of enemy powers, particularly if this happened in the north, could have serious effects for the Athenian population by causing high, often too high, corn prices. Its opponents, well aware of this weakness, provoked confrontations above all in the north. But as long as the Athenians were able to man enough triremes with skilled rowers, they had little to fear. Byzantium had to learn this the hard way when in 357 BC it disengaged itself from Athens and made others do the same.

The years 355 to 351 BC must have been particularly fortunate for Athens. Passage through the Hellespont had been restored to safety and the transport of corn was no longer endangered. Other products — luxury goods and timber — were imported without difficulty. Large numbers of merchantmen, identical to those of the fifth century BC, once again moored in Athens to unload or transship their goods. Eubulus, the driving force behind Athens' recovery, knew very well that successful trade and a strong war fleet were indissolubly linked with each other. The income from trade and commerce was spent on constructing new boathouses, completing the walls around Piraeus and above all on building new triremes.[7]

Eubulus' view would soon be proved correct. A new and unfamiliar enemy entered the scene, quite unlike Athens' former opponents. While the Greek cities were fighting one another, Macedonia, long considered a semi-barbarian land, had grown into a great power. Good roads traversed the land. Fortresses had been constructed at strategic points. The population, consisting of farmers and shepherds, had received a thorough military education, particularly after Philip II had come into power in 358 BC. Immediately after his accession he initiated an ambitious programme. The mining districts in the Pangaeus mountain range near Amphipolis, taken from Athens in 357 BC without the Athenians offering much resistance, provided funds to lay out more roads, found new cities, participate in the Aegean trade, establish colonies and improve military organisation. In Thebes Philip had become familiar with the new phalanx, which he altered by increasing the number of men and introducing the *sarissa*, a thrust lance of 3½ to 4 m in length. The hoplites in the phalanx were now supported on their flanks by heavily armed cavalrymen, a novelty in Hellenic military history, as well as by the peltasts.

These military innovations determined the outcome of both the confrontations with the Greek cities and of the struggle against Athens, whose power lay at sea. Convinced that his land forces were superior, Philip decided to occupy the harbour cities in Chalcidice, which offered important docking facilities for the Athenian corn ships. When the skilful Athenian skippers found ways to reach Athens without these supporting bases he was compelled to take further action. In the summer of 340 BC part of the Athenian grain fleet, anchored at Hieron Oros in the Propontis, was destroyed by a Macedonian military unit. Out of the fleet, consisting of 230 ships, 170 to 180 vessels were sunk.

Perhaps Philip hoped that the Athenians would give up their hostilities now that the grain supply was at risk. This attempt at intimidation was unsuccessful. The Athenians sent a fleet to Byzantium, which was besieged by Philip in the same summer. He had to abandon the siege.

It is doubtful whether this reverse caused Philip many sleepless nights; his progress in a southerly direction was too great for that. When in 338 BC the Greek cities finally formed an alliance and offered united resistance against the advancing Macedonians, it was too late. In that year the decisive battle of Chaeronea took place. And thus Philip defeated Athens without a single naval battle. The Athenian fleet fell into his hands untouched. In the near future this fleet could be of great use to him, for, not content with the conquest of Greece, he had greater plans. He was determined to 'liberate' the Greeks on the west coast of Asia Minor from the Persian king. Involvement of the Athenian fleet was badly wanted. Philip's death, however, changed the course of events. But whoever may have thought that the Macedonian domination would vanish was soon proved wrong. Philip's son Alexander turned out to be even more energetic than his father. His eyes were fixed on the east and he dreamt of distant journeys and great conquests. In his ideology there was no place for cities competing with and fighting against each other.[8]

The role of Athens was finished. An episode of Greek history had come to an end. Never again would cities such as Athens control the Aegean with a fleet of 200 to 400 vessels. Greek history became part of world history. The empires of the future would be huge, powerful and led by ambitious rulers. The death of Alexander would not set the clock back. When the Athenians received word of his death in 323 BC they made a last desperate attempt. A fleet of 170 vessels was dispatched to the Hellespont but was defeated at Amorgos. The harbour of Piraeus was occupied, the boathouses in Zea and Munichia were destroyed. In the future Athens would be an economic and cultural rather than a political centre.[9]

Notes

1. NAVAL INSTALLATIONS AFTER THE PELOPONNESIAN WAR: Isocr. 7.66; Lys. 30.22; *Hell. Oxy.* 1.1; cf. Morrison and Williams, 1968, p. 188. VICTORY OF CONON: Xen. *Hell.* 4.8.1–11.

2. TRADE IN THE FOURTH CENTURY BC: Pekáry, 1976, pp. 37–42 with other literature. BANKING OF PASIOON: Gomme, 1937, pp. 54–5; Casson, 1959, pp. 108–10. SECOND ATHENIAN LEAGUE: Cargill, 1981.

3. INVENTION OF QUADRIREME IN SYRACUSE: Diod. 14.41.3; 14.42.2; 14.44.7. INVENTION IN SIDON: Plin. *Nat. Hist.* 7.207; Clem. Al. *Strom.* 1.75.10; cf. Tarn, 1930, pp. 130–1; Anderson, 1962, pp. 21–2; Basch, 1969, pp. 240–1; Casson, 1971, p. 97; Morrison, 1980a, p. 32.

4. OARAGE: Anderson, 1962, pp. 21–30 offers a survey of various theories; cf. Basch, 1969, pp. 239–40; Casson, 1971, pp. 99–102; Morrison, 1980a, pp. 32–4.

5. NUMBER OF ROWERS: Polyb. 1.26.7; Morrison, 1980a, p. 41. DECK CONSTRUCTION: Morrison, 1980a, pp. 34–9. NAVAL BATTLE AT CATANA: Diod. 14.59–60; cf. Rodgers, 1937, pp. 202–3.

6. QUADRIREMES AND QUINQUEREMES IN ATHENS: *IG* 2² 1627.275–8; 1629.808–11. QUINQUEREMES IN SIDON: Diod. 16.44.6. INVENTION IN PHOENICIA: see note 3; Tarn, 1930, pp. 130–1.

7. INTRODUCTION OF QUADRIREMES IN ATHENS: Schmitt, 1974, pp. 80–90; cf. Morrison, 1941, pp. 41–3. MAINTENANCE OF THE TRIREMES IN ATHENS: Dem. 14.18; cf. *IG* 2² 1611.65–128. ATHENIAN NAVAL POLICY IN THE FOURTH CENTURY BC: Cargill, 1981; cf. Sealey, 1976, pp. 392–6; 410–14; 429–34.

8. CAPTURE OF THE GRAIN FLEET: *FGrH* III B 328 F 162; *FGrH* II B 115 F 292; Just. 9.1.5–6. SIEGE OF BYZANTIUM: Dem. 18.87–94; Diod. 16.74.2–16.77.3.

9. BATTLE AT AMORGOS: Diod. 18.11–17; Plut. *Dem.* 11.3. OCCUPATION OF PIRAEUS: Paus. 1.25.5.

Chapter Nine

The Rivalry of the Diadochi

When in the spring of 334 BC Alexander started out from Greece, crossed the Hellespont and left Europe behind him, he could not know that he was never to set eyes on it again. Nor was he to know that his expedition would mark the beginning of a new era in which the interaction of east and west would lead to the amalgamation of Greek and Oriental civilisation: the era of Hellenism, with Greek as the leading language of a transformed world. Firmly fixed in his mind was the liberation of the Ionian cities from Persian domination. But once he had achieved this, Alexander aimed higher. He wanted his expedition to be remembered as an act of vengeance for the miseries that 150 years previously had been inflicted on Greece by the Persian king Xerxes. The destruction of Xerxes' palace in Persepolis was to be the culmination of his conquests. But having overpowered the vast Persian empire and reduced its capital to ashes, he was still not satisfied. He led his army yet further eastwards into southern Siberia and the basin of the Indus: there, however, he had to give his mutinous soldiers his word that this was as far as he would go and that their hardships would come to an end. For almost ten long years they had marched through Asia and they wanted rest more than anything else.

It can be inferred from the foregoing that Alexander relied entirely on his land army consisting of Macedonians, Greeks and mercenaries recruited from various places; the huge empire was their accomplishment. The Persians were defeated in battles on land. The battle at the Granicus of 334 BC as well as the battles at Issus in 333 BC and at Gaugamela in 331 BC were decided by the tactical skill of Alexander's army. The fleet played no part at all. There was no naval battle between Alexander's ships and the Persian fleet. Alexander deliberately avoided a confrontation at sea. The Macedonian fleet was not strong and he was afraid to risk bringing in all ships of the Greek 'allies', suspicious as he was of the loyalty of the Greeks, in particular of the Athenians from whom he asked only 20 triremes. Bearing in mind that the Corinthian League, a confederacy of Greek city-states founded by Philip after his victory at Chaeronea, provided a total of 160 ships, this was a very small contribution.

The first plan for a Persian reaction to the Macedonian invasion was to have the fleet, consisting of 300 ships, cross over to the mainland of Greece and join forces with the more than 200 ships at anchor in Piraeus; then to occupy the Greek coasts and raise a rebellion against the Macedonians. The originator of this plan was Memnon, a Rhodian in Persian service, who had arrived at the Hellespont too late to prevent Alexander's invasion. The rivalry among the Persian satraps prevented the execution of this plan. Before they could finally come to an agreement Alexander's forces had taken possession of Miletus, the principal naval base on the Ionian coast. A great number of ships was captured by the Macedonians or escaped to Phoenician harbours. Memnon's death, shortly after this, put an end to the Persian threat.[1]

The only time the fleet was involved in the fighting, in 332 BC, was during the siege of the Phoenician city of Tyrus, the main Persian naval base in the Mediterranean. This harbour, for the greater part built on a small island a little over 1 km^2 in area and fortified with walls of *c.* 25 m high, managed to withstand Alexander's various attacks. Initially he attempted to construct a causeway in the narrows separating Tyrus from the coast. The closer the work moved to Tyrus the more dangerous it became, because the archers on the walls of the city could hit their targets with increasing accuracy. Moreover, the Tyrians brought their fleet into action; at the time it consisted of no more than 80 ships because the remainder were in Persian service elsewhere. The fleet approached the causeway on both sides, executed repeated attacks, thus compelling the workmen to wear armour. As a counteraction Alexander had high towers covered with hides erected on the causeway, so that his archers could keep the enemy fleet at a distance. The Tyrians, however, came up with an ingenious stratagem: they constructed a kind of fireship by equipping one of their vessels with fire devices on the prow and on the yard; they trimmed it up so that the prow was high above the surface of the water. Upon reaching the causeway, the crew immediately set fire to the towers, jumped into the water and returned safely to the shore under the cover of their own archers.

Alexander soon had the work restarted. The causeway was to be widened so that more battle towers could be built and a fleet was to be assembled in order to be able to resist Tyrian counteractions. Ships were sailed to Tyrus from wherever they were available. Rhodes, Lycia, Cilicia and Cyprus contributed the largest contingents. Even the Phoenician city of Sidon sent ships, showing once again the traditional disunity among the Phoenicians. Within a few weeks the Macedonians assembled a total of 250 ships, including quadriremes, quinqueremes and freighters. These heavier ships were particularly useful in the circumstances, because they could carry more men than the triremes; the latter were in some cases tied together in pairs in order to give more space for the soldiers.

At first the Tyrians intended to attack Alexander's fleet but changed their minds when they saw that they were outnumbered. Instead, they constructed even larger ballistic machines and cast heavy boulders into the water in order to obstruct the entrance and to prevent the approach of enemy vessels. Small Tyrian rowing boats made their way among the heavy Macedonian ships and confused the enemy even more. All the same these activities failed to produce the desired result. Heavy Macedonian ships dragged the boulders away to deeper water. Then the Tyrians brought in divers to cut the cables. Alexander, apparently not surprised by these actions, had the cables replaced by chains, thus enabling the siege to continue. At last the Tyrians resorted to a ruse. They pretended to have no intention of going out to sea but to be preparing a leisurely dinner on the beach, as was usual in the absence of immediate danger. In order to confirm the Macedonians in this idea they hung up the sails of most of their ships to dry in the sun. In the meantime they manned 13 ships with experienced crews, which attacked and partly sunk a Cyprian squadron. When Alexander observed how bad things were for that part of his fleet, he personally commanded a squadron in an attack against the Tyrians. Before the inhabitants of the city could warn them all these Tyrian ships were destroyed. The effect was considerable. From then on the Tyrian fleet, disconcerted by the unexpected turn of events, no longer took part in the fighting.

No longer interrupted by the Tyrian ships, the work on the causeway progressed, even though the Tyrians hurled burning torches at the besiegers. The decisive attack was a combined action of army and fleet. From the causeway and from specially prepared ships Alexander's elite of heavily armed soldiers attacked the south-eastern side of the city, which was taken to be the weakest. In order to conceal their strategy from the Tyrians the Macedonians also staged attacks on other fronts. Ships broke through the chains closing off the entrances to the two harbours. At the same time the remainder of the fleet circled round the entire island giving the impression that an attack would be made from all sides. The Tyrians, who had courageously withstood the seven month siege, fought desperately but could not get anywhere. The wall collapsed and Alexander's soldiers stormed into the city. Demoralised by this blow, the crews of the ships in the two harbours offered only unorganised resistance. When the northern harbour fell into Macedonian hands and further resistance was clearly pointless, the Tyrians surrendered. More than 10,000 were killed and 30,000 enslaved.[2]

The capture of Tyrus made Alexander lord and master of the south-eastern Mediterranean. In the near future, organised resistance was not to be expected. All the Phoenician ships had been seized by the Macedonians. To replace the ancient trade centre of Tyrus Alexander in 331 BC founded Alexandria, a new city named after himself, which in the following centuries would develop into a real metropolis. The location of this port on one of the mouths of the Nile leads one to surmise that Alexander was already thinking of seas other than the Mediterranean. The architect of the harbour, Democrates, was originally inspired by the architects who had designed the harbour of Syracuse. He connected the island of Pharos facing the coast to the mainland by means of a mole of 1400 m in length, thus creating a harbour on both sides. On the eastern side there was a natural bay with a narrow entrance which was to become a trade harbour. The western harbour was intended for naval purposes. From here the Ptolemies, Alexander's successors in Egypt, would send out their immense fleets.[3]

Continuing his expedition Alexander penetrated into the heart of Asia. It goes without saying that the fleet played a negligible role in these events. The only time ships are mentioned is in connection with the incidents of 326 BC when the Macedonian troops, exhausted by their long marches, the tropical heat, the monsoon rains and homesickness, wanted to turn back. At that moment they were in the eastern part of the Punjab. Forced by his soldiers' refusal to march any further, Alexander allowed them to build ships and to go down the Indus to the sea. Arrian, a second-century historian, relates that 80 triaconters were built, a number of unspecified small warships, freighters, supply ships and many river boats, all in all 800 ships. There is no mention of triremes. That the obsolete triaconter was preferred to the trireme is not surprising. Alexander's carpenters were skilled enough but unfamiliar with the singular construction of the trireme, so much more complex than that of the triaconter. Another reason for choosing the triaconter may have been that, in so far as information was available, no great fleets were to be expected.[4]

Having reached the coast of the Indian Ocean, Alexander's army split up. Craterus would return via the inland route, Alexander would march along the coast through the Gedrosian desert and Nearchus would take the sea-route. With 3000 to 5000 men, all the triaconters and a few smaller ships he set out from Patala, where the Macedonians were thinking of building a harbour; his arduous voyage produced a travel report from which later historians have abundantly drawn. Nearchus had no supply ships. Each day the crews had to search the inhospitable shores for food and water. Their meagre meals consisted mainly of fish and dates. After a voyage of 80 days the ships cast anchor in the mouth of the Amanis river. After a short meeting with Alexander and Craterus, Nearchus and his crews embarked once again, sailed along the coast and up the Tigris to Susa.[5]

Nearchus' report must have made a great impression on Alexander. On an ambitious scale he went ahead with the exploration of the seas to the south of the Asiatic continent. His goal was an unimpeded sea route from Egypt to India. The most difficult part would be sailing round the Arabic peninsula. In order to be ready for all eventualities, a large fleet was assembled in Babylon in which all current types of ships were represented. Carpenters were summoned to Babylon from Greece and Phoenicia in order to build ships on the spot. In addition some ships were transported by land from Phoenicia to Thapsacus on the Euphrates and from there to Babylon: two quinqueremes, three quadriremes, twelve triremes and about 300 triaconters. Rather than being conveyed in one piece on rollers, which was the usual way of transporting ships over short distances, they were sawn into sections and transported on carts drawn by horses. As for the triaconters, we know that they were sawn into three sections. Nothing is known about the other types. In Thapsacus the ships were reassembled.[6]

The expedition was, however, never carried out. Alexander died in the middle of the preparations, in the spring of 323 BC, when he was scarcely 33 years old. He had reigned for twelve years and eight months and had extended the Greek horizon to the Far East. His empire stretched from the Adriatic to the Punjab and from Tadzhikistan to Libya. Had he lived longer, Alexander could perhaps have welded this immense area into a whole. His death was followed by serious conflicts between the Macedonian generals Perdiccas, Antipater, Ptolemy, Antigonus, Seleucus and Lysimachus. They tried to acquire as great a territory as possible, which inevitably resulted in violent conflicts. These *Diadochi* ('successors') would fight one another over a period of more than 30 years, on land and at sea.

Among the Diadochi Ptolemy and Antigonus (nicknamed *monophthalmos*, the one-eyed), supported by his son Demetrius, were the most important. They not only dominated political history but also played a major role in the development of ship construction and naval warfare. Right from the beginning Ptolemy's position among the Diadochi was exceptional. Shortly after Alexander's death he had gained possession of Egypt and had since consolidated his position there. Antigonus had laid hold of a part of Asia Minor and aimed at control over the whole of Alexander's empire. By 315 BC he controlled almost the whole Asiatic part of the empire. Antigonus' success led to a coalition between Ptolemy, Lysimachus and the Macedonian king Cassander, the son of Antipater, who had been appointed by Alexander to look after Macedonia and Greece during his absence. In particular the occupation of the Phoenician harbour towns and the fact that the inhabitants had been ordered to construct a strong naval fleet enraged Ptolemy, who with a large part of Alexander's fleet dominated the eastern Mediterranean. On top of all this, Antigonus and Demetrius had also set their sights on the Greek cities; calling themselves 'liberators from the Macedonian yoke' they hoped to be able to take over the Greek fleet. In this same period Antigonus founded the League of Island Cities in the Aegean and his son started an ambitious shipbuilding programme. Yet, a great military confrontation between Antigonus and Ptolemy did not occur. In 311 BC a treaty was concluded, according to which Ptolemy would rule Egypt and Syria, Cassander would become 'supreme commander of Europe', Lysimachus would obtain Thrace and Antigonus would become master of all

Asia. The Greeks would live according to their own laws. This 'peace' could not last. Ptolemy wanted to establish an Egyptian/ Syrian empire, and to succeed he needed to dominate the eastern Mediterranean, which was prevented by Demetrius' presence in Tyrus. Antigonus, on the other hand, continued his attempts to gain influence in Greece, a strategy caused by his aspirations to control the entire Aegean.[7]

In the years following 311 BC it was clear that armed confrontations could not be avoided. Ptolemy attempted to increase his influence in Greece and in the spring of 308 BC sailed across the Aegean. But most of the Greek cities showed no inclination to join him and took sides with Antigonus, whose son in 307 BC 'liberated' Athens and temporarily restored democracy. Subsequently Demetrius sailed to Cyprus, intending to sever its trade contacts with Egypt. After Menelaus, Ptolemy's brother, had been defeated by Demetrius, Ptolemy himself appeared with a large fleet. The resulting battle at Salamis (Cyprus) in 306 BC is significant because Demetrius brought ships into action which up till then had been unknown.

During this naval battle Demetrius used ships that had not been tested till that moment — seven septiremes (Greek: *hepteres*, 'seven'), vessels which were rowed from one, two or three levels: by seven rowers per oar when there was only one level; by three or four rowers per oar when there were two levels; and twice two and once three rowers per oar when rowed from three levels. In total Demetrius had 118 ships at his disposal including 20 quinqueremes and 30 quadriremes. To oppose this fleet Ptolemy had 140 quinqueremes and quadriremes. It looks as if Demetrius, knowing that Ptolemy's fleet did not include any vessel larger than the quadrireme and quinquereme, concealed his true strength. For, if we are to believe the historian Diodorus, Demetrius and his father Antigonus had already even larger vessels at their disposal in 315 BC: three 'nines' and ten 'tens'. This fleet would at that time have consisted of 90 'fours', 10 'fives', 3 'nines', 10 'tens' and 30 smaller vessels, mainly open galleys.[8]

The heavier the ships and the greater the numbers of unskilled rowers, the greater the changes in naval tactics. The developments initiated by Dionysius of Syracuse were continued by Demetrius. High platforms were fitted on the ships and on them there was room for a great many soldiers, armaments, ballistic machines and catapults. Thus, although ramming tactics such as the old *diekplous* and *periplous* were still employed, boarding tactics became more and more important.

In choosing the site for the battle Demetrius clearly had the advantage. He was the first to reach the harbour of Salamis and could force a battle on his opponents. His ships were laid perpendicular to the coast, divided in two lines. The idea was that the left wing should force a decision. It consisted of 7 septiremes and 30 quadriremes in the first line and 10 sexiremes and 10 quinqueremes in the second line. The smaller ships, mostly triremes, had been placed in the centre and the right wing consisted of 10 quinqueremes and the remaining small, fast ships. Ptolemy's ships, on the other hand, were arranged in one long line. The left wing, which had to operate close to the coast, was reinforced, as a result of which the two strong left wings faced the 'weak' right wings.

During the first stage of the battle, both sides abundantly used their ballistic machines. Next the two fleets closed in on one another at great speed. Diodorus' report does not expressly state whether the aim of this manoeuvre was ramming or boarding. Both tactics are mentioned but it is not explained who used which. But it is probable that Ptolemy's ships intended to ram, since the crews of these ships consisted mainly of Phoenicians, who for generations had successfully used ramming tactics. Demetrius' strategy was presumably based on boarding tactics. His oarsmen were less well-trained and ramming with the heavy 'sixes' and 'sevens' would require superior skill. The battle was very complex. Demetrius' reinforced left wing broke through the enemy's right wing and, the large catapults continuously hurling rocks, drove it on to the shore. They then joined the centre which up to then had not been actively involved. The Egyptian left wing had also defeated their direct opponents but, while victoriously pursuing them, had lost contact with the rest of the fleet. When the captains of the pursuing ships discovered that the other ships were getting into trouble, they turned and tried to help. But it was too late. Demetrius' left wing had already taken up position between the Egyptian ships and the coast, followed by the centre. There was nothing left for the Egyptians to do but to flee. Forty of their ships were lost, 80 others so badly damaged that there was no way of repairing them quickly; 8000 men lost their lives. Only 20 ships of Demetrius' fleet suffered light damage.[9]

Despite this victory, which temporarily eliminated Ptolemy and enabled Demetrius to control the seas, he and his father encountered little success in the following years. When immediately after the victory at Cyprus they made an attempt to invade Egypt, they were driven back. Their next expedition, against the island of Rhodes, went even worse and resulted in considerable loss of face with the other competitors for supremacy in the Mediterranean. In 305 BC they attacked the island's port, which in the years following Alexander's death had grown into an important commercial centre. Favourably situated on the route from Egypt to Asia Minor and Greece, Rhodes was not only an excellent home base for its own ships but also a convenient port of call for numerous merchantmen. The only way to maintain this situation was to remain neutral. Therefore, the Rhodians had not taken sides in the conflict between Antigonus and Ptolemy, although their sympathy was with the Egyptians.[10]

The large-scale siege of the city in 305 BC — Demetrius brought with him 40,000 soldiers, 200 naval vessels and 170 freighters — did not produce the desired result. Whatever siege material Demetrius used, neither from the land side nor from the sea side did he succeed in occupying the city, a telling fact, since Demetrius was said to be the brightest designer of siege equipment. The support given to the Rhodians by Ptolemy and the summons of the Athenians for assistance against Cassander, who was advancing from Macedonia, finally compelled Demetrius to go back empty-handed.

The military coalition of Ptolemy, Cassander, Seleucus and Lysimachus against Demetrius and his by now 80-year-old father proved too much for them in the long run. In 301 BC the ambitions of father and son came to a sad end at Ipsus in Phrygia. Antigonus and Demetrius brought in 80,000 men and 75 elephants against the 75,000 men, 480 elephants and 12 chariots of their opponents. Antigonus was killed and Demetrius escaped to Ephesus with 9000 loyal troops.[11]

On land Demetrius' role was finished, at least temporarily, but at sea he was still powerful. Although he was no longer in control of an extensive area — this had been divided among the victors of Ipsus — he still had a powerful fleet and a large number of harbours at his disposal. From Ephesus he spread his influence once again over the harbours of Ionia, Caria, Cyprus and Phoenicia. In addition he could reckon on the support of the Greek cities which he had united in 302 BC in a Hellenic League.

However, as he pocketed more and more of the trade earnings himself the opposition against him increased. Demetrius needed the money to meet the expenses of his army and fleet. The construction of naval vessels had his special attention. Demetrius did not only launch great numbers of existing types but also designed and built new types. The ships grew larger and heavier. In addition to the 'nines' and the 'tens', 'elevens', 'twelves' (Fig. 9.1) and 'thirteens' were built, rowed from one, two or three levels.[12]

Figure 9.1 Oarage of a 'Twelve'

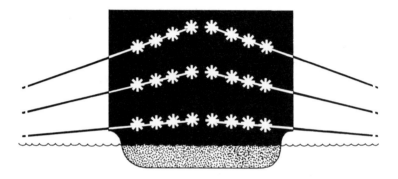

Supported by his strong fleet and taking advantage of the disunity among Cassander's sons, in 294 BC Demetrius succeeded in acquiring the throne of Macedonia, a position he maintained for almost six years. But he did not become very popular because he regarded Macedonia primarily as a foothold from which he might recapture Asia Minor, something which he actually tried to do in 289 BC. In Asia Minor, meanwhile, Lysimachus had not wasted his time. When in 288 BC Demetrius launched the 'fifteen' and the 'sixteen' (Figure 9.2), Lysimachus reacted promptly. In the years when the two rulers were still friends or at least not yet bitter enemies, Lysimachus had once written Demetrius a letter. In it he had asked Demetrius whether he could see the ships whose fame had spread throughout the world. After some hesitation Demetrius had consented; Lysimachus came to inspect the ships and departed in utter amazement, fully determined to build such a fleet for himself.[13]

In order to be able to resist Demetrius' 'fifteen' and 'sixteen', he constructed a ship, the *Leontophoros*, that would become famous

Figure 9.2 Oarage of a 'Sixteen'

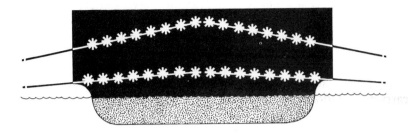

in the Hellenistic world for its 'size and beauty'. This in itself
uninformative statement comes from the historian Memnon, who
in the beginning of the second century AD wrote a history of his
mother city Heraclea; calling it an 'eight', he describes this ship,
which may have been built in Heraclea, as follows: 'in each file,
100 men rowed so that there were 800 in each part, 1600 in both,
those assigned to fight from the decks totalled 1200; there were
two helmsmen'. Memnon's description was initially assumed to be
incorrect. He must have meant a 'sixteen', for an 'eight' would not
quite be a match for the 'sixteen' of Demetrius. Some, willing to
accept that it was an 'eight', took it to be an exceptionally large
one rowed from three levels. But either way it is impossible to
explain the number of 1600 rowers. In view of the fact that the
maximum number of oarsmen on a 'five' was 300, an 'eight' cannot
possibly be supposed to have had 1600 rowers; a maximum of 400
to 500 would be more plausible. Moreover, a fighting-deck that
could accommodate 1200 men would be too large for a 'sixteen',
let alone for an 'eight'.

Since it had proved impossible to explain the *Leontophoros* as
described by Memnon on the basis of the traditional construction
techniques, L. Casson approached the matter from a different
angle. His starting-point is the assumption that the *Leontophoros*
was a catamaran, a ship whose hulls, in this case the hulls of two
'eights', were connected by cross-beams. In this way the Memnon
passage makes sense after all: the 1600 oarsmen were divided over
the two hulls: the 800 oarsmen in each hull were placed on two
levels: 4 men per oar, 50 oars on each side. The oarsmen on the
insides rowed below the platform which comprised the decks of
the two hulls and the space in between. This space was probably

rather large, because otherwise the inside oarsmen of the two hulls would have hindered each other and the fighting-deck would not have been big enough for 1200 marines. There was a helm in each of the wide hulls, which explains the two helmsmen, who co-operated in steering the ship. Casson's explanation is quite plausible, the more so since the basic idea of the catamaran was already known. During the siege of Tyrus vessels had been brought into action that consisted of two ships tied together carrying a platform with troops.[14]

A naval confrontation between Demetrius' mammoth ships and Lysimachus' *Leontophoros* never took place, for Demetrius' invasion of Asia Minor did not last long enough. Having been driven over the Taurus mountain range by Lysimachus he became engaged in a fierce battle with Seleucus, the satrap of Babylon, who was steadily rising in power. For a while it seemed as though Demetrius would be victorious and attain supreme political power in Asia. But when his Macedonian troops deserted him, he quickly lost ground. Before he could take refuge in his loyal fleet he was forced to surrender. He died in prison two years later.

On the Macedonian wharves the activities in ship construction went on as usual. The man who saw to this was Antigonus Gonatas, Demetrius' son, who had taken over the Macedonian throne. Because the greater part of his father's fleet had been lost to Lysimachus, he had to start all over again. But it was not Lysimachus who became his opponent, but Seleucus: in 281 BC Seleucus had crushed Lysimachus at Corupedium in Lydia and became master of all Asia, thereby establishing the tripartition of Alexander's empire. The sea did not particularly concern Seleucus. The fleet of Lysimachus, for which he did not care much, came into the possession of Ptolemy II. From Alexandria, which was slowly but surely becoming the most important harbour in the Mediterranean, he ruled the seas. Antigonus Gonatas' attempts to put an end to this failed. In a sea-battle in 280 BC about which we know next to nothing Ptolemy defeated his rival. One of the ships in his fleet was the *Leontophoros*.

Antigonus did not give up hope. Though hindered by internal difficulties in Macedonia, he did everything he could to inflict a defeat on the Egyptian fleet. In 258 BC he felt strong enough to fight the Egyptians at sea. He would not have been his father's son if he had not launched a new type of ship. In this battle near the island of Cos, he brought in a tremendously large ship that must have been superior to the *Leontophoros* but whose most important characteristics have not come down to us. The historians who studied the scarce data presume that this ship was based on the 'sixteen' of Demetrius. The improvement may have consisted in the addition of a third level of rowers on the fighting-deck, with nine oarsmen per oar. Dimensions and numbers of oarsmen and marines are not mentioned anywhere. The naval battle, in which this ship operated successfully, is equally badly documented; all we know is that Antigonus was victorious at Cos and that after the battle he consecrated the ship to Apollo in his sanctuary at Delos.[15]

The race as to who could produce the biggest ships was not finished with the *Leontophoros* and the mammoth galley of Antigonus. Athenaeus tells us that after his defeat at Cos, Ptolemy did not leave anything to chance anymore. If Athenaeus' reports may be trusted, then, shortly before his death in 246 BC, Ptolemy had at his disposal a gigantic fleet made up of 17 'fives', 5 'sixes', 37 'sevens', 30 'nines', 14 'elevens', 2 'twelves', 4 'thirteens', 1 'twenty' and 5 'thirties'. It seems fairly certain that from then on the mighty Egyptian fleet did not meet with any significant competition from the Macedonian fleet, which had to operate in small units along the coasts of Greece.[16]

The Egyptians, freed from the fear that new inventions from Macedonia would affect their hegemony at sea, could now give free rein to their imagination. Real showpieces were launched from the Egyptian wharves. The biggest ship, built during the reign of Ptolemy IV (221–203 BC), was the 'forty', about which Plutarch says: 'This ship was only for show. It scarcely differed from buildings which are rooted in the ground and had great difficulty in being put to sea.' Its dimensions prove Plutarch right, if at least the text of Athenaeus is correctly interpreted:

It was 280 cubits [*c*.129 m] long, 38 cubits [*c*.17 m] from gangway to gangway, and 48 cubits [*c*. 22 m] high to the prow ornament. From the stern ornament to the waterline was 53 cubits [*c*. 25 m]. It had four steering oars that were 30 cubits [*c*. 13.5 m] long and thranite oars — the longest abroad — that were 38 cubits [*c*. 17 m]. It was double-prowed and double-sterned, and had seven rams . . . During a trial run it took aboard over 4000 oarsmen and 400 other crewmen and, on the deck, 2850 marines.

Combining these data, it is impossible to come up with a reasonable solution without bearing in mind Lysimachus' *Leontophoros*. On a ship built according to the conventional construction principles, the 7250 crew members would have been sardines in a box. If, however, we take the *Leontophoros*, which, as we saw, had a catamaran construction, as a starting-point, then a great deal becomes clearer. The fact that the 'forty' had a double prow and stern increases the acceptability of this supposition. The dimensions of this gigantic catamaran would, with regard to breadth, have to be more than doubled. The breadth of 17 m applies to each of the hulls separately, which together supported the large deck that carried 2850 marines. The 4000 oarsmen were divided over both hulls, 2000 in each. As regards the placing of the 1000 oarsmen on starboard and on port of both hulls, there are various possibilities. Keeping in mind Athenaeus' mention of thranites, implying that there must have been thalamites and zugites as well, we may conclude that there were three levels of rowers. Taking into account the total length (129 m), rows of 50 men are the most logical, each having 20 rowers divided over three levels. A formation such as eight thranites, six thalamites and six zugites is as likely as 8, 7, 5 or 7, 7, 6 (Figure 9.3).[17]

Figure 9.3 Oarage of Ptolemy's 'Forty'

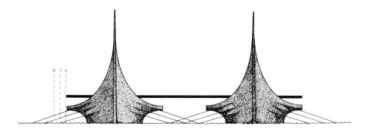

As we already observed, this ship was never tried in battle. There was no need, because in the latter half of the third century BC rivalry had died down in the east: the Antagonids in Macedonia were too preoccupied with the rebellious Greeks and the Seleucids in Asia did not have a strong fleet at their disposal. The possible threat from the west consisting of the Carthaginians or the

Figure 9.4 Two Reconstructions of the Oarage of a *Hemiolia*

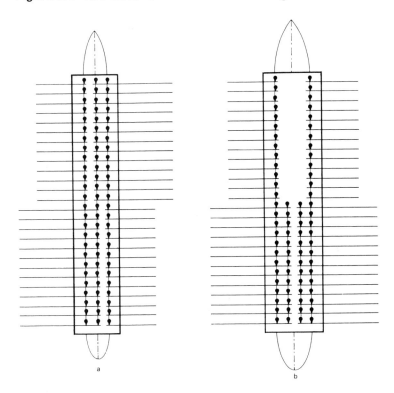

a

b

Romans was not yet taken seriously. In their desire for increasingly larger ships the Egyptians seemed to ignore a quite different but important enemy. Or rather, they recognised the danger but did not know how to deal with it. This danger was piracy: from their settlements spread along the inhospitable coasts of Crete, Cilicia and Illyria pirates made navigation a hazardous business. They were mostly exiles and lawless mercenaries. Many of these had once served in the fleet of Demetrius, for whom they had been particularly useful in plundering expeditions and in operations where heavy losses were expected. After Demetrius had been eliminated, their position became difficult and they became more aggressive.

The large, sluggish merchantmen with their rich cargoes were favourite targets. The pirates made use of a type of ship that, whatever the circumstances, would guarantee success. Its main characteristics were speed and manoeuvrability. In order to be fast enough to overtake a merchantman even when sailing close to the wind the pirates used ships that could sail and be rowed at the same time. The *hemiolia* ('one-and-a-half'), a type of ship that had already been in use with pirates as well as included in war fleets in the fourth century BC, adequately met these conditions. Since no reliable representations have come down to us, we have no information concerning the ship's dimensions. The oarage is also a matter of uncertainty. Until recently the *hemiolia* was believed to be a bireme. But J. Morrison has shown that it was presumably rowed with one and a half files of oars at one level. He indicated two possibilities (Fig. 9.4). Formation b is to be preferred because of the open space on the forepart of the ship providing room for fighting men.[18]

Whatever one may think of pirates, it is generally agreed that they were excellent sailors. In a time when the lack of skilled oarsmen had given rise to polyremes with more than one rower per oar, the pirates were able to maintain the principle of one man, one oar. To combat piracy the great Hellenistic powers included the *hemiolia* in their fleets, but this had little effect because of the acute shortage of trained oarsmen. Only the Rhodians were able to offer some resistance. They had succeeded in their efforts to remain neutral in the struggle among the great powers, despite various attempts of the Hellenistic rulers to change that situation. In other harbour towns the young were reluctant to serve on the galleys and mercenaries had to take their place at the oars; Rhodes, however, had at its disposal a great number of oarsmen. This enabled the Rhodians to form from their own ranks a navy which, though small compared to the fleets of Egypt and Macedonia, commanded respect. Like the pirates they mostly used ships that had only one rower at each oar.

Round about 300 BC the Rhodian wharves launched a ship that was a further development of the *hemiolia*: the *trihemiolia*. This ship may well have been intended as the Rhodian answer to the *hemiolia* used by the pirates. The *trihemiolia* probably had three files of oars on each side with one-and-a-half files a side arranged as in the *hemiolia* on each of two levels. In other words, the oarage of the *trihemiolia* differed from that of the *hemiolia* only in that there was a second level, the oarsmen at the upper level rowing above and in between those at the lower level. Although the *trihemiolia* resembled the trireme in having three files of oarsmen on each side, it obviously differed from it in having three files on two rather than three levels. Using the *trihemioliae*, the Rhodians cleared the seas of pirates. The Ptolemies eventually included the *trihemiolia* in their fleet, as did the Athenians.[19]

The successful elimination of the pirates allowed the Rhodian port to become a prosperous trade centre. In the third century BC Rhodian trade ranged from Egypt to the Crimea and from Mesopotamia to Italy, Sicily and Carthage. Rhodians settled in all leading centres of trade and commerce. They dealt in everything marketable, especially in corn, slaves, luxury goods and select wines. This wide-ranging trade resulted in great prosperity which was further enhanced by the revenues from tolls, harbour dues and dock charges. Public revenues of one million drachmae a year were not exceptional. Even though they were bound elsewhere and had to pay a harbour tax amounting to 2 per cent of their cargo, many skippers were willing to call on Rhodes. It was, after all, ideally situated as a port of call on the routes between Greece and Alexandria, one of the main centres of international trade and commerce.[20]

An inevitably tedious enumeration of all the products traded on the markets of Alexandria and other commercial centres would carry us too far. There was hardly a commodity that did not come into the market, but corn was sold more than anything else. Egypt and the cities of the Crimea were the most important suppliers. From Alexandria numerous corn ships found their way to Athens, Corinth and the Ionian cities in Asia Minor. In addition, Egypt exported papyrus, granite, glass, linen and wool. In exchange for the Egyptian corn the Greek cities exported their specialities: Athenian oil and honey and Ionian wines. Precious metals, marble, bronze statues, ceramics, ivory and purple garments became popular commodities. As a result of trade some cities underwent a rapid development. A transit-port to the west, Corinth experienced an economic revival as did Ephesus and Cyzicus.[21]

An unlimited growth of trade to the west was, however, impossible. East of Carthage the Hellenistic world reached its bounds. Syracuse and Massilia were the furthest points to the west of a network of trade routes that criss-crossed the Mediterranean and continually expanded because of the construction of new harbours. To the west of the line running from Carthage to the Spanish coast via the Balearics, the Carthaginians did not allow anybody who might interfere with their monopoly. Even the

Figure 9.5 Voyage of Pytheas

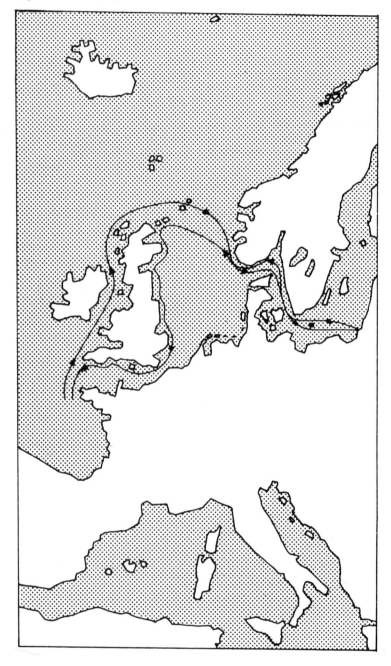

geographic knowledge of the area was kept a secret. In the course of 200 years, the discoveries made *c*. 500 BC by the Carthaginian Hanno along the African west coast down to Sierra Leone had hardly come to be known. In the spirit of Alexander, who had no respect for existing borders, Greek navigators tried to pierce the mist shrouding the west. One of the pioneers known to have sailed far to the west was Pytheas. He set out from Massilia in *c*. 300 BC, presumably backed by wealthy businessmen who wanted to explore trade opportunities. Without being detected by Carthaginian ships, he reached the Strait of Gibraltar and sailed the Atlantic Ocean in a northerly direction. He got as far as Brittany, from where he crossed to the British Isles. He called at Cornwall, skirted along the west coast of England and touched at the northernmost point of Scotland. At a distance of six days' sailing he saw the 'island of Thule' where the sun remains below the horizon for only two or three hours. Probably Pytheas did not mean Iceland, but had reached the west coast of Norway or Sweden. He also embarked upon an extensive exploration of the coast of northern Germany. When at long last, after a voyage of six months, he moored again at Massilia, he had covered more than 7000 sea miles and collected important scientific data, which would be worked out by scholars in Alexandria (Fig. 9.5).[22]

As yet merchants did not derive any benefit from Pytheas' explorations. The west remained sealed off because the Carthaginians denied entrance to everyone. So, the only way to open up the western part of the Mediterranean and the Atlantic Ocean was a naval war with the Carthaginians. But the Hellenistic powers, divided among themselves, were disinclined to make war.

Notes

1. NUMBER OF ATHENIAN SHIPS: Tod. 177; Diod. 16.89.5. MEMNON'S NAVAL WAR: Diod. 17.7.2; 17.22.5; 17.29.2–4.
2. SIEGE OF TYRUS: Arr. *Anab.* 2.16–24; Diod. 17.40–6; Curt. 4.2–4; for literature see Seibert, 1972, 102–3.
3. FOUNDATION OF ALEXANDRIA: Arr. *Anab.* 3.1–3; Curt. 4.8.6; Plut. *Alex.* 26.5; Fraser, 1972, is very exhaustive and gives many references.
4. CONSTRUCTION OF TRIACONTERS: Diod. 17.86.3; cf. 17.95.3–4; Arr. *Anab.* 6.1.1.
5. NEARCHUS' VOYAGE: *RE* XVI.2 col. 2132–54; Pédech, 1976, p. 82; 90–3.
6. TRANSPORTATION OF THE FLEET TO BABYLON: Arr. *Anab.* 7.19.3; cf. Strabo 16.741; Curt. 10.1.19; cf. Casson, 1971, p. 136.

7. STRUGGLE OF THE DIADOCHI: Will, 1975, II. pp. 349–67.
8. DEMETRIUS' FLEET IN 315 BC: Diod. 19.62.8. DEMETRIUS' FLEET IN 306 BC: Diod. 20.50.2. PTOLEMY'S FLEET IN 306 BC: Diod. 20.49.2; cf. Casson, 1971, pp. 137–8.
9. BATTLE AT SALAMIS: Diod. 20.49–52. Wallinga, 1956, suggests that the crews of Ptolemy's fleet were the ramming and the boarding side; cf. Hauben, 1976b, pp. 1–5.
10. RHODES AND THE DIADOCHI: Diod. 20.81.2–4; cf. Polyb. 30.5.8; cf. Berthold, 1984, pp. 59–66.
11. SIEGE OF RHODES: Diod. 20.81–8; 20.91–100; Plut. *Dem.* 21–2: see Berthold, 1984, p. 66–80. BATTLE AT IPSUS: Diod. 21.1; Plut. *Dem.* 28–30.
12. DEMETRIUS' SHIPS: Plut. *Dem.* 31.1; cf. Plut. *Dem.* 32.2.
13. 'FIFTEEN' AND 'SIXTEEN': Plut. *Dem.* 43.4–5. LETTER OF LYSIMACHUS: Plut. *Dem.* 20.4.
14. LEONTOPHOROS: *FGrH* III B 434 F8; Casson, 1969, pp. 185–93; Casson, 1971, 112–16; 137–40; contra: Morrison, 1980a, p. 46.
15. NAVAL BATTLE IN 280 BC: *FGrH* III B 434 F8; BATTLE AT COS: Athen. 5.209c; cf. Tarn, 1910, pp. 209–22; Casson, 1971, pp. 115–16.
16. PTOLEMY'S FLEET: Athen 5.203d; cf. *OGIS* 39.
17. SHIP OF PTOLEMY IV: Athen. 5.203e–204b; Casson, 1969, pp. 185–93; Casson, 1971, pp. 108–16; cf. Morrison, 1980a, pp. 45–6.
18. PIRACY: Ormerod, 1924, pp. 119–30; cf. Brulé, 1978. HEMIOLIA: Morrison, 1980b, pp. 121–6; contra: Casson, 1971, pp. 127–35.
19. TRIHEMIOLIA: Morrison, 1980b, pp. 121–6.
20. RHODES: see note 10; see also Pekáry, 1976, pp. 68–9; Finley, 1973, pp. 130–1.
21. GRAIN TRADE: Casson, 1954b, pp. 168–86. TRADE IN GENERAL: Pekáry, 1976, pp. 67–70; cf. Roztovtzeff, 1941, pp. 1238–301.
22. EXPLORATIONS OF HANNO: Cary and Warmington, 1929, pp. 47–52. EXPLORATIONS OF PYTHEAS: Cary and Warmington, 1929, pp. 33–40; Hawkes, 1975; Pédech, 1976, pp. 71–5; Dilke, 1985, pp. 136–7.

Chapter Ten

Rome's First Naval Adventures

The Romans who in the fifth and fourth centuries BC subdued the whole of Italy would never have expected that their descendants would sail out in great numbers to fight naval battles. They strongly disliked the sea and, after all, they had made very great conquests without a fleet. Starting out as a small agrarian community, it had taken them only two centuries to gain ascendancy over all Italy. This had been achieved without a single ship and they had never even so much as felt the want of a fleet. All those who had once meant a threat to Rome had to acknowledge its superiority. Latins, Volsci, Aequi, Sabines and Samnites had been defeated and their land had enlarged Roman territory. The dislike of the sea was in the Romans' blood. They were farmers and shepherds. When they felt threatened by peoples rushing down the surrounding mountains, they were quite willing to take up arms and defend themselves to the bitter end. And they had no qualms about teaching a potential enemy their strength, even if unchallenged.

There are hardly any traces in Roman literature of a real attachment to the sea. When the subject of the sea comes up, it is usually in the context of upper class landed estates situated on the coast. Climatic conditions and nautical manoeuvres are described in imprecise terms, as if observed by an outsider. Even when the Romans controlled large areas of the Mediterranean, they kept their distance. In this they were widely different from the Greeks. They, too, were originally farmers and suffered from a touch of hydrophobia, but in their case this was coupled with an attachment to the sea that grew stronger in the course of time. The Greeks sailed the seas themselves and the majority of the oarsmen in the war fleet were citizens. In Rome, serving in the navy was, if possible, left to foreigners. Certainly, during the time of the late republic Roman citizens did serve in the navy, but they were mostly *libertini* (former slaves) or naturalised foreigners, not Romans by birth. Roman citizens were called up to serve in the legions. Having to be an oarsman in the fleet was seen as a degradation.[1]

The Roman attitude towards navigation strongly contrasts with that of the Etruscans, with whom the Romans came into contact at an early stage and who in the sixth century BC dominated them. At that time the Etruscans had risen to a leading position at sea. Their thalassocracy in the area of the Tyrrhenian Sea resulted in military expeditions sometimes extending as far as the Aegean, which got them in Greek eyes the reputation of being pirates. When in the beginning of the sixth century BC the Phocaeans appeared and the Greeks discovered the routes to the west, the situation changed in that the Etruscan monopoly was threatened. They formed an alliance, both military and economic, with the Carthaginians. A confrontation between the allied forces of Etruria and Carthage and the Phocaeans took place in 535 BC at Alalia. Though the Greeks were victorious in this close battle the Etruscans remained masters of the Tyrrhenian. This thalassocracy was ended *c.* 60 years later in the battle of Cumae (*c.* 475 BC).

Figure 10.1 Etruscan Black Figure Hydria (*c.* 525–485 BC) with a Two-level Ship

The Etruscan fleet of the sixth century BC should not be belittled. Since the Etruscans were able to withstand the Greeks for a long time it is evident that they kept up with the developments in ship construction. Presumably they used the same type of ship as their Greek opponents: pentecenters rowed at two levels. This hypothesis is corroborated by a representation on a black figure hydria dated *c.* 525–485 BC (Figure 10.1).[2]

Though dominated by the Etruscans, the Romans acquired little nautical knowledge either from them or from the inhabitants of the Greek cities in southern Italy. One might be led to think that the Romans felt such a strong aversion to the sea that they had no ships at all. This was not the case, but their accomplishments at sea were minimal and were not taken very seriously by their opponents. A case in point is that of a Roman warship which was sent to Delphi in 394 BC in order to make a sacrifice to Apollo as a token of the Roman gratitude for the capture of the Etruscan city of Veii. The ship was intercepted by a patrol vessel from the Lipari Islands and taken to be an Etruscan pirate. When the Romans had managed to clear up this misunderstanding, the Liparians did not only allow them to continue their voyage but also escorted them to Greece and back; after all, they said, others might make the same mistake. Evidently the Romans were not very well-known among the seafaring nations. Fifty years later little had changed. When in 349 BC Greek pirates approached the coast of Latium the Romans were unable to fit out a fleet strong enough to defeat them. Instead, they stationed soldiers on the coast who prevented the pirates from landing.[3]

Whether they liked it or not, the Romans had to get involved in naval matters. The expansion of their territory to the south caused direct conflicts with the Greek cities and their well-organised fleets. Naples had been captured in 326 BC without naval support, but further expansion made a fleet absolutely necessary. In 313 BC a Roman colony was founded on the island of Pontia. The fleet did not play an important role in this operation, but its value was certainly recognised. Two years later two subordinate officials were appointed, each commanding a squadron of ten ships. In 310 BC one of these admirals, P. Cornelius, led an expedition against the rebellious league of Nuceria. The expedition was unsuccessful and only two years later Nuceria was subdued by the legions, an operation in which the fleet played no part at all. Yet, the Roman war fleet was born, even though it consisted of a mere 20 ships.

Initially no major feats were performed by this fleet, as became clear 30 years later. In 282 BC ten Roman triremes attacked the fleet of Tarente in the open sea and were sunk. Whatever serious consequences this defeat might have had, they were averted by the Roman legions, well-trained as a result of long campaigns. Tarente was defeated, in spite of the support of King Pyrrhus of Epirus who twice got the better of the Romans but was crushed in the third battle and left Italy empty-handed.[4]

The Roman conquests extended as far as Rhegium. Sicily, on the other side of the Strait of Messina, had for centuries been the scene of battles between the Greeks and the Carthaginians. The northernmost city of the island, Messina, had been captured by the Mamertines, Campanians who had served as mercenaries in the Syracusan army. They terrorised the city and engaged in large-scale piracy. Hiero, tyrant of Syracuse, attacked and defeated the Mamertines, but was unable to take possession of the city because the Mamertines asked the Carthaginians for help. A garrison was sent but, having installed itself in the city, remained there. Now the Mamertines turned to Rome. Following extensive de-liberations — the Senate was unable to reach a decision, but the Assembly voted in favour of an intervention — a Roman army was sent to Messina. This decision, taken in 264 BC, was the beginning of a conflict, the consequences of which could not possibly have been foreseen at the time either by the Romans or by the Carthaginians. The latter did not expect the Romans to come to Sicily and initially attempted to reach a diplomatic solution. The Romans considered the Carthaginian occupation of Messina a possible threat to southern Italy, a threat which could only be averted by capturing the city.

Polybius relates that, when the Romans decided to intervene in Sicily, they did not have a fleet of their own but only penteconters and triremes belonging to the Greek cities in southern Italy; no exact numbers are mentioned. Polybius' statement is probably not completely correct, but the Roman fleet was certainly much smaller than that of Carthage. The Roman decision to sail to Sicily was, therefore, a risky one. Carthaginian ships controlled the Strait of Messina and would doubtless intercept any troop trans-port. Moreover, if the Romans were defeated on Sicily the Carthaginians would have an excellent opportunity to cross over to Italy and threaten the coasts. When, however, the Romans put out from Rhegium the Carthaginians seemed to be overlooking this possibility. They did intercept the convoy consisting of merchantmen from the Greek cities, but, rather than destroying it, they forced it to return to its home port. The Romans ought to have realised that the Carthaginians had no aggressive intentions but wanted to comply with the existing agreements; in 279 BC they had even agreed upon mutual support against Pyrrhus of Epirus. But the Romans interpreted the Carthaginian strategy as a sign of weakness. Continuing their operation even more energetically, they managed to elude the Carthaginian ships in the darkness, took possession of the harbour of Messina and occupied the citadel. New armies were dispatched to Sicily and the war spread over the whole island, against the will of the Carthaginians. They were, at first, supported by Hiero of Syracuse, but when the Romans threatened to lay siege to his city he changed sides.[5]

Fortune continued to smile upon the Romans. The Carthaginians retreated to the fortified towns on the west coast of Sicily, leaving the inlands to the Romans. Agrigentum, after Syracuse the largest city of the island, was captured, albeit after a long struggle which took up seven months. Then — two years had passed since the initial intervention — the conquests came to a halt. However well-trained, the Roman troops were unable to take the remaining cities, which were safe behind their fortifications and received constant food supplies by sea. When, for the first time since the outbreak of the war, the Carthaginians began to consider countermeasures, thus giving up the possibility of a peaceful solution, the Romans even got into difficulties.

The powerful Carthaginian fleet had not yet been involved in the conflict, but after the siege of Agrigentum was given a central role in the Carthaginian strategy. In the spring of 262 BC a large fleet — the exact number of ships is not known — was sent to Sardinia; from there, it was to undertake attacks upon Rome and other cities in Latium. The Carthaginians expected the Romans either to leave Sicily altogether or at least to send part of their troops back to Italy. The Romans, however, adopted neither of these strategies but sent another army to Sicily. This came to nothing: though occupying most of the island, the Romans had to suffer the defection of several coastal cities to Carthage, a tendency which grew stronger when the Carthaginian fleet began operations everywhere along the Italian and Sicilian coasts.[6]

A difficult decision faced the Romans: in order to be successful in this war, which they themselves had started, they would have to build a fleet strong enough to bridle the Carthaginians. Yet, they realised that constructing such a fleet and recruiting capable crews was not an easy task. Good shipwrights, experienced in building quinqueremes, a type of ship which was very popular in the Carthaginian fleet at the time, would have to be looked for abroad. The Romans could probably have found such shipwrights as well as quinqueremes in Syracuse and possibly in Tarente and Locri; but, according to Polybius, the problem was solved by a stroke of unexpected good luck, as a result of which they were able to build a fleet themselves without any outside assistance. In 264 BC, in the course of their double attempt to cross the Strait of Messina, they had captured a grounded Carthaginian quinquereme and had towed it to a harbour. The ship had been carefully studied and now the Roman shipbuilders were ready to construct quinqueremes themselves. In 60 days a fleet consisting of 100 quinqueremes and 20 triremes was built. The Roman 'fives' were not quite identical to the Carthaginian quinqueremes. They were heavier and more sluggish, but the Romans did not consider this a serious drawback; they may even have seen it as an advantage in view of the boarding tactics which they would have to resort to.[7]

Yet, ships alone do not make up an effective fleet: the recruitment of rowers posed new problems. Neither Rome nor the cities of Latium had any kind of rowing tradition. Great numbers of capable oarsmen were, however, needed. A regular 'five' required at least 300 rowers, so that at full complement the Romans would have to have 100×300 or 30,000 men to man the quinqueremes and 20×170 or 3400 for the triremes. From later sources we know that the crews were mostly levied from the *socii navales*, the inhabitants of the allied Italian cities. These crews were, however, by no means sufficient to man the entire fleet, not even combined with rowers from the cities of Latium. All over Italy, therefore, the Romans attempted to recruit rowers, even among the Samnites, though they had only recently fiercely fought the Romans and had no naval tradition. Slaves serving on the fleet are not mentioned, but considering the enormous lack of manpower it cannot be excluded that they were assigned to the galleys. Roman citizens did not serve as rowers, but were recruited as marines. The crews were thoroughly trained. They were given elementary instruction seated in temporary platforms constructed on land. Since on a quinquereme one oar was manned with two or three rowers, only one capable oarsman was required per oar. Presumably the recruits from the coastal cities of Latium and Italy were selected for this task, while the others were mainly trained to increase their muscle power in order to be able to keep up with the beat set by the stroke oarsman.[8]

This hurriedly assembled Roman fleet sailed along the Italian coast to Sicily, commanded by Cn. Cornelius Scipio. With a squadron of 17 ships he attempted to occupy Lipara, a Carthaginian naval base, but was captured by the Carthaginians. Weakened by this setback, the morale of the Romans suffered yet another blow when, after executing an irresponsible manoeuvre, a Carthaginian squadron of 50 ships managed to escape due to the lack of speed of the heavy Roman vessels. As things stood now, the Roman admirals were less experienced than their Carthaginian opposite numbers and the Roman ships and crews were inferior to those of their opponents. Considering all this, and convinced that they were better soldiers than the Carthaginians, in 260 BC the Romans introduced a weapon which added a completely new dimension to the existing boarding tactics. The boarding bridge, which must have been designed on the basis of extensive experiments on the Italian wharves, had two important characteristics: firstly, it could be used to catch and immobilise an enemy ship and was heavy enough to prevent the enemy from cutting it loose; secondly, the marines could, in formation, safely board the enemy ship, because a kind of gangway was created.

As to the construction of the boarding bridge, the inventor of which is unknown, information is supplied by Polybius. His description is, however, not clear on all aspects of the construction. Much ink has been spilled on the problem of reconstructing the design of the boarding bridge on the basis of Polybius' text. The most elaborate and most satisfactory reconstruction is that of H. T. Wallinga, who extensively describes the mechanism of this new boarding bridge, generally referred to as the *corvus*, as well as its implications for naval tactics (Fig. 10.2). He translates and elucidates the relevant passage from Polybius as follows:

A round pole stood on the prow, four fathoms (7.20 m) long and three palms (0.23 cm) in diameter. [That is to say: 7.20 m of the pole was visible above the prow. It had been stepped into the keel, so as to give it firmness, and its real length therefore was about 12 m]. That pole had a tackle-block at the top

Figure 10.2 Reconstruction of the Boarding Bridge

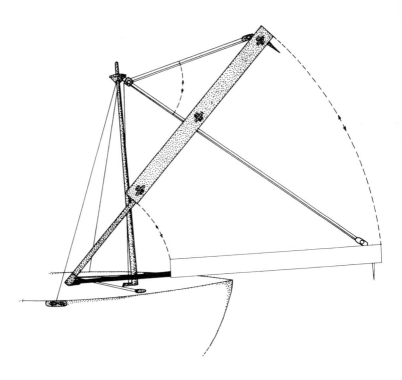

[perhaps a many-sheaved, but probably a simple one]. Round it was put a ladder on which cross-planks had been nailed, [so that the result was a gangway] 1.2 m wide and 10.80 m long. [This gangway had a weight of about 1150 kg.] The aperture in the planking was oblong [a slot, that is, about 0.25 m wide], and it went round the pole right after the first two fathoms of the ladder [i.e. the slot was 3.60 m long. It was closed at the end of the gangway by means of a detachable cross-bar which served to enable the Romans to mount the bridge and to jettison it if need came. The principal function of the slot as slot, that is in contradistinction from a much shorter oblong hole, was to give the bridge sufficient play for all its movements]. The gangway had also a railing along each of its long sides, as high as a man's knee [not however over the full length of the sides, but only to the point where the slot began, so as not to prevent the soldiers from stepping on the bridge near or past the pole]. At its end [that is the gangway's end] was attached something like a pointed pestle, made of iron [probably about one meter long and 0.10 m in diameter], at the upper end of which there was a ring, so that the whole looked like the machine used in working corn. To that ring was fastened a rope with which, as soon as the ships charged, they [the Romans] raised the ravens by means of the tackle-block on the pole [and a capstan or, less probably, by means of the compound pulley it was part of] and dropped them [by means of a trigger-mechanism] on the deck of the enemy ship, sometimes forward, sometimes bringing them round [by means of two tackles, the blocks of which were attached to the rear-end of the bridge and to two points near the ship's board, rather more forward than the bridge's rear-end] to meet flank-attacks.[9]

The Carthaginians, as yet ignorant of the new weapon, repeatedly challenged the Romans, convinced as they were that the Romans would not be able to offer any effective resistance. The Roman commander, the consul C. Duilius, did not avoid a confrontation. The Roman fleet of 145 ships — reinforced by contingents from Massilia and Naples — sailed to Mylae; here the Carthaginians had concentrated their activities. When the Carthaginians spotted the Roman fleet they confronted it with only 130 ships, though they could easily have manned 200, a decision which clearly illustrated their excessive self-confidence. They did not even take the time to line up their ships but attacked in disorder, attempting to ram the Roman ships. This strategy was not very successful. When the Carthaginian ships were about to ram, the Romans put the boarding bridges into operation. Within seconds the iron pins penetrated the decks of the enemy ships and the Roman marines occupied the Carthaginian vessels. When, after a short but vehement fight, the Carthaginians retreated they turned out to have lost 31 ships, including their flagship, a 'seven'.

The first naval battle between the Carthaginians and the Romans was not over yet. The Carthaginians now resorted to the well-tried tactic of the *periplous*, which they expected to be very effective against the sluggish Roman ships and to prevent the Romans from using the boarding bridges. But the Carthaginians had only 99 ships left whereas the Romans had not suffered any appreciable losses; consequently, the latter were able to resist the Carthaginian *periplous*. When the Carthaginians attacked the

Roman ships, the Romans formed a second line consisting of over one-third of their fleet. The Carthaginians did, indeed, manage to encircle the first line of Roman ships and attacked them from all sides. This was, however, what the remaining Roman ships had been waiting for; they fell upon the Carthaginians and successfully employed the awesome boarding bridges. Again, the Carthaginians could offer no resistance and were put to flight.[10]

The Roman victory at Mylae had by no means put an end to the Carthaginian naval supremacy. During the years 260–259 BC the Romans did not dare attack the west coast of Sicily, from Lilybaeum in the west to Panormus in the north; their naval bases were too far away for them to operate successfully in this area. Thus the Carthaginians were given a chance to repair their losses. It did not take them very long to rebuild their fleet and there was an increasing chance that they would again take the offensive. In 256 BC, the Romans, therefore, decided to undertake a rather risky venture, albeit not without considerable hesitation. Rather than attempting to gain control of the west coast of Sicily in order to keep the Carthaginians at a distance, they began preparations for an invasion of Carthage itself. This strategy was well-chosen. The Carthaginians were hated by the other inhabitants of northern Africa, whom they kept in subjection with the aid of violence. The Romans hoped that their invasion would induce these nations to rebel. The Carthaginians knew very well that the position of their empire in Africa was rather weak and attempted to prevent the Roman invasion, of which they had been informed by scouts. Rather than the coast of northern Africa, which they felt was too long to be defended effectively, they chose the southern coast of Sicily as the scene of battle. Considering that the Roman fleet would sail along the coast as far as possible before crossing to Carthage they expected that the enemy would in any case pass the south coast of Sicily in the environs of Heraclea. At Ecnomus they would confront the Romans.

Polybius' estimate of the number of ships involved in this battle is probably too high. He mentions 350 Carthaginian and 330 Roman ships; according to modern scholars the Carthaginian fleet probably consisted of 200 ships and the Roman fleet of 230, mostly quinqueremes (Fig. 10.3) and some sexiremes. Polybius' high estimate of the total number of ships may presumably be explained by the fact that he included the transport vessels. He states that the quinqueremes were rowed by 300 men at three levels: two files of thalamites, two of zugites and one of thranites on each side. The numbers may have been 2 × 29, 2 × 29 and 1 × 34, adding up to 92 oars on each side. Assuming that there were 120 marines per ship, the total number of Roman marines must have been 230 × 120 = 27,600. The Roman admirals, the consuls M. Atilius Regulus and L. Manlius Vulso, had devised a special formation. The fleet was divided into three lines. The first line consisted of 80 quinqueremes, spread over two wings which were commanded by the two consuls. A second line, made up of an equal number of ships, was to prevent the Carthaginians from attacking the first line in the rear, and, at the same time, it was given the difficult task of taking the transport ships in tow. A third line of 70 ships covered the transport ships in the rear. When the Carthaginians spotted this formation — according to Polybius from a distance of

Figure 10.3 Reconstruction of the Bow of a Carthaginian Quinquereme

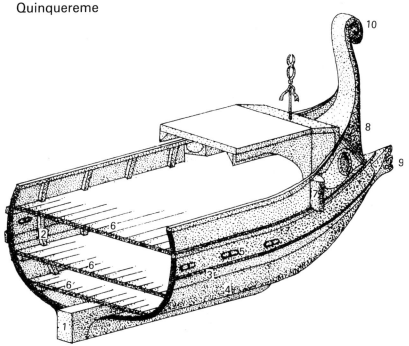

1. keel   2. frames   3. wale   4. strakes   5. oarport   6. decks   7. forward face of the outrigger   8. sternpost   9. ram   10. ornament atop the sternpost

five miles — they immediately adapted their strategy. They intended to isolate the first line of the Roman fleet. Hamilcar, the Carthaginian counterpart of the Roman consuls, ordered the centre of his fleet to retreat slightly, in the hope that this manoeuvre would entice the first line of the Roman ships to attack, thus enabling the Carthaginian wings to execute a *periplous*. When Hamilcar felt that the distance between the first and second lines of Roman ships had become large enough for the Carthaginians to attack the first line in the rear without any danger from the boarding bridges of the ships in the second line, the Carthaginian centre took the offensive.

Theoretically speaking, Hamilcar's strategy was well-devised. He intended to confront the first line of the Roman fleet first and only afterwards to take on the second and third lines, rather than fighting the entire fleet at the same time. But the Romans could not be lured into a trap so easily. Contrary to the expectation of the Carthaginians, the Roman first line did not attack in line abreast formation, but while the centre pursued the enemy at full speed the wings advanced more slowly, thus creating a wedge-shaped formation. As a result of this manoeuvre the centre of the first line had lost contact with the second line, but the wings were still close enough to prevent a Carthaginian *periplous*. Moreover, the ships in the second line rid themselves of the transport vessels which they had in tow. Left without protection, the sluggish freighters were aided by a favourable wind and managed to escape to a safe harbour before the Carthaginians could reach them.

Increasing confusion reigned among the Carthaginians as they realised that the battle was not proceeding according to Hamilcar's plan. The Carthaginian wings in particular did not know what to do. The distance between the first and second lines of the Roman fleet was by far not as great as they had expected. Fear began to prevail: vivid memories of the boarding bridges kept them from attempting to encircle the first Roman line. They attacked the second and third lines, thus completing the failure of Hamilcar's strategy; if his plan had worked, the entire Carthaginian fleet of 200 ships would have confronted a mere 80 enemy vessels (the first line). Now, however, the battle was fought on three fronts, on each of which the Romans were numerically superior. First, the weakened Carthaginian centre was dealt with by the Roman first line and, after losing several ships, took to flight. The Romans took the captured ships in tow and sailed back to support their third line against the right wing of the enemy. Here, too, the Carthaginians were routed. Finally, the entire Roman fleet fell upon the ships of the Carthaginian left wing, which seemed to be getting the better of the Roman second line: now they, too, were put to flight. The disastrous outcome of this battle for the Carthaginians is best illustrated by the fact that they lost 94 ships, almost half of their fleet. The Romans had lost 24 of their 230 ships and were now clearly superior to the Carthaginians; moreover, the Romans had captured 64 Carthaginian vessels, 20 of which they repaired and added to their own fleet.[11]

The Roman winning streak did not go on for ever. The year 255 BC brought several disappointments. An expedition to Africa, made possible by the Roman victory at Ecnomus, was a great failure. It was not the fleet and its crews, who played a minor role in the events in the Carthaginian territory, who were to blame. Initially, a Roman defeat did not seem at all likely. Having landed at Clupea they defeated a Carthaginian army, and Carthage seemed ready to surrender. However, the harsh terms stipulated by the Romans made the Carthaginians decide to continue the struggle. In the spring of 255 BC they defeated the Roman army. The consul Regulus was taken prisoner, many others were killed and 3600 men retreated to Clupea. In Rome the newly elected consuls, who were already busy preparing a new invasion of Africa, were ordered by the Senate to change their plans and merely to evacuate the Romans from Clupea. Invigorated by their successes on land, the Carthaginians attempted to intercept this fleet. Within a few weeks they constructed a new fleet, which was, however, by no means comparable to the fleets that up to 260 BC had dominated the seas. Both the ships (more than 200) and the hurriedly levied crews were of poor quality. At Cape Hermaeum the two fleets confronted each other. In the ensuing battle, the Romans crushed their opponents and captured 114 Carthaginian ships. Polybius does not give any detailed information as to how exactly this battle developed. All we know is that the poorly-trained Carthaginians sailed too close to the coast, afraid to be encircled by the Romans, who were numerically superior. This strategy turned out to be ill-advised, for it allowed the Romans to advance in line abreast formation. The threatening boarding bridges drove many Carthaginian ships on to the shallows near the coast or fastened themselves to the decks, after which the Roman marines dealt with the crews. After this battle the Romans under siege in Clupea were evacuated without any difficulty.[12]

At that moment the Romans seemed to dominate the waters between Africa and Italy. Including the 114 ships captured from the Carthaginians the Roman fleet totalled 364 ships. The Carthaginian fleet, on the other hand, had been reduced to less than 100 ships as a result of the failure at Cape Hermaeum. According to the Romans, no danger was to be expected from the Carthaginians in the near future. But they were overlooking one important factor. Up till then they had hardly ever operated in unfavourable weather. Neither their limited naval experience nor their ships, less seaworthy due to the heavy boarding bridges, had been put to the test by the elements. When, returning from Africa, the Romans were rounding the south-eastern promontory of Sicily they were caught in a violent storm. All but 80 of their ships went down in the whistling wind or were dashed to pieces against the rocks. Great numbers of oarsmen and marines were drowned. According to Polybius, the obstinacy and lack of experience of the Roman consuls are to be blamed for this massive shipwreck. They had disregarded warnings from experienced sailors not to round the cape. Thus the end of the year 255 BC saw two decimated fleets.[13]

Both parties spent the following years rebuilding their fleets. In the year after the disaster the Romans already had 220 ships, identical with those that had been lost, at their disposal, as well as new crews. The Carthaginians, on the other hand, were faced with problems. Regulus' invasion into Africa, though a failure, had induced a rebellion of the nations under Carthaginian domination, so that the Carthaginians were compelled to keep a large army in Africa. As a result, the fleet and Sicily were slightly neglected. The Romans took advantage of the situation and occupied Panormus, on the north coast of Sicily. Having regained confidence, they undertook some minor expeditions to the coast of northern Africa, which were, however, by no means comparable to Regulus' invasion. The reappearance of the Carthaginian fleet took the sting out of these attacks, and they came to an end after a new shipwreck of 150 Roman ships between Sicily and Rome.[14]

The struggle on Sicily was slowly approaching a new climax. Initially the Romans had been fearful of the elephants which the Carthaginians had brought into action, but after some time they found ways to effectively fight these animals, got the upper hand and drove the Carthaginians back to the west coast. In order to achieve their goal of 'liberating' Sicily from the Carthaginians the

Romans would have to occupy one of the two major fortified cities on the west coast, Drepana and Lilybaeum. In 250 BC they laid siege to Lilybaeum, both from the sea and from land. Three years had passed since the capture of Panormus, a delay caused by the fact that the Roman fleet had to be rebuilt after the shipwreck. Now four complete legions, *c.* 32,000 men, and 120 fully manned ships were brought into action. The surrender of the 7000 mercenaries, reinforced by 10,000 soldiers, seemed only a matter of time. But contrary to the expectation of the Romans, who considered themselves far superior both on land and at sea, they did not succeed in taking the city.

Why were the Roman attempts unsuccessful? First of all, Lilybaeum, situated on a promontory, was almost impossible to reach by land or by sea. The harbour, defended from the fortified city, was small and could only be entered through a narrow fairway. Only very experienced sailors could safely sail into the harbour. But a much more important factor was the lack of experience on the part of the Romans. A siege under these circumstances required a close co-operation between fleet and army, a requirement with which Roman military forces had rarely been confronted. While the army had succeeded in preventing access to the city over land, the blockade at sea was far from secure. If, in fact, the Roman fleet had been able to close off the city, the intensive siege would doubtless have been effective. But now the Carthaginians repeatedly managed to slip through the Roman blockade and provide the city with food and military reinforcements.

During this siege the Romans became painfully aware of the fact that their ships, however useful in naval battles at close quarters, were not sufficiently effective in a situation such as this. The boarding bridge was of little use but made the ships less seaworthy and less manoeuvrable. Moreover, after their defeats at Mylae and Ecnomus, the Carthaginians had spared no effort in designing ships able to defeat the Roman vessels. The Roman sailors were dumbfounded at the sight of Carthaginian quinqueremes, even faster and lighter than the original type, breaking through their blockade. In a direct confrontation with the Roman quinqueremes these new ships would no doubt have run into difficulties, but the Carthaginians made every effort to avoid such a confrontation. They waited for a favourable wind and then, sailing and rowing at full speed, attempted to elude the enemy. They were all the more successful because the Romans, afraid to get trapped in the narrow fairway, did not want to come too close to the entrance of the harbour. In this way Carthaginian squadrons repeatedly managed to reach Lilybaeum.[15]

The failure of the siege of Lilybaeum caused significant developments in Roman ship construction. The new Carthaginian quinquereme was looked upon with a mixture of envy and appreciation. Then, a stroke of good luck, comparable to that which had enabled the Romans to build their own quinqueremes, caused another fast Carthaginian ship to fall into their hands. A quadrireme, leaving the harbour of Lilybaeum at night with messages for the Carthaginian senate, ran aground in the dark and was captured by the Romans. They repaired and manned the ship, and noticed that it was fast enough to overtake a quinquereme sailing at full speed.[16]

This discovery made the Romans realise that if they wanted to follow the development of ship construction in Carthage, they would have to do away with the boarding bridge. Besides, the disastrous shipwrecks of 255 and 253 BC had made it painfully clear to what extent the boarding bridges impaired the quinqueremes' seaworthiness. But the Carthaginians, who were quickly building great numbers of new ships, did not leave them enough time to construct a balanced fleet. In 249 BC, when the Roman legions were still besieging Lilybaeum, the Romans learnt that a Carthaginian fleet of 110 ships, anchored at Drepana, would soon be reinforced by another 70 ships, which had just been launched from the wharves. The Roman consul P. Claudius Pulcher was faced with a difficult decision. On the one hand, he could confront the Carthaginian fleet at Drepana before the arrival of the reinforcements. On the other, any delay would be to the advantage of the Romans. Many oarsmen had died at Lilybaeum and the 10,000 new men, recruited from Italy, were untrained and would be of little use in a full-scale naval battle.

In the end, Pulcher decided to take the offensive, though with ships of the old type (presumably the boarding bridges had been removed) manned with oarsmen who hardly knew how to row. Initially he hoped to be able to surprise the Carthaginians in the harbour of Drepana, but the Carthaginian commander Adherbal soon saw through the Roman plans and took countermeasures. He ordered his fleet to leave the harbour immediately, so that the Romans could be confronted in the open sea; here the

Carthaginians would be able to take full advantage of their light and fast ships. The sight of the Carthaginian fleet, in line ahead formation, caused considerable confusion among the Romans. Pulcher, who was nowhere to be seen in the front ranks, could not do anything to allay the panic which seized his men. Though at first the Romans were able to offer some resistance, they soon had to retreat. Now the absence of the threatening boarding bridges made itself felt. The fast Carthaginian galleys circled around the Roman ships on all sides. Because Pulcher had stationed his ships just off the coast the retreat ended in a disaster. The battle resulted in a complete victory for Adherbal. Of the 123 Roman ships 93 were lost, and the first naval defeat of the Romans by the Carthaginians was a fact.[17]

As a direct consequence of their victory, the Carthaginians had restored their hegemony at sea, a position which had been challenged by the Romans since 260 BC. Roman ships, freighters and warships alike, were repeatedly intercepted by Carthaginian galleys. On top of all this, a large Roman squadron sunk in a storm at the same spot where in 255 BC a fleet had suffered shipwreck. One setback followed another, and in 249 BC the Roman fleet, which a few years earlier had consisted of 240 ships, had been reduced to 20. Public opinion in Rome turned against those who advocated a naval war at all costs. It was clear that in the near future the Romans were not likely to take any initiatives.

When the Romans seemed ripe for the assault, the Carthaginians did not attack. If ever they had a chance, it was in 249 BC: Carthage had a vast numerical superiority of 170 against 20 war vessels. But internal crises which threatened to break up the African empire demanded attention, and the Carthaginians felt that a war on two fronts would be too much. The Carthaginian senate decided to postpone the struggle against the Romans on Sicily until the war in Africa had been brought to an end. A large part of the troops on Sicily were transferred to Africa, and the crews of the fleet passed their days in idleness in the harbours of Lilybaeum and Drepana. Training, necessary to keep up physical condition and rowing techniques, was neglected. After all, nobody expected the Romans to reappear at sea in the near future.

In Africa the Carthaginians were slowly but surely regaining control and could begin developing plans for war against the Romans, who still occupied large parts of the Sicilian inlands. In 247 BC the new Carthaginian commander Hamilcar Barca recommenced hostilities. When his initial attempts to drive the Romans off the island failed — he was unable to ease the pressure on Lilybaeum and Drepana — he started a guerrilla war: the coasts of Sicily and south-west Italy were subjected to nocturnal Carthaginian attacks. But this strategy came to nothing. The Romans did not give up any territory. Even when Hamilcar occupied the city of Eryx, west of Panormus, he was unable to extend the area under Carthaginian control.

This war would no doubt have continued for a long time, if in 243 BC the Romans had not decided on a new ship construction programme. The moment was well-chosen, because most of the Carthaginian ships had left the Sicilian waters and the Carthaginians did not at all expect the Romans to renew their naval activities in the area. Serious financial problems due to the previous wars were solved by patriotic Roman citizens: very rich citizens personally financed one quinquereme each, others who were less well off co-operated in subsidising the construction of one ship.

Most of the vessels that were launched were quinqueremes. These new 'fives' hardly resembled their predecessors of the beginning of the war. The boarding bridge had disappeared from the design and the emphasis was on speed, manoeuvrability and seaworthiness, characteristics the absence of which had been made painfully clear by the shipwrecks of the past 15 years. In training the rowers much more attention was given to ramming manoeuvres.

It was with great surprise that the Carthaginians learnt of the launching of the new Roman fleet. Their own ships lay unused in the harbours of Sicily and Africa and the crews still had not resumed rowing practice or had been consigned to the army in Africa. In July of 242 BC the Roman fleet, consisting of 200 new ships, sailed to Sicily and, without meeting with any resistance, blockaded the harbours of Lilybaeum and Drepana. Only eight months later, in March of 241 BC, the Carthaginian fleet, the size of which Polybius does not mention, appeared. Both ships and crews were ill-prepared for battle. The vessels were undermanned and heavily laden with supplies for the besieged cities.

Before the Carthaginian admiral Hanno was able to carry out his plan to postpone the impending battle until after he had disposed of the supplies and taken on board new troops, the Romans took the offensive. They waited for the Carthaginians to cross to

Drepana from Hiera, the westernmost of the Aegates Islands, where they had cast anchor. In spite of the presence of the Romans the Carthaginians continued their course, apparently assuming that the strong westerly wind would keep the Romans from intercepting them. But the Roman fleet was no longer manned with sailors who were afraid of the elements. Now the removal of the boarding bridge, though victorious in many battles, proved useful. As soon as the Carthaginians put out, sailing before the westerly wind, the Romans confronted them. No details are known concerning the ensuing battle, but presumably the Romans had the upper hand from the very beginning. The Carthaginians were crushed; they lost 120 ships, 20 of which were captured by the Romans.[18]

The defeat of the Carthaginian fleet put an end to the resistance of Lilybaeum and Drepana. No more supplies were delivered, and hunger, thirst and disease spread rapidly. The Carthaginians did consider constructing a new fleet but rejected this plan when they realised that it could by no means be accomplished in time to save the two cities. Instead, the Carthaginian senate decided to attempt to conclude a reasonable peace treaty. They had already expected to be forced to give up Sicily, and the tribute of 3200 talents, to be paid in 20 yearly instalments, was not considered excessive. But the most serious consequence of their surrender was the loss of face. The Carthaginian naval supremacy had come to an end. Their authority was no longer taken for granted. Many nations took up arms against Carthage, whose domination had involved considerable violence. The mercenaries, who had fought so many battles on land and at sea for the Carthaginians, were robbed of the pay due to them and rebelled. It took the Carthaginians over three years to defeat them. The Carthaginian garrison on Sardinia, strategically situated opposite the west coast of Italy, mutinied. Supported by the local population they asked Rome to take over on the island. At first the Romans refused, but when the request was repeated they took possession of Sardinia and, soon afterwards, Corsica. Even in the far west Carthage suffered losses. The silvermines in northern Spain were lost, probably due to the inhabitants of Massilia, who were faithful allies of the Romans.

The defeat of Carthage also affected trade in the western Mediterranean, which had for a long time been reserved for Carthaginian freighters. Now foreign traders had complete access to the area, apart from the coasts of northern Africa and southern

Spain in the vicinity of Gibraltar. Massilia in particular profited by the disappearance of the Carthaginian monopoly and founded new trade settlements in Spain.

Notes

1. ROMAN ATTACHMENT TO THE SEA: De Saint Denis, 1935; Thiel, 1946, pp. 1–16.
2. ETRUSCAN EXPANSION AT SEA: Liv. 5.33.7–10; cf. Heurgon, 1969, pp. 110–11; Hus, 1980, pp. 258–62. ETRUSCAN SHIPS: Morrison and Williams, 1968, p. 112 and p. 162; Biers and Humphreys, 1977, pp. 153–6.
3. SITUATION IN 394 BC: Diod. 14.93.7; Liv. 5.28.1; App. *It.* 8; Plut. *Cam.* 8; cf. Ormerod, 1924, p. 157; Thiel, 1954, pp. 6–7. SITUATION IN 349 BC: Liv. 7.25.3–4; 7.25.12–13; 7.26.10–15.
4. PONTIA: Liv. 9.28.6. DUOVIRI NAVALES: Liv. 9.30.4. NUCERIA: Liv. 9.38.2–3. TARENTE: App. *Sam.* 7; Liv. *Per.* 12.
5. CAUSES OF WAR: Pol. 1.10–11; cf. Thiel, 1954, pp. 128–43. FLEET OF THE GREEK CITIES: Polyb. 1.20.13–14. TREATY BETWEEN ROME AND CARTHAGE IN 279 BC: Polyb. 3.25.1–5.
6. CARTHAGINIAN ATTACKS ON SICILY: Zonar. 8.10.1.
7. GROUNDING OF A CARTHAGINIAN QUINQUEREME: Polyb. 1.20.15. CONSTRUCTION OF A ROMAN FLEET: Polyb. 1.20.9; cf. De Saint Denis, 1975, pp. 62–6.
8. RECRUITMENT OF ROWERS: Thiel, 1954, p. 41 and pp. 73–6. TRAINING OF THE ROWERS: Polyb. 1.21.2; cf. De Saint Denis, 1975, p. 68.
9. BOARDING BRIDGE: Wallinga, 1956, spec. pp. 69–70. LATIN NAME CORVUS: Wallinga, 1956, pp. 73–4; see also Poznanski, 1979, pp. 652–61. Tarn, 1907, p. 51 note 9 doubts the existence of the boarding bridge.
10. BATTLE AT MYLAE: Polyb. 1.21–3; Flor. 1.18.8–9; cf. Rodgers, 1937, pp. 276–7; Thiel, 1954, pp. 115–28. NUMBER OF SHIPS: Tarn, 1907, pp. 48–60.
11. STRENGTH OF THE FLEETS AT ECNOMUS: Polyb. 1.26.8; Tarn, 1907, pp. 48–60; Thiel, 1954, p. 84; pp. 209–10. De Saint Denis, 1975, pp. 72–3 accepts Polybius' numbers. BATTLE AT ECNOMUS: Polyb. 1.25.7–29.1.; cf. Rodgers, 1937, pp. 278–91; Thiel, 1954, pp. 212–53.
12. BATTLE AT CAPE HERMAEUM: Polyb. 1.36.11–12; cf. Thiel, 1954, p. 121 and pp. 232–5.
13. FIRST SHIPWRECK OF THE ROMAN FLEET: Polyb. 1.37.3–10.
14. SECOND SHIPWRECK OF THE ROMAN FLEET: Polyb. 1.39.6; cf. Diod. 23.19; Zonar. 8.14; Oros. 4.9.11.
15. SIEGE OF LILYBAEUM: Polyb. 1.41–8; Diod. 24.1–4.
16. CARTHAGINIAN QUADRIREME VERSUS QUINQUEREME: Polyb. 1.47.5; 1.59.8.
17. BATTLE AT DREPANA: Polyb. 1.50–1; cf. Thiel, 1954, pp. 272–81.
18. ROMAN BUILDING PROGRAMME IN 243 BC: Polyb. 1.59.6–8. BATTLE AT THE AEGATES ISLANDS: Polyb. 1.60–1; cf. Thiel, 1954, pp. 311–14.

Chapter Eleven

Roman Supremacy at Sea

After the first Punic War the Romans ruled the western Mediterranean. They had a fleet of over 250 heavy warships, including captured Carthaginian vessels. Between 240 and 230 BC no naval activities were required, not even in the conquest of Sardinia and Corsica, because the Carthaginians had fewer ships, particularly smaller triremes and penteconters.

It is uncertain why Teuta, queen of Illyria, risked a war with the Romans. One reason may be that up till then the Romans had mainly sailed the seas west of Italy and had paid little attention to the activities of the Illyrian pirates in the Adriatic. The inhabitants of the Greek cities in Italy, however, did worry, because maritime trade between the cities of Magna Graecia and the mainland of Greece suffered as a result of Illyrian attacks on merchantmen. Like the Cretan and Cilician pirates, the Illyrians used light rowed galleys, the so-called *lembi*. This type of ship, of which many variations existed, was characterised by its speed and man-oeuvrability. Some *lembi* had 50 rowers, others only 16. Some were rowed at one level, others at two. Due to their speed they could surprise their victims and quickly board them. The Italians frequently complained to the Senate about the Illyrian pirates, but their grievances were ignored. When, however, the Illyrians had killed a large number of Italian merchants and captured many others the Romans went into action. The immediate cause of their initiative was the death of one of the two envoys who had been sent to Teuta in 230 BC. A fleet of 200 ships (almost the entire Roman fleet) and an army of 20,000 troops and 200 cavalry crossed the Adriatic. Without encountering any appreciable res-istance the Romans occupied Corcyra, Epidamnus and Apollonia. They hoped that, as a result, the safety of the trade routes would be guaranteed. At first this was, in fact, the case. But after the departure of the Romans, Demetrius of Pharus, a local dynast who had allied himself with the Romans in 229 BC, began to engage in large-scale piracy, thus violating the existing agreements. He was supported by the Macedonians, who feared a permanent Roman influence in the Balkan. When Demetrius invaded the protectorate which the Romans had established in 229 BC on the south coast of Teuta's territory the Romans went into action once again. The exact number of ships which crossed the Adriatic in 219 BC is not mentioned in the sources but it is likely not to have been lower than in 229 BC. No significant resistance was offered. Demetrius fled by sea to the Macedonian king Philip V; Pharus and his other properties were added to the Roman protectorate.[1]

Rome had enlarged its territory but, at the same time, gained an enemy: the Antagonids, dynasts of Macedonia. If the enemies of the Romans were to form a coalition, especially if such a coalition were to have both a powerful fleet and a strong army at its disposal, a rather dangerous situation might arise. Carthage and Macedonia were perfectly suited to undertake combined action against the Romans. The latter strongly resented and feared the increasing Roman influence in the eastern Mediterranean, while the Carthaginians longed for a restoration of their naval supremacy. Their expansion in Spain did not sufficiently compensate for the losses they had suffered in the Punic War.

A new conflict between Rome and Carthage became inevitable when the Romans allied themselves with the city of Saguntum in Spain. In 226 BC a treaty had been concluded with the Carthaginians in which the river Ebro was agreed upon as the dividing-line between the territories of the two nations. The Roman alliance with Saguntum, situated south of the Ebro, constituted an overt violation of this agreement. The Carthaginians considered this an act of aggression; under the command of Hannibal, they captured the city after a long siege.

Considerable attention has been devoted to Hannibal's heroic journey across the Pyrenees and the Alps to Italy. It is less well-known that Hannibal chose this route because of Roman naval supremacy. An expedition by sea, which would have saved a great deal of time and effort, was out of the question. In 218 BC the Carthaginians were unable to man a fleet strong enough to confront the Romans. The Carthaginian fleet was merely assigned the task of guarding the coasts of northern Africa and Spain, while Hannibal marched to Italy across the Alps. The entire fleet, which was stationed in Spain, consisted of no more than 50 quinqueremes, two quadriremes and five triremes, whereas the Romans had 220 quinqueremes at their disposal. Sixty vessels were assigned to P. Cornelius Scipio in Spain and 160 to Ti. Sempronius Longus, who was stationed in Sicily. The latter was to carry the war into Africa. It is, therefore, not surprising that the Carthaginian fleet was extremely reluctant to confront the Romans and that, as a result, no major naval battles like the ones at Mylae, Ecnomus and the Aegates Islands took place in the second Punic War.

Initially the Romans were rather unsuccessful. An attempt to intercept the Carthaginian army near Massilia failed; Hannibal invaded Italy and thrice defeated the Romans: at the river Trebia, at Lake Trasimene and, finally, at Cannae in 216 BC. Yet, these Carthaginian successes did not bring about the complete surrender of the Romans. They continued to fight, encouraged by several minor naval victories, as a result of which Carthaginian troop transports by sea were cut off. Hannibal's attempts to occupy the harbours of Naples, Puteoli and Cumae failed.[3]

The invading troops plundered and devastated large parts of the Italian countryside. Gradually starvation became a serious problem in the cities of Italy, particularly in Rome. If the Romans had not been superior at sea, Rome would perhaps have been starved out and forced to capitulate. But now freighters could freely transport grain to the city and relieve the shortage of food, all the more serious because large numbers of people flocked to Rome from the countryside. In the spring of 216 BC a fleet of transport vessels from Sicily unloaded 300,000 *modii* (*c.* 2000 tons) of grain at Ostia, the port of Rome.

These large-scale grain transports to Rome did not require extensive preparations. After the Roman naval successes navigation had become increasingly safe and Sicily had become the granary of Italy. The ships that were used to transport the grain were presumably larger than the normal freighters; reliable data are, however, lacking. The only evidence is provided by Athenaeus (third century AD) in a description of the *Syracusia*, a superfreighter built before 221 BC by Hiero II of Syracuse, probably following a design of Archimedes. According to Moschion, Athenaeus' source of information, this ship was the largest merchantman in antiquity, manned by a crew of 700 oarsmen. Unfortunately, no dimensions are mentioned, but the ship's cargo on its maiden trip is said to have consisted of 60,000 *modii* (400 tons) of grain, 10,000 jars of pickled fish, 20,000 talents of wool and 20,000 talents of miscellaneous items. Modern estimates range from 1900 to 4200 tons. It ought to be realised that the fact that more than four centuries later Athenaeus decided to describe this ship indicates that it must have been exceptional and cannot be viewed as representative of the grain ships of the late second century BC. The *Syracusia* cannot possibly have moored at Ostia, because the river port was not at all suited for ships of that size. If the *Syracusia* did, in fact, take part in the grain transports to Rome, the grain must have been transferred to smaller ships at Puteoli. Probably, however, smaller grain ships, of the order of 200 to 400 tons, brought the grain from Sicily and unloaded it out at sea on to smaller vessels, which took it ashore.[4]

The Romans suffered a serious blow when in 215 BC their loyal ally Hiero II died and was succeeded by his grandson Hieronymus. After some hesitation, he took sides with Carthage. A new war on Sicily had thus become inevitable. The situation became even more difficult for the Romans when the Macedonians, too, allied themselves with Hannibal. In order to preclude a Macedonian invasion a squadron of 25 ships was sent to Calabria. Due to the unpopularity of the Macedonian king Philip V his attempts to block the sea lanes along the Greek coast failed, in spite of the support of several cities in Achaea. As a result, the increasing trade contacts between Italy and Pergamum, Rhodes and Egypt were not endangered. The long route to Egypt was particularly important to the Romans, now that the imports from Sicily stagnated.[5]

Sicily did, indeed, become the scene of battle, but only on land. The Carthaginians seemed to have accepted Roman naval supremacy, though the fleets of the two nations were almost equal in size. Apart from some minor engagements no real naval confrontations occurred. Between 218 and 214 BC the Romans had the opportunity to build many new ships to replace older ones. The Roman fleet had a threefold task: it plundered the African coast, protected the Italian coast and intercepted Carthaginian convoys which supplied Hannibal with food, money and troops. It engaged in military activities when in 214 BC the Roman commander M. Claudius Marcellus laid siege to Syracuse, using 130 ships. At first this siege, both from land and from sea, was not very successful. The Roman attack over land was directed against the northern part of the city, because there the fortifications were less strong than elsewhere. However, the Syracusans effectively withstood the Romans by means of Archimedes' ingenious ballistic machines which hurled large rocks down the slopes. The Roman fleet attacked the eastern walls of the city, which extended into the sea. The first line, consisting of the oldest ships, advanced to the coast as far as possible; there heavily-armed marines disembarked and stormed the walls. Slingers, archers and javelin-throwers on a second line of ships provided cover. Moreover, the Romans also had four special siege vessels, consisting of two ships tied together and rowed by the outside files of rowers. These catamarans were provided with ladders, the so-called *sambucae*, ending in a platform which accommodated four persons. Upon approaching the walls these ladders were pulled up by means of pulleys, so that the platform was at the same height as the enemy soldiers on the walls. Marines on the platform fired at the enemy while others attempted to reach the walls by means of gangplanks.

Any other city would not have been able to hold out. But thanks to Archimedes' inventions Syracuse was hardly affected by the Roman attacks. The troops were sheltered from enemy missiles in trenches. Moreover, the Syracusans had at their disposal large cranes which would unexpectedly appear above the walls and either drop large rocks on the Roman ships or grab a ship by the stern, lift it up and drop it again, causing it to capsize or to take water.

In the end the Romans managed to take the city. While the Syracusans were celebrating a festival in honour of Diana they occupied the strategically situated heights of Epipolae. In addition, the commander of the citadel, Euryalus, defected and surrendered to the Romans. Carthaginian attempts to relieve the city failed. When contagious diseases broke out, particularly in the Carthaginian army, their attacks ceased completely. Then a commander of Spanish mercenaries betrayed his employers and enabled the Romans to occupy Syracuse. Archimedes, whose inventions had delayed the Roman victory, was killed, against the will of the Roman commanders. The city was plundered and ransacked. Large numbers of Greek artefacts were transported to Rome in order to decorate the houses of the aristocracy.[6]

As was noted above, this Punic War took place on land. Roman naval supremacy was not affected, not even by the Macedonians, upon whom the Carthaginians had built their hopes. As a result, the Carthaginians could not possibly win the war of attrition. While the Romans were always able to send troops and supplies to threatened areas, the Carthaginians had to take the difficult routes over land. Thus the Romans managed to overcome initial setbacks in Spain and capture Carthago Nova, the capital of the Carthaginian empire in Spain. Hasdrubal, however, was compelled to make a long detour through the Pyrenees and the Alps in order to relieve his brother Hannibal, who had finally been driven into a corner by the unyielding Roman forces. His expedition was an utter failure. He was intercepted, defeated and killed.

One would have expected the Romans to attempt to maintain their preponderance at sea. They did so only to some extent. As soon as an agreement had been concluded with the Macedonians and Hasdrubal had been defeated, the active fleet was reduced. The consequences of this decision became evident in 204 BC. Under the command of the young P. Cornelius Scipio the Romans were preparing an expedition to Africa in order to finish off the Carthaginians on their own ground. Though the Romans knew that the Carthaginian fleet in the African harbours consisted of 100 ships, Scipio took only 60 war vessels to Sicily, only 40 of which he was able to use in the expedition to Africa. The Romans optimistically assumed that the Carthaginian fleet was not prepared for battle and would not be able to offer any resistance. They were proved right. The Carthaginians did not challenge Scipio's fleet. Yet, whatever the final outcome, sailing a fleet of 400 transport vessels to Africa with an escort of a mere 40, mostly old warships was a rather hazardous venture.[7]

The way in which the Romans made use of their war fleet during their stay in Africa also illustrates that, in spite of their naval supremacy, they still lacked real seamanship. After a failed attempt to storm and occupy the city of Utica the Romans had to entrench themselves for the winter. They chose a rocky peninsula, where, however, they were not very well protected against repeated attacks of the Carthaginians, who had now brought their fleet into action. The Roman fleet of 40 ships was not at all sufficiently large to resist the Carthaginians. The Romans, therefore, resorted to a special defensive strategy. They arranged the transport ships around the warships, in three files. The freighters were tied together and, after masts, rigging and any other obstacles had been removed, covered with planks, so that a large deck was created. On this 'battlefield' the Romans felt more comfortable. A few narrow channels were left open, in order to allow fast ships to pass through. The crews of these ships were to attack any Carthaginian ship that had lost contact with the fleet.

This strategy failed. The Carthaginians were able to advance and reached the wall of transport ships. With grapnels they broke open the first line and captured 60 transport ships. But in spite of this success they did not continue their attack. Thus Roman neglect of a sound naval policy was spared a catastrophe.[8]

The Romans did not increase the size of their active fleet until Hannibal was forced to leave Italy and returned to Africa. Now, too, they missed a chance to intercept Hannibal. They did not assemble a fleet to prevent Hannibal's disorganised and demoralised troops from crossing over to Africa. It was not until Hannibal had reached Africa and was preparing himself for the battle which would be decisive for Carthage's position as a major power that they were stirred into activity. The year 202 BC saw tremendous naval activity in the African waters. Scipio's 40 warships were reinforced by a fleet of 120 vessels. Fear and respect for the energetic Carthaginian general had moved the Roman Senate to take this measure. It was not ruled out that in spite of their apparent superiority the Romans would be defeated, in which event the fleet would be needed to evacuate the troops and to prevent the war from being transferred out of Africa once again.[9]

These precautions turned out to be superfluous. Thanks to the Numidian cavalry the Romans were victorious, albeit after a hard battle. Carthage's role as an imperialist power was over. A tribute of 10,000 talents, the loss of its territory apart from the city itself and its immediate surroundings and the surrender of the entire war fleet except for ten triremes precluded any aspirations in the near future. A most humiliating condition was added: any military activity would have to be approved of in advance by the Romans.[10]

Rome now dominated the western Mediterranean, but had paid a high price for its victory. The countryside had been devastated and the farms were undermanned. After years of military service many farmers stopped trying to make their business pay and moved to Rome, where they lived a humble life, dependent on the aristocratic elite. The latter bought up the land and planned to grow olives and grapes and to graze cattle, activities which they considered to be more profitable than the cultivation of grain. As a result of this development Italy, and Rome in particular, became dependent on other areas for its grain. A certain amount could be imported from Sicily and Sardinia, though these islands had suffered considerable devastation during the war. Livy relates that several times during the 30 years following the second Punic War the annual tithes from Sicily and Sardinia were not sufficient to feed the increasing population of the city. It became more and more necessary to find new suppliers of grain, which were most likely to be found in the east. Soon Asia Minor, Egypt and northern Africa exported large quantities of grain to Italy.[11]

Macedonia, only recently a direct opponent of the Romans, disapproved of any Roman influence in the Aegean. The Seleucids in Syria equally opposed any change in the balance of power in the eastern Mediterranean. When in 204 to 202 BC the Macedonian king Philip adopted an aggressive attitude towards Pergamum and Rhodes the Romans jumped at the opportunity and sent their naval squadrons to the east. First Philip incited Cretan pirates to attack Rhodian merchantmen. The Rhodians reacted to the hostilities and at the outset were confronted by most of the cities of Crete. As president of the Cretan confederacy Philip was obviously injured by the Rhodian action against Crete. While extending his influence in the Aegean and the Propontis he attempted to harm Rhodian interests as much as possible. The occupation of four cities in the Propontis made a conflict inevitable. The capture of Miletus, a short time later, also caused King Attalus of Pergamum to declare war on Macedonia. Both nations, as well as Philip, prepared their fleets. In 201 BC a Macedonian fleet consisting of 53 warships, mostly quadriremes and quinqueremes, but also several 'sixes', 'eights', 'nines' and one 'ten' as well as 150 fast Illyrian *lembi*, sailed to the island of Chios. The fleet of Rhodes and Pergamum consisted of 65 warships, quadriremes and larger types, and only three triremes and nine *trihemioliae*.

The naval battle at Chios is worthy of mention because it marks the end of an era, being the last major confrontation in which the Romans were not involved. On both sides tactical errors abounded. Ramming and boarding manoeuvres were executed in complete disorder. The battle must have given the impression of a wild, disorganised struggle. Since the fleet of Rhodes and Pergamum was caught somewhat off guard the ships were unable to go into action all at the same time. Two separate battles developed, one between the Macedonian right wing and the fleet of Pergamum and the other between the Rhodian ships and the Macedonian left wing. Both sides suffered extensive losses. The

Macedonians lost 28 large warships, among which their flagship, the 'ten', which was destroyed at the very beginning of the battle, three lighter vessels and half the *lembi*. Rhodes and Pergamum lost fewer ships, five large galleys and two lighter vessels, but did not dare to proclaim themselves victors. Philip did, in spite of his considerable losses and the fact that during the winter of 201/200 BC he was trapped at Bargylia by a blockade of the fleet of Rhodes and Pergamum. It was not until the following spring that he could escape with his battered fleet.[12]

After the battles Rhodes and Pergamum expected Philip to rebuild his fleet and to try again to get the upper hand. Afraid to have to give up their independence, they resorted to a course of action which was, in view of the circumstances at the time, by all means understandable. They wanted to preserve the balance of power at sea and in the autumn of 201 BC requested help from the Romans, the only nation which could be expected to be powerful enough to defeat the Macedonians. The Romans granted the request, moved by bitter resentment over Philip's alliance with Hannibal and by the desire of leading senators to obtain a glorious command against Philip.[13]

The war between Rome, supported by Rhodes and Pergamum, and Macedonia was mainly fought on land, due to the enormous difference in naval strength. The Romans had several hundred quadriremes and quinqueremes, which could be made ready for battle within a few weeks. The Macedonians, on the other hand, had lost half their fleet at Chios. Though no exact numbers of ships are known, it may be assumed that the Macedonian fleet was inferior by far. Apparently the Macedonians were well aware of this. When the Romans crossed the Adriatic and established several naval bases in the Balkan the Macedonian fleet remained in the harbour of Demetrias and dared not put out to sea, a situation which would remain unchanged throughout the war. Had this not been the case, then conducting a war in Macedonia would have posed far greater problems for the Romans. Now transports of troops and supplies from the west could proceed unhindered.

The lack of a good fleet made it practically impossible for the Macedonians to develop an effective strategy. Now the Roman fleet would operate along the west coast and the army in the east, now the fleet would sail into the Aegean and the army would move into western Macedonia. Philip had to be everywhere at the same time. When in 199 BC Aetolia and the small states of the Aegean took sides with the Romans, induced mainly by the threatening fleets of Rome, Pergamum and Rhodes, Philip's position became practically hopeless. He was forced to fight. In 197 BC the Macedonian army was defeated by the Roman legions commanded by the consul T. Quinctius Flamininus at Cynoscephalae. For over three years Philip had been able to hold out in this unequal struggle.

The conditions imposed on the Macedonians by the Romans were severe, but had to be accepted: a tribute of 1000 talents and surrender of the entire fleet. Moreover, the Macedonians had to give up all their possessions abroad, both in Greece and elsewhere in the Aegean. As a result, the Greek cities would be free and autonomous. A curious aspect of these conditions is that the Romans demanded the surrender of the Macedonian fleet, which consisted of little more than 20 real warships, but left the Macedonian army untouched. They probably considered the Macedonian strength a useful buffer against nations advancing from the north and were confident that, if need be, they would easily be able to defeat Philip, since he had no fleet.[14]

The defeat of the Macedonians and the weakening of the Egyptian empire had upset the balance of power in the eastern Mediterranean. Antiochus III, king of the Seleucid empire, saw an opportunity to increase his power. He ordered the construction of a fleet of 200 triremes and larger types and 200 smaller ships, mainly *lembi*. With this fleet he began operations in the Aegean, and soon took possession of large parts of the west coast of Asia Minor as well as areas north of the Hellespont and in Thrace. Pergamum and Rhodes watched these conquests with increasing uneasiness, Pergamum because it feared to be conquered as well, and Rhodes because its trade interests were at risk. But Antiochus wanted to avoid a confrontation with the Rhodians, who would be supported by the fleets of Rome and Pergamum.

It is misleading to assume that the Roman intentions were entirely pacific. By proclaiming the freedom of the Greek cities subject to Antiochus Rome had interfered in his affairs. In 192 BC the Aetolians decided to summon Antiochus to liberate Greece and to arbitrate between themselves and the Romans, who laid claim to several cities in Thessaly. War broke out. Before the Romans had realised what was happening, Antiochus crossed to Greece, with a fleet of 100 warships, triremes, quadriremes and smaller galleys, as well as over 200 transport ships. His army consisted of 10,000 infantry, 500 cavalry and six elephants. Initially, the Romans underestimated Antiochus' intentions. Only 25 quinqueremes were sent out to prevent the enemy from landing near Demetrias. As a result, Antiochus met with little resistance and was able to establish a foothold on Euboea. He did not, however, get much support. The Achaean League remained faithful to the Roman cause and even Philip of Macedonia preferred his lukewarm friendship with the Romans to an alliance with Antiochus. The Aetolians, who did support Antiochus, could only muster 4000 soldiers. When in 191 BC a Roman army of 22,000 men landed at Apollonia Antiochus' optimism rapidly disappeared. One by one cities were forced to surrender to the Romans. Finally, Antiochus built his hopes on stopping the Romans at Thermopylae, the passage into Greece. But he did not succeed in preventing the Romans from continuing their advance. He was defeated, fled to Chalcis on Euboea and sailed back to Asia Minor, where he cast anchor off Ephesus.[15]

In the first part of the Syrian War the fleet played a minor role, but later on its involvement was of extreme importance. If the Romans wanted to finish off Antiochus for good they would have to fight the Syrian king in Asia. This would only be possible if the Romans gained control of the Asian waters, a goal they could only reach if they eliminated Antiochus' fleet. Now this was easier said than done; Antiochus had enlisted a Rhodian exile, Polyxenidas, who had competently embarked upon the construction of a fleet which was to be a match for the Romans. Meanwhile, the king himself had sailed the ships that were already prepared to the Thracian Chersonnesus in order to block the advance of the enemy.

In August 191 BC the Romans appeared in the area of the island of Delos with a fleet consisting of 81 triremes and quinqueremes, and 24 lighter ships. Unfavourable weather, however, prevented them from continuing on to the coast of Asia Minor to join the fleet of Pergamum. When they were able to leave, Antiochus had, in the meantime, left the Hellespont and set sail to Ephesus; he arrived before the Romans had made contact with the Pergamene forces. Polyxenidas' fleet now consisted of 70 triremes and 130 lighter ships. His opponents did, however, join forces when Polyxenidas had cast anchor at Cissus, half-way between Phocaea and Ephesus. Reinforced by 24 heavy ships — presumably quadriremes and quinqueremes — and 26 light ships from Pergamum, the total fleet opposing the Syrians now consisted of 105 quinqueremes, quadriremes and 50 open light ships.[16]

A confrontation was inevitable. In line ahead formation the Romans sailed through the strait of Chios. Rounding Cape Argennum they spotted the enemy fleet, which was approaching them. Somewhat surprised by this quick development they began preparations for the imminent battle. Sails and masts were lowered, marines were stationed on the decks and rowers on the benches. The Romans, led by C. Livius Salinator, turned aside on to the open sea to confront the reinforced right wing of the Syrian fleet, which was commanded by Polyxenidas himself. The Pergamene ships, under the command of Eumenes, remained close to the coast and formed the right wing.

As has been noted several times already, naval battles are not very well documented. The battle of Cissus is no exception to this rule. More is known about individual exploits than about the battle as a whole. But, comparing and combining the information given by Polybius, Appian and Livy, we may attempt an overall description. The Romans on the left wing and Polyxenidas' ships first joined battle. Immediately a Roman ship was lost as a result of an attack by two enemy vessels, but as the battle proceeded the Romans got the upper hand. They patiently withstood the raging attacks, let the Syrian triremes and light ships execute the *periplous* and the *diekplous* but repeatedly struck their decks with grappling-irons and boarded them. These iron 'claws' are in no way comparable to the boarding bridges which the Romans had introduced at Mylae. In the 50 years that had passed since then the Romans had followed the development of ship construction and had realised that the tendency toward lighter triremes and quadriremes excluded the boarding bridge, for reasons of stability. But in a surprise attack the grappling-irons were extremely effective. Thus, boarding tactics got the better of ramming: ten Syrian ships were sunk and 13 captured, while the Romans lost only that one ship.[17]

With the remainder of the fleet Polyxenidas fled to Ephesus, wisely ignoring Roman provocations to renew the fighting. As a result, the Romans controlled the waters of Asia Minor. Antiochus had given up the Hellespont and Polyxenidas' fleet was caught in the harbour of Ephesus. Much further to the south, Syrian squadrons lay in the harbours of Cilicia and Phoenicia, but at least for the time being, they could not yet directly threaten Roman superiority.

The Roman victory seemed to have settled matters at sea; but Livius and his successor L. Aemilius Regillus made some tactical mistakes. They did not maintain the blockade of Ephesus nor did they send the remainder of the fleet (reinforced by 25 Rhodian ships, mostly triremes, and 50 newly built quinqueremes and triremes) to the south to confront the rest of Antiochus' naval forces, commanded by Hannibal, who had fled from Carthage. Instead, in 190 BC the Romans transferred their military headquarters to the Hellespont; they intended to secure safe passage for L. Cornelius Scipio, who was marching to Asia Minor via Thessaly, Macedonia and Thrace. At that moment, however, Scipio was still at a considerable distance from the Hellespont. In the meantime, Polyxenidas had increased his fleet to 47 triremes, 18 quadriremes and quinqueremes, nine 'sixes' and five 'sevens' and felt strong enough to leave his shelter. His spirits rose even further when he managed to capture a Rhodian squadron which was on its way to the Romans in the north: having pretended that he was planning to defect to Rhodes, he had attacked them from all sides during the night.[18]

There was a serious danger that Polyxenidas' ships in Ephesus and the fleet which was assembling in increasing numbers in the harbours of Cilicia and Phoenicia would join forces. In the Roman naval headquarters on Samos, the admirals were facing a difficult decision. It would be too risky to split up the allied fleet of Rome, Rhodes and Pergamum in order to fight both Polyxenidas and the fleet commanded by Hannibal at the same time. The Roman fleet of 125 ships was strong enough to check Polyxenidas, but that was all. Moreover, part of the allied fleet would not be sufficient to take effective action against Hannibal, whose fleet had become a great deal stronger. Antiochus had learnt his lesson from the Romans and had reinforced the fleet with large numbers of heavier ships, particularly several 'sixes' and 'sevens'.

The position of the Romans did not improve when the Roman army was reported to be approaching the Hellespont; measures would have to be taken to ensure a safe crossing to Asia Minor. Seleucus, Antiochus' son, was awaiting his chance in northern Asia Minor. In June 190 BC, therefore, Eumenes was sent northwards with 23 ships. Only recently all Roman troops had been withdrawn from this region because of the increasing hostilities in the south, a neat illustration of the day-to-day strategy of the Roman commanders. Though initially the Romans intended to keep the remainder of the fleet together, they were forced to change plans once again. Hannibal's squadron was aproaching at a higher speed than had been expected, and, in spite of the limited number of ships, the fleet had to be split up. The Rhodians were given the difficult and dangerous task to check the fleet advancing from the south. Their commander, Eudamus, put out with only 15 quadriremes, which were joined by 17 other 'fours' and six open ships from Rhodes: thus, the squadron amounted to a mere 38 ships. In addition, they were reinforced by four triremes and two quinqueremes from Cos and Cnidus. The fleet which they had to confront consisted of 47 warships: 3 'sevens', 4 sexiremes, 30 quinqueremes and quadriremes and 10 triremes. The odds seemed to be against the Rhodians: they were numerically inferior and had lighter ships. The Syrians, with their heavier ships, expected to be able to imitate the Roman strategy at Cissus, but they underestimated the Rhodians, who were very experienced in the use of triremes. When, at the end of July, the two fleets confronted one another off Side (on the south coast of Asia Minor), the Syrians were prepared to attack immediately, convinced that their opponents would offer little resistance. They were already lined up in formation while the Rhodians were still sailing line ahead. The Rhodian commander Eudamus must have panicked slightly at the sight of this strong fleet. He turned away towards the open sea, allowing the ships following him to catch up. This manoeuvre was, however, executed in a rather clumsy fashion, as a result of which the ships which were supposed to form the right wing on the land side did not have enough room. The enemy, numerically superior as it was, jumped at the opportunity and encircled the Rhodian formation, which did not extend far enough towards the open sea. And when Eudamus, disregarding his function as commander of the entire fleet, suddenly fell upon the enemy with five ships the situation seemed to become even more unfavourable. Fortunately, Pamphilidas and Chariclitus, who commanded the centre and right wing of the Rhodian fleet, remained calm. A number of ships, which due to lack of room could not join the formation, were directed to the other wing in order to assist Eudamus. He badly needed some support, because the Syrians had already started encircling and boarding his ships. On the other wing and in the centre the Rhodians were in control; due to the inexperience of the Syrians and the excellent seamanship of the Rhodians the Syrian attempts at boarding failed. The fast Rhodian triremes could easily outmanoeuvre the badly steered sluggish ships of the Syrians and even got the better of them through a successful *diekplous*. Many ships were rendered ineffective, though only a few were sunk. Most of the enemy fleet turned about and took to flight. Seeing this, the crews on the other wing lost courage and felt incapable of resisting the Rhodians attacking them from all sides. They sailed off, having lost twelve ships.[19]

Not surprisingly, the Romans and their allies were quite satisfied with their victory. Polyxenidas and Hannibal had been successfully and definitively prevented from joining forces. As a precaution a Rhodian squadron continued to patrol the coasts of Cilicia. In particular, they kept a close watch on the Syrian naval base at Patara in order to prevent the enemy fleet from putting in there for necessary repairs (almost all the Syrian ships had incurred some kind of damage). The Syrians, on their part, were seriously demoralised. Polyxenidas' strategy had depended upon joining forces with Hannibal, so that they could have attacked the Romans together. He had passed up the opportunity to fall upon the Romans while the Rhodian ships were away, though he must have realised that he had more ships at his disposal in Ephesus than the Romans had at Samos.

King Antiochus realised that a naval battle could no longer be avoided. Unless the Syrians managed to defeat or at least drive back the Roman fleet, which had been restored to its former strength, the entire Roman fleet would be able to sail to the Hellespont and nothing would prevent the invasion of the Roman army. It was unlikely that the Roman admiral, aware of the favourable developments in the south (the naval victory at Side) and in the north (Eumenes' superiority in the Hellespont), would readily take the offensive. Therefore, Antiochus decided to attack the city of Notium, an ally of the Romans, situated close to Ephesus, in the hope that the Roman fleet would leave its base at Samos and thus offer Polyxenidas an opportunity to go into action. The Roman ships did, in fact, put out from Samos but, contrary to Antiochus' expectation, did not sail directly to Notium. They suffered from a serious shortage of food, a problem which they considered more urgent. In September they sailed to nearby Teos, which had, in the past, supplied Antiochus with large quantities of food. At the sight of the Roman fleet the inhabitants of this island asked for forgiveness and offered supplies to the Romans, who cast anchor in the harbour of Geraestum, just north of Teos. When it was reported to Polyxenidas that the Roman fleet was in the narrow harbour of Geraestum, surrounded by two mountain chains, he went into action immediately. He intended to station ten ships on either side of the narrow entrance to the harbour and to disembark the crews of the remaining ships; he wanted to attack from two sides, a strategy which had proved successful against the Rhodians at Panormus. Now, too, he would have been likely to get the upper hand, but at the last moment the Roman fleet sailed to the harbour of Teos, which was ill-suited for such an attack.

All the same, Polyxenidas took the offensive, at noon on the following day, when the Roman crews were in the city. But, once again, his plans were thwarted by bad luck. A farmer from the environs of Myonessus reported to the Roman commanders that the enemy fleet was preparing an attack. At once, the crews were called back and the ships were made ready for action. The Roman admiral Regillus immediately put out from the harbour and sailed to the open sea, while the rest of the fleet followed in line ahead formation. The Rhodian ships, which were supposed to be the fastest, brought up the rear. In total 58 Roman and 22 Rhodian vessels confronted Polyxenidas' fleet, which consisted of 89 ships.

The situation was unique in that neither fleet had anticipated a battle such as the one they were about to fight. Polyxenidas had not expected to face a fleet in line abreast formation (Regillus on the right wing on the open sea and the Rhodians on the left wing near the coast) while his own ships were still sailing line ahead. However, the Romans did not operate according to any planned strategy. Regillus, confronted by Polyxenidas, had already engaged his opponent while, on the other wing, the Rhodians were still advancing. Almost at once the Syrians got the upper hand and even threatened to encircle Regillus' squadron. Eudamus, however, turned about and came to the rescue. The first Rhodian ships had large fires on their stems, at the sight of which the oarsmen of Polyxenidas' fleet, who were already rejoicing in their victory, were struck with fear. Many captains were so frightened of the fires that they turned their ships away from them, offering the vulnerable flanks of their vessels to the rams of the enemy. From all sides the Rhodian triremes, superior in speed and manoeuvrability, fell upon the Syrians. Some ships caught fire and got in the way of the others. Polyxenidas' encircling strategy failed completely, as did his boarding tactics. In the bitter fights of ship against ship, man against man, the Roman marines turned out to be stronger. Only on the land side did the Syrians not suffer any losses, due to the fact that the Rhodians had left their position to assist the Romans on the other wing. Polyxenidas' order to retreat to the harbour of Ephesus meant a serious disappointment for the Syrians. A different strategy was, however, out of the question: half of the fleet had been lost; 13 ships had been captured by the Romans and 29 had been sunk.[20]

This combined victory of the Romans and Rhodians put an end to Antiochus' naval aspirations. Antiochus realised that the Romans, having defeated both Hannibal and Polyxenidas, would send the greater part of their fleet to the Hellespont, since they had little to fear elsewhere. He concentrated on his land forces and allowed the Roman army of 28,000 troops and 2800 cavalry to cross the Hellespont. The final confrontation took place a few months after the naval battle at Myonessus. Near Magnesia Antiochus' army, though numerically superior, was defeated by the experienced and well-trained Roman legions. Apart from considerable tributes the Hellenistic ruler was forced to surrender all but ten of his warships to the Romans. Syrian activities at sea could only take place to the east of Cilicia, and their ties with Greece and Macedonia were severed.

Within a few decades the Romans had defeated Carthage, Macedonia and Syria and now dominated the Mediterranean from the Spanish beaches to the coasts of Asia Minor. In the east they did not enlarge their empire but even put Rhodes and Pergamum in control of several cities in Asia Minor. The Romans were not eager to control the seas themselves. The Hellespont was Pergamene, the west coast of Asia Minor was either free or under Rhodian control, and Rhodes was master of the Aegean through its trade and its position as leader of the Nesiotic League. Rome, however, was the decisive power in the affairs of Greece and Asia Minor.

After a new war from 171 to 168 BC against the Macedonian king Perseus, who strove to restore the kingdom of his father Philip to its former glory, the true intentions of the Romans became clear. The war itself, started by the Romans out of fear of Perseus and a possible Macedonian/Syrian coalition, was fought mainly on land. After all, the Macedonians had very few ships. In 196 BC Philip had been forced to surrender almost all his heavy ships to the Romans, and since then the Macedonian fleet mainly consisted of *lembi* and other light ships, which were no match for the Romans and their allies. A small fleet of 40 to 65 ships was sufficient to prevent Macedonian naval activities, though in the beginning of the war a rather careless attitude on the part of the Romans had allowed the Macedonians to gain a few minor successes, such as attacks on Roman transport vessels escorted by warships. The fleet primarily acted as support for the army, which in June 168 BC won the decisive battle at Pydna. Macedonia was divided into four separate, independent republics, which were not even allowed to have any trade contacts with one another.

After this victory the Romans devoted their attention to all those who had obstructed them, who had offered too little co-operation or who had remained neutral. This included the Rhodians. The ruling aristocracy had always been in favour of the alliance with Rome, but the people had inclined to Perseus. As a result of the struggle between the pro-Roman and the pro-Macedonian groups Rhodes had hardly participated in the last war. In 171 BC only six ships had been contributed to the Roman fleet and in the following years none at all. During those years the Rhodians had been busy restoring the important grain shipments from Egypt, which had been severely disturbed by increasing piracy. The Roman Senate considered this behaviour a sufficient reason to subject the Rhodians. No military action was required. Rhodes was ordered to give up Lycia and Caria, 20 years after it had been put in control of these regions; this condition was not unexpected, considering the expansionist tendencies of the Romans. Rhodes' position as a trade centre was severely impaired as a result of the establishment of Delos as a free port, a measure which did not only have economic but also political consequences. The Rhodian domination had come to an end. Levantine traders, carrying products from the east, would now bypass Rhodes and its harbour dues and prefer the more lucrative markets of Delos, where they could do business with Italian merchants without interference from the Rhodians. Only grain continued to be traded in Rhodes, whose harbour had in the past been adapted to the large grain ships. Rhodian revenues plummeted, according to Polybius from one million to 150,000 drachmae. As a result, the war fleet could no longer be maintained: there was not enough money to replace old ships and train crews. Now that the Rhodian fleet had disappeared and Pergamene ships patrolled the Aegean in the name of the Romans, no threats from organised fleets needed to be expected. Rome's continued expansion no longer required naval activities.

Small squadrons sailed out occasionally, but the other ships of the fleet remained in the harbours. Even in the enormous Roman offensives from 150 BC onwards, as a result of which Macedonia, Greece and northern Africa were definitively annexed, the fleet played only a minor role. Wars were decided on land.[21]

Notes

1. ILLYRIAN PIRATES: Polyb. 2.8.2–4; Dell, 1967, pp. 344–58. ROMAN INTERVENTIONS IN 229 BC: Polyb. 2.8–11; Harris, 1979, pp. 195–7; cf. Holleaux, 1935, pp. 99–100; Gruen, 1984, pp. 359–68. ROMAN INTERVENTION IN 219 BC: Polyb. 3.16–19; Gruen, 1984, pp. 369–73.
2. CARTHAGINIAN FLEET IN 218 BC: Liv. 21.21–2. ROMAN FLEET: Polyb. 3.41.2; Liv. 21.17.
3. ACTIONS OF THE FLEETS IN 218–216 BC: Thiel, 1946, pp. 33–64; De Saint Denis, 1975, pp. 76–7.
4. CORN SUPPLY IN 216 BC: Liv. 23.21.5–6. SYRACUSIA: Athen. 5.206d–209b; Casson, 1971, pp. 184–9; pp. 191–9; cf. Hopkins, 1983, pp. 98–9.
5. SHIPS TO CALABRIA: Liv. 23.32.17. TRADE IN SECOND PUNIC WAR: Frank, *ESAR*, I, pp. 100–8.
6. NEW SHIPS: Liv. 24.11.5. TASKS OF THE FLEET: Liv. 24.8.14. SIEGE OF SYRACUSE: Rodgers, 1937, pp. 336–41.
7. SCIPIO'S FLEET: Liv. 29.25.10–11; cf. Thiel, 1946, pp. 156–7.
8. DEFENCE OF THE ROMAN CAMPS: Liv. 30.9.10–10.21.
9. ROMAN NAVAL POLICY IN 203–202 BC: Thiel, 1946, pp. 170–182.
10. PEACE CONDITIONS: Polyb. 15.18; Liv. 30.37.3.
11. CORN FROM SICILY AND SARDINIA: Rickman, 1980, pp. 36–45. EGYPTIAN CORN: Casson, 1954b, pp. 168–87.
12. RHODES' CHOICE FOR ROME: Berthold, 1984, pp. 106–7. CRETAN WAR: Brulé, 1978, pp. 34–56. FLEETS IN THE BATTLE AT CHIOS: Polyb. 16.2.9–10. BATTLE AT CHIOS: Polyb. 16.3.1–7.6; cf. Berthold, 1984, pp. 117–18.
13. EMBASSIES: Polyb. 16.25.3; Liv. 31.2.1–2; App. *Mac.* 4.2; cf. Gruen, 1984, pp. 390–8.
14. ROMAN NAVAL POLICY IN 200–197 BC: Thiel, 1946, pp. 200–46.
15. CAUSES OF SYRIAN WAR: Harris, 1979, pp. 219–33. ROMAN FLEET IN 191 BC: Liv. 36.42.7; Thiel, 1946, pp. 258–61. ANTIOCHUS' FLEET: Liv. 35.43.3.
16. ROMAN FLEET AT DELOS: Liv. 36.42.8; 43.12–13; 45.5; App. *Syr.* 22. SYRIAN FLEET: App. *Syr.* 22; Thiel, 1946, pp. 273–4 goes into the information of the ancient authors, which is very different.
17. BATTLE AT CISSUS: Liv. 36.44; App. *Syr.* 22; cf. Rodgers, 1937, pp. 398–410; Thiel, 1946, pp. 305–9.
18. VARIOUS MANOEUVRES OF THE FLEETS: Thiel, 1946, pp. 309–81; cf. Rodgers, 1937, pp. 401–8.
19. BATTLE AT SIDE: Liv. 37.22–4; cf. Rodgers, 1937, pp. 408–12; Thiel, 1946, pp. 338–44; Berthold, 1984, pp. 157–9.
20. BATTLE AT MYONESSUS: Liv. 37.24.10–30.10; App. *Syr.* 27; Flor. 2.18.2; Rodgers, 1937, pp. 412–17; Thiel, 1946, pp. 350–7; Berthold, 1984, pp. 159–61.
21. ROLE OF THE FLEET IN THE MACEDONIAN WAR: Thiel, 1946, pp. 370–412. RELATION BETWEEN ROME AND RHODES: Berthold, 1984, pp. 179–212. FALL OF INCOME IN RHODES: Polyb. 30.31.12.

Chapter Twelve

Trade and Piracy

Now that the Romans had conquered large parts of the Mediterranean and the competing enemy powers no longer needed to be feared, trade increased rapidly. The inhabitants of Rhodes, Massilia and the cities on the Greek and Italian coasts transported diverse cargoes. Recently some light has been thrown on the increase of trade by underwater excavations in the Mediterranean. Up to 1980 538 wrecks have been investigated in the western Mediterranean. Of these, 68 date from the period 300–150 BC, 130 from 150–1 BC, 142 from AD 1–150 and 67 from AD 150–300. These numbers (which are of little significance for the extent of trade in the eastern Mediterranean) indicate that in the last two centuries of the Roman republic and in the first two centuries of the principate trade was more extensive than in the centuries preceding and following these periods. In the case of wine trade, this is undoubtedly so. The numbers of amphoras found in the wrecks clearly show that in the second half of the second century BC Roman wine exports began to expand. In special amphoras wines from Etruria, Latium and Campania were transported to Greece, Asia Minor and Africa and, in the first century BC, also to Gaul and Spain. In addition, considerable quantities of olive oil were exported in special round jugs, in particular from Baetica in Spain. Most other agricultural products, apart from dried fruits and grain (see p. 188), were transported by sea only in small quantities, since in most areas the local production was sufficient.

In Rome raw materials from all parts of the empire were offered for sale. Almost all cities had a speciality of their own which found a ready market among the elite in Rome. Alexandria provided the Roman aristocrats with papyrus, Pergamum supplied parchment and Sidon glass. Marble was shipped from the island of Paros as well as from Athens and Euboea. Purple-yielding molluscs and sponges were imported from the Aegean, but the finest purple came from Phoenicia. Even ivory from India made its way to

Rome, via Alexandria and Delos, as well as precious metals and stones.

The infusion of wealth and Hellenistic influence caused an increase in the construction of town and country houses as well as new forms of public buildings, as a result of which heavy building materials were also shipped to Rome. Wood was largely supplied by Italy itself; only luxury woods such as citrus were imported from Africa. Marble for building and sculpture reached Rome from Greece and Numidia, supplies which included large monolithic columns. Sarcophagi, hollowed out and roughly shaped, were shipped from Egypt, Asia Minor and Greece. Along the coasts of Italy, Greece and Tunisia several wrecks have been found which illustrate the increasing significance of the transport of sarcophagi and marble from the second century BC onwards. The tonnage of these ships is unknown. The condition of the wrecks found at the Greek island of Anticythera and at Mahdia in Tunisia, which transported marble and sunk in the first century BC, does not allow any conclusions to be drawn. The length of the wreck at Mahdia, *c*. 30 m, might indicate that the ship was a sailing vessel of more than 200 tons.[1]

As the urban population increased in the second and first centuries BC grain imports became more and more necessary. From the middle of the Roman republic onwards the locally produced surplus did not suffice to feed the inhabitants of Rome (see p. 169). As the elite used more and more land for the cultivation of crops of higher value than cereals and the number of people living in the city amounted to *c*. 800,000, grain imports were of vital importance for the state. From the end of the third century BC onwards there had been a system for tapping the corn resources of Sicily and Sardinia. A striking aspect of this system was the lack of any direct state involvement, though there was a certain amount of supervision. The provinces had to surrender a tenth part of their grain harvests by way of tax. These tithes were sold to private traders, and the money earned in this way permitted the Romans to buy as much grain as they needed. Moreover, the Romans reserved the entire grain production of Sicily for themselves by forbidding the Sicilians to sell to anyone else. The transport of the grain to Rome was also put out to private shippers, who had contracts with the state.[2]

The size of the grain transports during the last two centuries of the republic can only be estimated. Supposing the level of minimum subsistence to be 220 kg of grain per annum, the entire population of the city would require at least 175,000 tons. Local production amounted to 20,000 tons at the most, so that more than 150,000 tons had to be imported by sea. The average tonnage of freighters being 300 tons, a minimum of 500 grain ships moored at Ostia each year.[3]

In other areas of commerce the involvement of the Roman Senate was minimal. The state played no part in the increasing trade. It is more difficult to determine the attitude of the individual senators. They seemed to comply with the *Lex Claudia* of 219/218 BC, which forbade any senator or senator's son to own a seagoing ship, that is, a ship larger than 300 jars. Any pursuit of gain was thought unsuitable for senators. Even for a member of the elite participation in commercial enterprises provoked negative reactions. It was unthinkable for senators actively to engage in buying and selling merchandise. Those who sailed the seas and earned their living from trade were Romans of the lower classes and foreigners. Yet, there was some indirect involvement of the elite, often in co-operation with men of equestrian rank. Plutarch throws light on the nature of this indirect senatorial involvement; his description of Cato Maior's financial interests is a detailed account of the organisation of business:

> His method was as follows. He required his borrowers to form a large company, and when there were fifty partners and as many ships for security, he took a share in the company himself and was represented by Quintio, a freedman of his, who accompanied his clients in all of their adventures. In this way his entire security was not imperilled, but only a small part of it, and his profits were large.

Testimonies of this kind are rare. In literary sources the names of distinguished men are not found, and inscriptions likewise mostly contain names of insignificant persons. The higher someone's rank, the more rarely his name is mentioned. However, it seems unlikely that the elite shunned involvement in commerce as a matter of principle. It is not without cause that Cicero writes that small-scale trade is dishonourable, but that large-scale trade should by no means be looked down upon.[4]

The one sector of commerce which directly concerned the interests of the elite was slave trade. War and expansion created favourable conditions. The enlarged landed estates (*latifundia*) required great numbers of workers, a need which was met by slave labour. From the first Punic War onwards massive acts of enslavement took place. After each Roman campaign many thousands of slaves were brought to Italy: in 209 BC 30,000 from Tarente, in 204 BC 8000 from Africa, in 174 BC 40,000 from Sardinia, in 167 BC 150,000 from Epirus and in 146 BC 50,000 from Carthage. Many slaves were directly transported to Italy, but large numbers were offered for sale on the huge slave market of Delos, where the daily turnover could amount to 10,000 slaves.[5]

In the second century BC the demand for slave labour increased to such an extent that wars alone did not supply sufficient numbers; as a result, slave trade developed with regions outside the Roman provinces. Pirates were important suppliers of slaves. Some areas in the Mediterranean were perfectly suited for piracy: they had good harbours or sheltered coves, ample supplies of timber, and safe places of refuge where pirates could hide after attacks. Three places met these conditions to a high degree: the Rif Atlas mountains on the north-west coast of Africa, the Dalmatian coast and the spurs of the Taurus mountain range on the coasts of Lycia and Cilicia. The Cilicians had for centuries already been pirates of some reputation. From their fortified bases, of which Coracesium was the strongest, they gradually increased their influence in the Mediterranean. In the early stages they primarily operated along the coasts of the Levant, but the absence of a Roman naval fleet in the east allowed them to increase their range. Rhodes and Pergamum could do little to prevent this development. Soon the plundering Cilicians were dreaded along all the coasts of Asia Minor. The slaves which they captured in rapid surprise attacks on coastal cities were sold on Delos as well as in Side, only 40 km from their main base. Many powerful men from east and west came to their market. Other commodities they acquired by means of a clever method: Cilician agents posed as representatives of bona fide trade companies and readily found out the destinations and cargoes of ships. Their fast *hemioliae* and *liburnae* could then intercept the merchantmen without any difficulty. The Cilicians had a remarkable way of dealing with Roman citizens of some distinction captured during attacks on merchantmen. They treated such prisoners with great respect, apologised for their 'mistake', dressed them in their toga and sandals, let down a ladder and wished them a good journey home. Some Romans, however, managed to outwit the pirates in such critical situations, such as C. Julius Caesar. During a journey from Rome to Rhodes his ship was intercepted by Cilician pirates. When forced to pay 20 talents in order to avoid the traditional 'walking tour on the water' Caesar replied that he was worth at least 50. Greatly surprised, the pirates consented to wait for the money to be sent from Rome and, in the meantime, treated their prisoner extremely well. When the ransom was actually paid they were overjoyed and did not listen to Caesar's angry threats; a few months later, however, he returned with a small fleet and put an end to their happiness.[6]

Even when the pirates extended their activities as far south as Cyrene and as far west as the Peloponnese no steps were undertaken against them. The Romans left it up to the local inhabitants to take countermeasures. The Roman attitude may in part be explained by negligence, but was to some extent also caused by political considerations. The pirates were important for the Roman elite, because they supplied the slaves necessary to cultivate the ever growing *latifundia*. Especially when the Roman conquests were coming to a halt and co-operation with the pirates was the only way to acquire slaves the Roman senators would certainly not benefit by the elimination of the pirates. The Senate finally did decide to take measures against piracy, but only when the grain transports to Rome were threatened. It was no coincidence that a corn shortage in 104 BC was followed in 102 BC by an expedition against the pirates under the special command of the praetor M. Antonius. We have no information concerning his activities along the Cilician coast, but his expedition resulted in the establishment of naval bases on the south-west coast of Asia Minor. Warships were stationed there in order to prevent the Cilician ships from sailing into the Aegean. As a result, the route from Cilicia to Delos was cut off and the profitable slave trade came to an end.[7]

The change in the Roman attitude caused the Cilician pirates to turn to Mithridates Eupator, king of Pontus, who had already made extensive conquests both in easterly and in westerly directions and was now eager to expand his territory towards Asia Minor and Greece. A conflict with Rome was inevitable, especially after at his instigation the local population had killed 80,000 tax collectors and merchants from Italy. Mithridates was, therefore, quite pleased with the support of the Cilicians. They did not operate in separate squadrons but were closely identified with Mithridates' fleet. According to Appian, the Cilician units did not at all look like a fleet of pirates. Mithridates trusted the Cilicians unconditionally, for when once his ship threatened to sink he continued his journey on board a Cilician ship without any hesitation. The exact number of vessels contributed to Mithridates' fleet by the pirates is difficult to determine, but we know that Mithridates started the war against Rome with 400 triremes and a considerable number of lighter ships, *hemioliae* and *liburnae*, which had presumably been supplied by the pirates.[8]

Before the Romans realised how serious the situation was, hostilities had spread over the entire Aegean world. The devastation of Delos, repeated several years later, was a slap in the face for the Romans. The very same pirates who had once co-operated with them in bringing slaves to the market of Delos now destroyed this free port. The Romans were forced to react. In 88 BC the consul L. Cornelius Sulla was sent to Greece to fight Mithridates and the pirates. On land the Romans were successful, but due to the lack of a good fleet they were unable to do much about the pirates. Sulla could not prevent them from continuing their plundering expeditions; during his presence in the east they attacked and ransacked Iassos, Samos, Clazomenae and Samothrace.[9]

The reactions of the Roman Senate to this growing expansion were not in the least effective. In 77 BC P. Servilius Vatia was sent out to attack the strongholds of the pirates in Cilicia itself. Unfortunately, we do not know how Servilius set about this. The strategy probably included a naval attack combined with a simultaneous advance by land along the northern face of the Taurus mountains. Increased activities of the Cilicians in the following years lead to the conclusion that Servilius was unsuccessful. M. Antonius, who in 74 BC was given unlimited authority to fight the pirates of Cilicia and Crete, was equally unable to bridle their aggression. Some nations considered Antonius a greater menace than the pirates. His most important achievement was the invasion of Crete, as a result of which he was given the title 'Creticus'. But the Cretan pirates were not by far as dangerous as the Cilicians. Around 70 BC the latter were active in the Strait of Messina, the junction of the sea lanes from east to west. Verres, the governor of Sicily, whose policies and character Cicero described with some disapproval, was unable to take effective measures against them. A Roman squadron of six undecked vessels and one quadrireme fell an easy prey to the pirates. Around 67 BC the problem became particularly pressing because the Cilicians had disrupted trade to such an extent that the corn supply of Rome was threatened once again. The pirates dominated the Adriatic, the coasts of Sicily and, in the end, also the Tyrrhenian. Their most spectacular feat was beyond doubt the raid on the harbour of Ostia. A Roman naval unit was captured and destroyed. Fear reigned everywhere, not in the least among the crews of the large grain ships who were utterly defenceless against the surprise attacks of the fast pirates.[10]

So many corn ships were intercepted by the Cilicians that Rome was threatened with a famine. Supported by the urban population and the members of the equestrian rank, a proposal made by the tribune Gabinius to entrust Cn. Pompey with a special command was carried. This appointment inspired so much confidence that the prices on the markets of Rome fell. Pompey was given three years to achieve his goal. Everyone, even the proconsuls and propraetors in the provinces, had to obey Pompey's commands. Within a few months he assembled a fleet of 200 warships and 70 fast vessels. The warships were largely built in Italy, unlike the fleets that had been used in emergencies in the recent past, which usually consisted of ships contributed by the seafaring nations in the east. Evidently the Romans took the matter rather seriously, also considering the fact that an army of 120,000 men was levied in order to be able to pursue the pirates on land as far as necessary. In the early spring of 67 BC the fleet put out in 13 different directions, each squadron to a specific part of the Mediterranean and Black Seas. Even the waters along the Spanish coasts were to be searched carefully. Pompey's most pressing task was to reopen the sea lanes between Rome and the corn producing regions. He therefore concentrated his activities first of all on the routes to Sicily, Sardinia, Egypt and Africa. The Roman squadrons took the offensive in all regions at the same time. As a result, the pirates were unable to support one another. Within 40 days the western Mediterranean had been cleared. The pirates were driven back to the east, until finally they had to withdraw inside their fortified strongholds, which were besieged by the Romans from all sides. A naval battle was their last resort. They confronted the Romans off Coracesium, their main base, but were crushed by Pompey's fleet. More than 1300 ships were set on fire and the pirates collectively threw themselves on Pompey's mercy. To most of them he offered land in the inlands of Asia Minor, far away from the coast, in the hope that they would forget their original occupation.[11] The elimination of the Cilician pirates and Mithridates — in a successful war shortly after Pompey's victory — resulted in the definitive annexation of Asia Minor and Syria. Once again, the trade routes from Rome to the east were busy and the supply of food in Rome was, at least for the time being, safeguarded. Yet, a revival of piracy could not be ruled out. Only a permanent fleet would really guarantee safety at sea. Upon his return to Italy Pompey proposed the establishment of such a fleet to the Senate. As a result, in 62 BC the Adriatic and Tyrrhenian Seas were patrolled by permanent naval units. And in the same year Flaccus, the governor of Asia, collected funds from the coastal cities for the maintenance of an Aegean squadron, which cruised in two units along the west coast of Asia Minor. Incidental references show that piracy had not disappeared completely. Ships sailing along the Syrian coast continued to be threatened.[12]

Notes

1. WRECKS IN THE WESTERN MEDITERRANEAN: Parker, 1980, p. 50. TRADE IN MARBLE: Ward-Perkins, 1980, pp. 325–55. TONNAGE OF THE SHIPS: Casson, 1971, p. 190.
2. TITHE SYSTEM: Rickman, 1980, pp. 37–42.
3. Cf. Hopkins, 1983, p. 98, who gives an equal speculation for Rome at the end of the last century BC when Rome had a population of nearly one million people; cf. Garnsey, 1983, pp. 118–19.
4. LEX CLAUDIA: Liv. 21.63.3–4. CATO'S BUSINESS ARRANGEMENTS: Plut. *Cat. Mai.* 21.5–6. CICERO'S APPRECIATION OF DIFFERENT PROFESSIONS: Cic. *Off.* 1.150–1; cf. D'Arms, 1981, pp. 22–44.
5. PARTICIPATION IN SLAVE TRADE: Harris, 1979, pp. 80–5. SLAVES FROM TARENTE: Liv. 27.16.7. SLAVES FROM AFRICA: Liv. 29.29.3. SLAVES FROM SARDINIA: Liv. 41.28.8. SLAVES FROM EPIRUS: Polyb. 30.15; Liv. 45.34. SLAVES FROM CARTHAGE: App. *Lyb.* 130. NUMBER OF SLAVES AT DELOS: Strabo 14.666.
6. CILICIAN PIRACY: Ormerod, 1924, pp. 190–247. SALE OF SLAVES IN SIDE: Strabo 14.664. CAESAR AND THE CILICIAN PIRATES: Plut. *Jul.* 2; *Crass.* 7; Suet. *Jul.* 4; Vell. 2.41.
7. THREATENING OF THE CORN SUPPLY: Casson, 1954b, pp. 168–87; Rickman, 1980, p. 50. COMMAND OF ANTONIUS: *IGRR* 4.1116; cf. Cic. *Orat.* 1.18.
8. RELATIONS BETWEEN MITHRIDATES AND THE PIRATES: Plut. *Pomp.* 24; App. *Mithr.* 63; *Sic.* 6.1. MITHRIDATES ON PIRATE SHIP: App. *Mithr.* 78; Plut. *Lucull.* 13; Oros. 6.2.24. STRENGTH OF THE FLEET: *FGrH* IIIB 434, p. 358; App. *Mithr.* 63.
9. DESTRUCTION OF DELOS: Athen. 5.215; App. *Mithr.* 28. DESTRUCTION OF OTHER CITIES: App. *Mithr.* 63.
10. SERVILIUS VATIA: Oros. 5.23; Cic. *Verr.* 2.1.56; *Leg. Agr.* 2.50; M.

ANTONIUS: Vell. 2.31; Sall. *Hist.* 3.2. VERRES AND THE PIRATES: Liv. 5.28.2; Cic.
Verr. 2.4.144; 2.5.42ff. THREAT OF THE CORN SUPPLY: Plut. *Pomp.* 25; Cass. Dio
36.23.1; App. *Mithr.* 93; Liv. *Per.* 99. RAID ON OSTIA: Cic. *Leg. Man.* 33; Cass. Dio
36.22.
    11. POMPEY'S FLEET: App. *Mithr.* 94; Plut. *Pomp.* 26; Liv. *Per.* 99; POMPEY'S
SUCCESS: Cic. *Leg. Man.* 34; 56; Plut. *Pomp.* 27–9; Cass. Dio 36.37; App. *Mithr.*
95; Liv. *Per.* 99.
    12. ARRANGEMENTS FOR PERMANENT FLEETS: Cic. *Flacc.* 27–33. PIRACY: Cass.
Dio 39.59.2.

Chapter Thirteen

Fleet and Civil War

In the late republic the fleet was brought into action also for purposes other than checking foreign powers and pirates. In the turbulent final decades of republican Rome the fleet became an important means of power. The struggle for hegemony in Rome, up till then fought among politicans supported by loyal land armies, extended itself to sea. Primarily responsible for this development was Pompey. During his expeditions against the pirates and against Mithridates he had learnt to appreciate the value of a well-organised fleet. Pompey was so popular among his former crew members that they would undoubtedly respond *en masse* if called upon to support him. In 49 BC this did, in fact, happen. Pompey had adopted an implacable attitude towards C. Julius Caesar, with whom he had collaborated only a few years earlier in a triumvirate together with M. Licinius Crassus. Now Caesar had been declared an enemy of the state.

Several points were in Caesar's favour. His power was based on his eleven well-trained legions, which had helped him to overcome many difficulties in Gaul. Pompey, the Senate's candidate, had at his disposal the army and the fleet of the Senate but had to comply with the senators' wishes. In total he had nine legions, seven in Spain and two in Italy, but these were less well-trained than Caesar's. At sea, however, Pompey did not expect any appreciable resistance. All over the Mediterranean the fleets could be brought into action at any moment.

Having been declared an enemy of the state by the Senate Caesar immediately took the offensive. He crossed the river Rubicon, which constituted the dividing-line between Cisalpine Gaul and Italy. Many joined his army, and before Pompey could raise new troops in addition to his two legions Caesar had conquered Italy. The only thing Pompey could do was to flee from Italy, cross over to the Balkan, assemble a new army and attack Italy from all sides, a plan which he felt capable of carrying out in view of his superiority at sea. Caesar pursued him to Brundisium, from where Pompey was planning to put out. In spite of the fact that the town was blockaded on the land side and dams were thrown up before the entrance to the harbour the evacuation could not be prevented. Pompey departed to the east and Caesar stationed his troops in the various ports of southern Italy.[1]

If Pompey had acted immediately and combined his seven legions in Spain with the rest of his army on the Balkan, the situation might have developed in a completely different way. But Pompey allowed Caesar to take the initiative; the latter went into action at once. A few weeks after he had restored order in Italy, Caesar went to Spain in order to fight Pompey's legions stationed there. Using transport ships he sailed along the coast. Massilia, Rome's loyal ally in the Punic Wars, wished to remain strictly neutral in this civil war and did not allow Caesar's fleet to enter the harbour. Caesar had little time to force his way into the city, but, on the other hand, access to Massilia was necessary because from there corn and other supplies could be shipped from Gaul to Caesar's army in Spain. Caesar himself continued on to Spain, but a contingent commanded by D. Junius Brutus remained in the environs of this strategically important city. Then the Massaliotes openly took sides with Pompey, who, however, offered them little support. On a small island off the coast of Massilia Brutus set up a naval base and began preparations for a naval confrontation, since the Massaliotes would undoubtedly try to settle the issue at sea. Just before his departure Caesar had ordered ships to be built because no warships could be found in the area. In Arelate (Arles) twelve triremes were built within 30 days, a force inferior in number to the 17 galleys and many fast light ships of the Massaliotes.

Between the Massaliotes and Brutus' ships, on which well-trained soldiers served as marines, a disorderly battle developed. The Massaliotes tried to take full advantage of the speed of their ships and the seamanship of their crews. They attempted to encircle the Roman fleet but failed; then several Massaliote ships attacked one Roman ship and tried to ram it. Brutus' crews opposed them with boarding tactics. Their ships, heavier and more sluggish than those of their opponents, were equipped with grapnels. These penetrated the decks of the enemy ships, allowing the marines to board them and transform the fight into a land battle. The Massaliotes were unable to offer any resistance and fled, leaving six ships behind. They could, however, hardly believe that they had been defeated by a fleet manned with land troops and soon renewed the attack. Any vessel which was at all sea-worthy was sent out, stimulated by the prayers of the citizens, who were watching the battle from the quays. Now too, however, the Roman boarding tactics got the better of the manoeuvres of the Massaliotes. A crushing defeat ensued, but they still refused to give up. Only after the Romans had captured the walls on the land side as well did they realise how futile further resistance would be and surrendered.[2]

The capture of Massilia was a relief for Caesar. The food supplies to his army in Spain were no longer at risk. Many tribes in southern Gaul and northern Spain decided to take Caesar's side and offered to provide foodstuffs. The campaign in Spain was equally successful. Without having to fight a real battle Caesar managed to break the resistance of Pompey's supporters within 40 days. As a result, the Mediterranean to the west of the Adriatic was now dominated by Caesar.

In the meantime, Pompey was preparing to return to Italy in order to attempt to recover his position. All over the eastern part of the Roman empire troops were levied on a large scale; from all directions ships were assembled in which the army was to cross to Italy. Warships from Macedonia and Syria were gathered, fixed up and sent to Dyrrhachium in Illyria. Together with the vessels constructed in the dockyards of the Balkan this fleet amounted to 500 ships in the autumn of 49 BC. The crews would be kept busy reconnoitring the coasts until the invasion of Italy, planned to take place in the spring of the following year.[3] But nothing came of Pompey's plans, in spite of his powerful fleet. Once again Caesar's talents of improvisation proved more effective than Pompey's lengthy preparations. In Italy Caesar was getting ready for a surprise attack on Dyrrhachium. Unexpectedly, against all pro-gnoses, he crossed the Adriatic in January 48 BC. No winter storms, against which he had been warned by experienced seamen, occurred. An army of 15,000 troops and 600 cavalry, accompanied by only twelve warships, landed in Illyria *c.* 130 km south of Dyrrhachium, to the surprise and irritation of M. Calpurnius Bibulus, Pompey's naval commander. Caesar immediately sent the transport fleet back to Italy to fetch more troops and supplies, but on the way back 30 ships were intercepted and sunk. The crews were killed. Because Pompey's ships were now patrolling the coasts more frequently Caesar could no longer count on reinforcements. Attempts to take Dyrrhachium before Pompey's return from Macedonia failed. Caesar did capture Oricum and Apollonia but could profit little by these successes, because the cities were controlled from the sea by Pompey's fleet.[4] If the Adriatic had been effectively controlled this expedition might well have been Caesar's last. But the blockade by Pompey's fleet was not secure. In March 48 BC M. Antonius succeeded in crossing with an army of 20,000 troops and 800 cavalry and joined Caesar's forces. Caesar's army, however, now consisting of 35,000 men, suffered from increasing shortages of food as Pompey's fleet blockaded the coastal cities and prevented supplies from being delivered. The siege of Oricum was of particular significance because there a large part of Caesar's fleet had taken shelter. Caesar's admiral M. Acilius Caninianus could not beat off the attack on the harbour. He had sunk a freighter loaded with rocks in the harbour mouth, anchored another vessel on top of it and built a defence tower on this colossal construction; Pompey's son Gnaeus, however, broke through these improvised fortifications after divers had removed the rocks from the sunken ship. He now attacked Caesar's squadron from two sides and destroyed it. Shortly afterwards he also succeeded in setting fire to 30 freighters in the harbour of Lissus. Caesar's troops attempted to lay siege to Dyrrhachium in order to capture the foodstuffs stored in the city but failed, because Pompey landed troops behind Caesar's lines. The loss of a considerable part of the fleet was a severe setback for Caesar: now a potential invasion of Italy by Pompey could hardly be prevented. It cannot be ruled out that if at this stage Pompey had actually invaded Italy, he would have been successful and considerably changed the course of the struggle for hegemony.[5]

Pompey chose to continue the war on the Balkan and attempted to starve out Caesar's army. The latter was compelled to move inland to search for fertile areas. He hoped to find an abundance of foodstuffs in the plains of Thessaly. Pompey followed him and forced a battle, but at Pharsalus his army was defeated by Caesar's well-trained legions and retreated to the camp, which was taken after a short battle. Over 15,000 men were killed, *c.* 24,000 surrendered and many others fled to the naval base at Dyrrhachium and from there to Corcyra. Under the command of Cato many sailed to Africa to continue the war from there.

Pompey himself fled to Egypt, but while leaving his ship he was treacherously murdered by order of Ptolemy XIII, whose father

Pompey had once put into power. Caesar, who had followed Pompey to Egypt, took advantage of internal strife between Ptolemy and his sister Cleopatra, whose charms soon got the better of him. The inhabitants of Alexandria, for the most part supporters of Ptolemy, laid siege to the royal palace, which overlooked the harbour. For quite some time the palace and some strategic places which Caesar and Cleopatra had managed to occupy were under siege, protected by an army which was by far numerically inferior to the Alexandrians. In this difficult situation reinforcements were badly needed, but without access to the open sea they would be of little use. A large number of ships lay at anchor in the harbour of Alexandria: 35 galleys of Caesar's fleet, 50 quadriremes and quinqueremes of the Egyptian squadron which had assisted Pompey but had returned to base after his defeat, and 22 other Egyptian warships. If Caesar's opponents had managed to make these 72 galleys ready for battle they would have dominated the sea and put Caesar in an even more difficult position. This was, however, prevented because Caesar's troops set fire to the entire squadron. But in a smaller harbour of Alexandria, the Eunostus harbour, the Egyptians had another fleet which was now enlarged to 22 quadriremes and a great number of smaller ships of unknown types. The Romans succeeded in entering this harbour and a bitter fight took place, during which the Egyptians lost five ships. The battle dragged on for quite some time: in an attempt to occupy the island of Pharos, strategically important because from there the entire harbour could be controlled (see p. 130), the Romans lost 400 soldiers and 400 oarsmen. Finally, thanks to the support of a naval unit from Asia Minor, the resistance of the Egyptians could be broken.[6]

After the war in Alexandria the scene of battle moved to the coasts of Africa, where Caesar's opponents had gathered. In this phase the fleet played only a minor part. Small naval units took part in sieges of coastal cities, accompanied convoys of freighters and executed raids in hostile areas. All the same, the fleet was an important factor in the war. It was in part due to the numerical superiority of Caesar's fleet — it was said to consist of over 100 ships — that in the spring of 46 BC troops and supplies could be escorted to Thapsus, the scene of the decisive confrontation between Caesar and his republican opponents.[7]

The fleet played a very important part in the renewed power struggle which followed Caesar's assassination in 44 BC. This was primarily due to the activities of Pompey's son Sextus, who upheld the Pompeian cause in Spain. While Caesar was alive he had led the life of a pirate and had threatened the safety of the sea lanes in the western Metiterranean. In 43 BC the Senate, a majority of which was in favour of the republic, rehabilitated Sextus Pompey and appointed him admiral of 'the fleets of the republic'. He was to counterbalance the increasing power of Octavian, Antonius and Lepidus, who had formed a triumvirate in the same year. After the republican army under the command of Brutus and Cassius had in 42 BC been defeated at Philippi by the army of the triumvirate part of the fleet had come into Antonius' possession. Sextus Pompey had acquired 100 ships. As a result, he now controlled the western Mediterranean, a situation which aroused Octavian's envy because he desired a position equal to that of Antonius, who did have a large fleet at his disposal.[8]

Sextus Pompey lost a large part of the popularity which he had originally enjoyed. Because of the large-scale proscriptions by Octavian and Antonius, Sextus Pompey's fleet did not only become a refuge for those who had managed to escape persecution but also attracted large numbers of discontented people such as slaves, former pirates and disillusioned farmers. The fleet expanded to 300 ships. Sextus Pompey no longer upheld the legal authority in the western Mediterranean, the task originally assigned to him, but operated as a pirate from Sicily and Sardinia. His crews repeatedly attacked heavily laden cornships. The grain supply was seriously threatened. Though even his mother begged him to stop these activities because he would lose public sympathy, he could not be persuaded. The attacks continued and increased, bringing together Octavian and the Senate. Nothing came of the treaty of Misenum between Octavian and Sextus Pompey, in which it was agreed that the latter would control Sicily, Sardinia and Achaea on condition that he would no longer disturb the grain transports to Rome and put an end to his piratical activities. Sextus Pompey's crews could not be curbed. In the end, the Senate was compelled to construct a new fleet and fight him at sea.

At first, Octavian was rather unlucky. Part of the new fleet, built in the dockyards of Ostia and Ravenna, was destroyed off Cumae by Sextus Pompey in 38 BC and, shortly afterwards, again in the Strait of Messina. Sextus Pompey's fleet, numerically superior and manned with oarsmen more capable than Octavian's hurriedly levied crews, thus kept control over Sicily and the Strait of Messina.[9]

It soon became clear that only a thoroughly prepared campaign of a large fleet supported by an army would be able to defeat Sextus Pompey, whose troops were reinforced by an ever increasing number of adventurers. Octavian entrusted the construction of the new fleet to M. Vipsanius Agrippa, an outstanding military man and a good friend of his. Agrippa immediately set to work and designed a fleet which would put Sextus Pompey's fleet in the shade both qualitatively and quantitatively. The latter's ships were light and fast — presumably triremes and *hemioliae* — and his crews well-trained and experienced, so that Agrippa decided not to build light, fast and easily manoeuvrable ships; ramming, the favourite strategy of real oarsmen, would not enter into his plans. Besides triremes, therefore, also quadriremes, quinqueremes and sexiremes were constructed, a process which took up the entire year 37 BC. In Portus Julius, a harbour close to Puteoli, rowers from all parts of the empire gathered to be thoroughly trained before serving on the fleet. In the spring of 36 BC, the ships, built on dockyards in the entire Mediterranean, assembled in the harbour of Portus Julius. Moreover, Octavian was supported by Antonius and Lepidus, his partners in the triumvirate. As a result, Agrippa now commanded a fleet of 370 ships, which was to attack Sicily, the centre of Sextus Pompey's activities, from three sides: Lepidus would land on southern Sicily from Africa, and T. Statilius Taurus, commander of the 120 ships contributed by Antonius, would attack the east coast of the island while Octavian and Agrippa would invade the north coast. Only Lepidus was successful, the other two attempts failed due to unexpected storms.[10]

Sextus Pompey already supposed that he would be safe for the rest of the year — it was now August — and went around in a dark-blue cloak, indicating that he considered himself the 'beloved son of Neptune', who had protected him from the recent attacks. The campaign could, however, not be postponed: starvation spread rapidly in Rome and quick action was required. Within 30 days the damage incurred in the storms was repaired and a new invasion could be attempted. To prevent this Sextus Pompey had concentrated his fleet and most of his army in the north-east of Sicily. Agrippa and Octavian did not cross together: Agrippa was to keep Sextus Pompey's fleet occupied while Octavian crossed over from Italy. When Agrippa wanted to land near Mylae he was confronted by a fleet of 155 warships, over 40 more than he had himself. It did not seem sensible to wait for reinforcements to arrive, because now Octavian had a chance to cross over without encountering any appreciable resistance. In the ensuing battle between Sextus Pompey's light and fast galleys, manned with excellent seamen, and Agrippa's heavier ships, defended by heavily armed soldiers, neither party got the upper hand, though Agrippa's troops succeeded in landing on the island. Meanwhile, Octavian had been less successful. He had not reckoned with any considerable resistance because Sextus Pompey was occupied in the battle against Agrippa. But the latter had noted the absence of Octavian at Mylae and suspected that he would attempt to cross elsewhere. Sextus Pompey left Mylae, sailed to Messina and from there to Tauromenium, where Octavian had begun to disembark his troops. Thirty of Octavian's ships were sunk and presumably another 30 seriously damaged. The strategy used by Sextus Pompey and the losses which his fleet incurred are unknown. This unexpected confrontation prevented Octavian from landing all his troops. Many of his captains panicked and made for the Italian coast. Three legions had reached the shore and, after an exacting voyage along the north coast, managed to join Agrippa's army; a base was set up at Tyndaris. Within two weeks the army was enlarged to 21 legions, thanks to reinforcements from Italy which Sextus Pompey could not prevent from landing, and to the arrival of an army commanded by Lepidus, which had made its way to the north from Lilybaeum in the west, escorted by the fleet of 200 ships. Octavian himself, too, was able to join the army at Tyndaris. With regret Sextus Pompey watched his hegemony on Sicily disappear. The only way for him to force a continuation of the war was to eliminate the Roman fleet; in that case the supplies for the Roman army would be cut off and he would be able to conclude a treaty on favourable conditions. Moreover, he wanted to confront his opponents at sea, because after the hard lesson at Mylae he had reinforced the boards of his ships with heavy covers and had built towers on the largest vessels of his fleet. Agrippa had also added a piece of equipment to his ships, the *harpax*, an iron grapnel, which could be hurled at an enemy ship by means of a catapult. Once the grapnel was firmly fastened, the enemy ship was hauled in with a winch until the marines could board it across a wooden plank of 2 to 3 m in length which was covered with strips of iron.

Confidently Sextus Pompey confronted his opponents near

Naulochus in a battle in which more than 300 ships were involved on both sides. He had, however, not thought of a way to counteract the new weapon of the Romans, so that the grapnels could do their destructive job. The course of this battle is not known, but the sources do tell us that after the initial skirmishes Sextus Pompey's crews either quickly sailed away or surrendered or, something which happened more and more frequently now that the days of Sextus Pompey's naval power were numbered, took sides with the Roman fleet. Twenty-eight of his ships were sunk, many others were set on fire or captured. Sextus Pompey himself fled to Asia Minor with 17 ships. There he was captured and killed while assembling troops for yet another war.[11]

As a result of the successful outcome of the war against Sextus Pompey trade in the western Mediterranean was restored and Octavian came into possession of a fleet which consisted of *c.* 500 ships and could be considered equal to Antonius' fleet in the east. When Lepidus, a rather powerless figure, was removed from the triumvirate it became clear that both Antonius and Octavian were striving to acquire absolute power and an open rupture between them seemed to come closer. A struggle developed between the east, where, in spite of some setbacks in Armenia, Antonius' position had became practically unassailable, and the west, which largely supported Octavian. The rivalry between them was all the more vehement because of some personal developments. Antonius, married to Octavian's sister Octavia, sent her back to Rome and chose Cleopatra as his partner. From her he hoped to receive love, but also money to maintain his enormous army and fleet with which he wanted to sail to Italy before long. Thus, however, he became dependent on the will of this capricious woman, who was hoping to restore the empire of the Ptolemies to its former glory. When Antonius went so far as to entrust parts of Armenia, Parthia, Media, Syria and Cilicia to Cleopatra, her son and his own son, the breach between him and Octavian was definitive. Yet, there were still people in Rome who put more trust in Antonius than in Octavian, among whom were both consuls and many senators. They went eastwards and joined Antonius. Now the entire Roman Senate, rid of the supporters of Antonius, was on Octavian's side.

In the autumn of 32 BC Antonius began to assemble and prepare his army and fleet in order to start for Italy in the early spring of the next year. From all over the east ships and troops were sent to

Figure 13.1 Relief from Palestrina with a Roman Bireme, probably a Quadrireme (Second Half First Century BC)

Patras on the Peloponnese, where he had set up his headquarters. Over 100,000 men and 500 warships gathered. The fleet evoked memories of the fleets of the Ptolemies and the Antagonids two centuries previously: heavier types of ship predominated. The flagship was a 'ten', presumably one left over from the glorious past. All types from triremes to 'nines' were present in large numbers. Evidently such a fleet was most suitable for boarding tactics. The ships had, therefore, been covered with iron plates, to prevent an immediate catastrophe as a result of ramming by the enemy.

During the winter of 32/31 BC, when a compromise between Antonius and Octavian had become impossible, Agrippa took charge of the preparations in Italy. The army amounted to 80,000 men, slightly smaller than Antonius'. Octavian's fleet, however, made the difference: though 100 ships smaller than that of Antonius, it mainly consisted of biremes, triremes and quadriremes (Fig. 13.1); the heaviest type represented was the sexireme. Most of the biremes were *liburnae*, narrow open galleys with two files of rowers. They had, though on a small scale, been introduced in the battle at Naulochus and had proved their mettle due to their speed.[12]

When considering the events leading up to the decisive battle at Actium one is struck by the fact that Antonius grossly neglected his fleet and naval strategy. During the winter many of his oarsmen had fallen ill or died due to the terrible conditions in which they had to live and were replaced by farmers and shepherds, who were given hardly any training. The fleet was not sufficiently involved in the guarding of the long routes from Asia to Actium on the Gulf of Ambracia in north-west Greece, where Antonius set up his naval base. Agrippa, who did recognise the value of separately operating naval units, succeeded in occupying important ports of call such as Methone and Corinth shortly after putting out from Brundisium. As a result, Antonius' supply routes were threatened.

Soon Octavian's fleet felt superior and proceeded to blockade the enemy fleet, which had retreated into the harbour of Actium. The only entrance to this harbour was a narrow fairway, a mere 400 m in width. Initially, Antonius was not inclined to attempt to break through the blockade, hoping that he would be able to defeat Octavian's army first. Agrippa, on the other hand, avoided a confrontation on land. In view of the circumstances, this was a wise decision. Antonius' army received no supplies as a result of the occupation of several ports of call by Octavian's troops. Only supremacy at sea could make the supply routes from the east safe again, but in order to achieve that aim Antonius required his fleet, which was locked up in the harbour of Actium.

All things considered, Antonius was in a difficult situation, and it was not surprising that he changed his strategy. To conquer Italy by storm, as he had originally planned, was out of the question. His decisions were strongly influenced by Cleopatra, who had accompanied him. She had hoped that, if Antonius were victorious, the Ptolemies would be restored to power in Egypt. Now that such a victory seemed unlikely, she advised Antonius to withdraw over land to Asia Minor and to concentrate on the east. In this way, she thought, Antonius being completely dependent on her, she would be given control over Egypt and parts of Asia and Africa. Cleopatra's egocentric view sharply contrasted with that of most of the Roman officers and defected senators, who felt that a defensive war from Asia would come to nothing. They were in favour of breaking through the blockade — an action advocated by Cleopatra as well, but in her case with the sole purpose of fleeing to the east — and confronting Agrippa's fleet. If this battle were successful the situation would change completely and Octavian would be forced by a shortage of food to take the offensive on land.

Antonius' dilemma is reflected in the preparations for breaking the blockade of the harbour of Actium. Contrary to normal practice the crews were ordered to take the sails on board, supposedly in order to be able to pursue Octavian's fleet in the case of an offshore wind. The oarsmen, however, interpreted this as an order to flee, an impression which was reinforced when the treasure chests were brought on board the fastest ships. Next to these fast vessels Cleopatra's Egyptian squadron was stationed. Many Roman officers lost faith in Antonius and defected to Octavian. Without any exaggeration it may be said that, even before the actual hostilities had begun, the battle had been decided. Antonius was already handicapped by his lack of self-confidence due to the events preceding the battle, but he had also wrongly expected to be confronted by a fleet of heavy ships, which he intended to fight with even heavier ones. Instead, Octavian brought into action light ships manned with capable seamen.

On 2 September 31 BC both commanders made the customary speeches to their troops, emphasising that only victory would be an acceptable outcome, and put out to sea. Octavian's fleet, unhindered by the obstacles which Antonius had to pass when sailing through the narrow fairway, was first to take position in front of the entrance to the harbour. Octavian himself commanded the right wing, assisted by M. Lurius, L. Arruntius was in charge of the centre while Agrippa led the left wing. Antonius could not but follow suit and likewise split up his fleet in three parts. He himself took charge of the right wing, which lay opposite Agrippa, C. Sosius, one of the defected consuls, was in command on the left wing and the centre was commanded by M. Insteius and M. Octavius. Cleopatra's Egyptian squadron remained behind close to the harbour mouth, supposedly in order to be able to offer support in case of a breakthrough.

The battle proper commenced when the wing commanded by Antonius advanced towards Agrippa's wing. The latter immediately reinforced the left flank of his squadron in order to take advantage of his numerical superiority (260 vs 120) by encircling the enemy. As a countermeasure Antonius' ships sailed at greater distance from one another than was usual. Now, however, Agrippa's fast galleys were able to sail between Antonius' ships and to ram them. The crews of the threatened ships attempted to defend themselves by hurling missiles at the enemy but the fast moving *liburnae* and triremes were a very difficult target.

Antonius' wing had incurred its first losses, when, to everyone's amazement, around noon the Egyptian squadron suddenly appeared. At full speed it sailed right through the centre of both fleets and rapidly disappeared from sight. Antonius' reaction was even more surprising. He left his position on the wing, went on board a fast ship and with 40 ships followed Cleopatra in the direction of Egypt. In spite of their commander's disappearance the crews did not immediately surrender but continued to fight. Yet, a crushing defeat was inevitable. Only rarely did the disorderly manoeuvres of Antonius' mammoth vessels result in the boarding of one of the enemy ships, which fell upon them from all sides. Their opponents' ramming tactics, however, were executed with such accuracy that many ships were left completely helpless, robbed of their oars. Though the crews of the ships in the centre and on the left wing had as yet hardly been involved in the battle they realised that all hope was lost and either returned to the harbour or surrendered.[13]

At first, Antonius' army remained faithful to the cause. The troops could not believe that Antonius had really fled for good and refused to give up. But when, a week later, it was reported that he had, in fact, arrived in Egypt they felt betrayed and surrendered *en masse*.

After a short intermezzo in Italy, where he claimed land as a reward for his veterans, Octavian sailed to Egypt and occupied Alexandria. Antonius' resistance was negligable, for his last troops finally deserted him. Shortly afterwards he committed suicide, as did Cleopatra, who was unable to persuade Octavian to take an interest in her cause.

For over two years, Octavian remained in Egypt and the east to restore order. Then he returned to Rome, a powerful man commanding an enormous fleet. Land and sea were safer than ever before. Agriculture, cattle-breeding and trade flourished. The battle of Actium had laid the foundations for a period of unity, albeit created by force by one man. But at the time this did not concern the Roman population. After almost a century of civil strife they could now live in peace. To signify that the war had come to a definitive end, the doors of the temple of Janus could, for the first time in centuries, be closed.

Notes

1. CROSSING OF POMPEY: Caes. *Bell. Civ.* 1.25–8; Plut. *Pomp.* 62–3; Cass. Dio 41.12.
2. NAVAL BATTLES AT MASSILIA: Caes. *Bell. Civ.* 1.56–58.2; 2.3–7; 2.22.
3. PREPARATIONS OF POMPEY: Caes. *Bell. Civ.* 3.4–5; Cic. *Att.* 9.9.2; App. *Bell. Civ.* 2.201.
4. CROSSING OF CAESAR: Caes. *Bell. Civ.* 3.18; Oros. 6.15. CROSSING OF M. ANTONIUS: Caes. *Bell. Civ.* 3.26–9. CAPTURE OF THE HARBOURS OF ORICUM AND LISSUS: Caes. *Bell. Civ.* 3.39–40; Cass. Dio 42.12.
5. CONFRONTATIONS IN THE HARBOURS OF ALEXANDRIA: Caes. *Bell. Civ.* 3.107–11; *Bell. Alex.* 12–13; cf. Rodgers, 1937, pp. 462–71; Viereck, 1975, pp. 210–12.
6. FLEET AT THAPSUS: Caes. *Bell. Afr.* 62.
7. NAVAL COMMAND OF SEXTUS POMPEY: Cic. *Phil.* 13.50; App. *Bell. Civ.* 4.84–5; Cass. Dio 46.40.3; cf. Starr, 1941, p. 5.
8. TREATY OF MISENUM: App. *Bell. Civ.* 5.73; Cass. Dio 48.38. DESTRUCTION OF THE ROMAN FLEET IN STORMS AND BATTLES: App. *Bell. Civ.* 5.77–92; Suet. *Aug.* 16.74; Cass. Dio 48.45–8.
9. NEW FLEET OF AGRIPPA: Cass. Dio 48.49–51. UNSUCCESSFUL INVASIONS OF SICILY: App. *Bell. Civ.* 5.98–100.
10. NAVAL BATTLE AT MYLAE: App. *Bell. Civ.* 5.105–8; Cass. Dio 49.2–6.3; Vell. 2.79; Suet, *Aug.* 16.1. UNSUCCESSFUL DISEMBARKATION OF OCTAVIAN'S TROOPS: App. *Bell. Civ.* 5.109–10; Cass. Dio 49.5. NAVAL BATTLE AT NAULOCHUS: Plut. *Ant.* 32; App. *Bell. Civ.* 5.118–22; Cass. Dio 49.9–11; cf. Rodgers, 1937, pp. 503–12; Viereck, 1975, pp. 220–1.
11. STRENGTH OF THE FLEETS: Plut. *Ant.* 56; 61; 66; Flor. 2.21.
12. BATTLE AT ACTIUM: Plut. *Ant.* 64–72; Cass. Dio 50.31–5; cf. Tarn, 1931, pp. 173–99.

Chapter Fourteen

Maritime Policy in the Roman Empire

The Imperial Fleets

In 27 BC the Senate conferred upon Octavian the title Augustus. This was an honorary title without any concomitant constitutional rights. Formally the authority of the Senate had been restored and Augustus was only the first among the leading Romans. Augustus himself emphasised this aspect of his position. He did not want to be considered a military dictator, but a *princeps*, albeit a *princeps* who enjoyed such prestige and held so many functions that he put all others in the shade. The most important of these functions was the *imperium*. The title of *imperator*, which he even used as cognomen (*Imperator Caesar Augustus*), endowed him with the supreme command over army and fleet. The army was organised in 28 legions and consisted of 150,000 Roman citizens and an equal number of auxiliaries, so that the total strength was 300,000 troops. The legions were mostly stationed along the borders of the empire: one in Africa, three in Egypt, three in Syria, three in Macedonia, two in Dalmatia, three in Pannonia, seven in Germania and six in Spain. In the centre of the empire there were hardly any troop concentrations.

The fleet, on the other hand, was deliberately stationed in the centre of the empire (Fig. 14.1). First of all it was to maintain peace and order along the coasts of the Mediterranean. Since these coasts were all in Roman hands and the local inhabitants no longer had fleets of their own, this was not a difficult task. The military role of the fleet was confined to ensuring quick and safe transport of troops to threatened areas. Furthermore, it served as an important preventive weapon against piracy. Unlike the previous century, during which many pirates had been active, the two centuries from Augustus until Septimius Severus (AD 193–211) were characterised by a striking absence of piracy, with the ex-

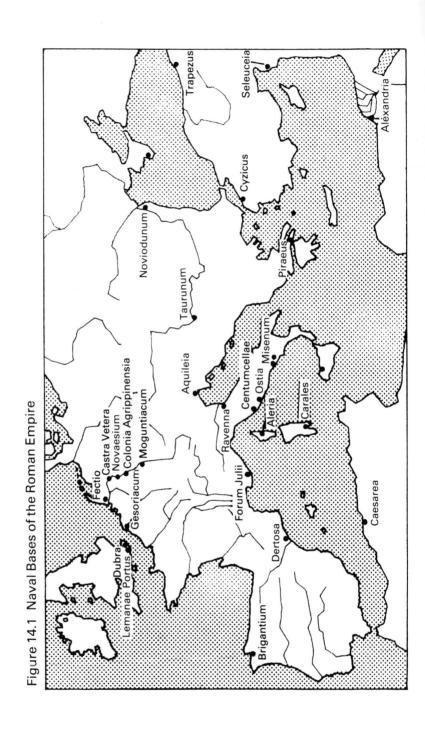

Figure 14.1 Naval Bases of the Roman Empire

ception of the far west. The trade routes and particularly the corn supply routes, vitally important for the city of Rome, were, of course, given special attention by the commanders of the fleet. The construction of a permanent fleet, already planned by Pompey in 62 BC, was begun immediately after the battle of Actium. At that time, Augustus had over 750 ships at his disposal, including Antonius' fleet. The heavy ships of this fleet were considered too sluggish and impossible to manoeuvre; they were burnt or otherwise destroyed. The remainder were added to Augustus' new fleet. After making a sacrifice to Apollo, consisting of one ship of each type, Augustus chose a new naval base, Forum Julii (now Frejus), a colony on the south coast of Gaul. From this base the coasts of Gaul and Spain could be controlled. Soon, however, it became clear that Italy could be much better defended from the motherland itself. Finally, probably advised by Agrippa, Augustus decided on two harbours, one on the west and one on the east coast of Italy: Misenum, on the northern headland of the Bay of Naples, and Ravenna, on the Adriatic. The most important base was undoubtedly Misenum. Here the largest part of the Roman fleet was stationed, the *classis Misenensis*. Its range of action was great: ships from Misenum patrolled the coasts of Gaul, Spain, Mauretania, Egypt, Sardinia and Corsica. The important corn supply routes were controlled by this fleet. The wide range of action required the establishment of temporary bases on the coasts mentioned above. In Ostia, the port of Rome from the reign of the emperor Claudius (AD 41–56) onwards, a large contingent of the Misenian fleet was stationed. The remaining bases were temporary and could be moved to other ports if necessary. Inscriptions have proved the presence of the fleet in Aleria, the capital of Corsica, and Carales, the main port of Sardinia. It is striking that in Spain and Gaul little evidence has been found of involvement of the fleet there. The fleet based in Ravenna, the *classis Ravennas*, may have been smaller than the Misenian fleet but covered almost as large an area of the Mediterranean. Units from Ravenna patrolled the coasts of Epirus, Macedonia, Greece, the Black Sea, Syria, Crete and Cyprus. The selection of Ravenna as a second naval base had not been a difficult one. Surrounded by marshes the city was well-protected against attacks over land; the fleet, on the other hand, could reach the river Po via the *Fossa Augusta*, a canal dug during Augustus' reign, in order to support the army in the case of an invasion from northern Italy. The harbour could easily be reached from Rome over land.[1]

Smaller fleets were mainly stationed on the frontiers of the enormous empire, far from the waters of the Mediterranean and completely outside the range of the fleets based in Misenum and Ravenna. On the rivers Rhine and Danube, which Augustus had made the definitive northern borders of the empire, Roman naval bases were established. The Germans offered little resistance, so that the activities of the fleets could be restricted to patrolling the rivers. They also provided the armies protecting these borders with food and materials. The Danube was controlled by two fleets, the *classis Moesica* and the *classis Pannonica*. The Rhine frontier was defended by the *classis Germanica* whose most important bases during the century following Augustus' reign were Colonia Claudia Ara Agrippinensium (Cologne), Novaesium (Neuss), Castra Vetera (Xanten) and Noviomagus (Nijmegen). Other, smaller bases were situated on the Rhine in Holland. During the reign of the emperor Claudius, who successfully invaded Britain, two new bases were established on both sides of the English Channel. The most important task of the *classis Brittannica*, based in Gesoriacum (Boulogne) and Dubrae (Dover), was to ensure the safe passage of troops and supplies to and from Britain.

The ships used on the northern borders were quite different from the Mediterranean types. Their design must have been influenced by local traditions. Wrecks of Roman ships found in and along the Thames and the Rhine show a different construction. These ships, both those used at sea and river craft, were practically flat-bottomed and drew little depth; the boards were set on the bottom at an angle of almost 90 degrees. The planks, which partly overlapped, were joined to one another and to the ribs by means of long iron nails. The high stem and stern of the ships which were used on the North Sea and the Channel markedly differed from the usual Roman ships but closely resemble the ships of the Veneti (Brittany) described by Caesar in his *De Bello Gallico*.[2]

In the Mediterranean, too, Augustus' successors established new naval bases: Alexandria in Egypt, Seleuceia in Syria and Caesarea in Mauretania became the home ports of fleets which controlled the surrounding waters. The establishment of a fleet in Egypt is readily understandable from an economic point of view. The grain suplies had to be protected at all cost. During periods of internal crisis in Egypt the *classis Alexandrina* even sailed up the Nile in order to assist the river patrols in restoring law and order. The Syrian fleet was probably formed at the same time, though it

Figure 14.2 Detail of Trajan's Column with a Trireme

is not mentioned in the sources until the reign of the emperor Hadrian (AD 117–38). Seleuceia, in Hellenistic times already an important export harbour of precious goods from the east, flourished once again. It became the centre of the preparations for the numerous Roman wars against the rebellious Parthians, who inhabited the area around the river Euphrates. The activities of the fleet based in Seleuceia, the *classis Syriaca*, extended from the Syrian coasts to the inner Aegean. It was undoubtedly effective, as may be deduced from the lack of reports of unrest in the regions patrolled by this fleet. In difficult situations it could be assisted by the *classis Pontica*, the fleet of the Black Sea, which was based in Cyzicus on the coast of the Propontis. By far the most difficult task had been assigned to the fleet of Mauretania, which consisted of units of the *classis Alexandrina* and the *classis Syriaca*. The coasts and the hinterland near its home port Caesarea were so inaccessible and inhospitable that the local inhabitants could hardly be pacified. Because the rocky soil yielded very little for them to live on they went to sea and engaged in piracy. The Roman fleet was continually at loggerheads with these pirates, whose activities extended as far as southern Spain, during the empire an important producer of olive oil and wine.[2]

The fleets of the Mediterranean consisted of various ships, predominantly smaller types. The battle of Actium had shown that quadriremes, triremes (Fig. 14.2) and *liburnae*, manned with capable oarsmen, were preferable to quinqueremes and even heavier types. Augustus' preference for the smaller ships was also partly caused by the fact that the permanent nature of these fleets made it possible thoroughly to train the crews. A comparison with the Athenian fleet at the time of Pericles easily comes to mind. Then the trireme was the most popular type, Athens had a fleet which was continually active and much attention was devoted to the training of the oarsmen.

In general, the organisation of the Roman fleet betrayed a strong Greek influence. In the late republic it had become customary to recruit rowers from the Hellenistic world. With these crews the Greek jargon for naval officers, boatswains and oarsmen was introduced. The commander of a naval unit was called *navarchos*, the captain of a ship *trierarchos*. The *kubernetes* (*gubernator*) supervised the steersmen and the rowers on the after end. Another important man was the *keleustes* (*celeusta*), who beat the time for the rowers, as well as the *proreus* (*proreta*), who supervised the rowers on the fore part of the ship. In addition, there were several originally Roman administrative officials, such as the *beneficiarius*, an assistant to the *trierarchos*, and the *scriba*, who kept the log-book for the supreme naval command at Misenum or Ravenna. The *scriba* was aided by the *adiutor*, an administrative assistant, and by the *librarius*, who took care of financial matters.

By analogy with the organisation of the army in legions, maniples and *centuriae* each ship of a fleet constituted an independent unit, a *centuria*. The purpose of this organisation was to train the crew of a ship as a *centuria* for close combat on land or of ship against ship. The need for such training had arisen because Augustus no longer wanted to let soldiers from the legions serve on the fleet as marines, as had been customary during the republic. Both the fleets guarding the boundary-rivers and those fighting pirates or rebellious coastal nations derived considerable profit from this training. Our scanty sources do not state whether the entire crew or merely selected members were educated in military science. It is equally uncertain whether military operations were led by a *trierarchos* or by a *centurio classicus* recruited from the army for this purpose. In view of the fact that the *trierarchos* was a real sailor without knowledge of military matters it is mostly assumed that special *centurio*'s were added to the crews.

Roman citizens rarely served on the fleet. The Italians, who during the republic had supplied large numbers of rowers, preferred the legions. This may be explained by the low social status of sailors, most unlike that of soldiers in the legions. The benches on the ships were filled with foreigners, inhabitants of the provinces subjected to Rome. The Hellenistic world in particular supplied many oarsmen. More than half came from Greece, Asia Minor, Syria and Egypt. A minority came from the western half of the empire. They were taken from the middle and lower strata, mostly free citizens or freedmen. Very few slaves served on the fleet. Crew members had very limited chances to work their way up to higher functions, and only within the organisation of the ship on which they served. The low status of the sailors may perhaps best be illustrated by a passage from Cassius Dio, a third-century historian. He relates how a soldier was punished for ill conduct by being degraded and sent to the fleet, rather than to the auxiliaries, who also lacked citizenship but still enjoyed some social status.

The terms served by sailors were long: 26 years, ten years longer than those of the soldiers in the legions and also longer than the period of 22 years served by the auxiliaries. Most sailors, however, did not complete their terms. They lived a hard life on the galleys. The exacting training programme often proved too much, especially for the older men. Conditions on the fleet were not conducive to long terms, least of all during expeditions to places far away from the known ports. But even in their home port the crew members did not live in comfortable circumstances. Only very few fortunate sailors were honourably discharged after their term, granted Roman citizenship and allowed to take up permanent residence in one of the ports. There they had to earn a meagre livelihood as carpenters, masons or dock-hands, as they had done during the winters while still serving on the fleet.

In spite of all this young men in the eastern part of the Mediterranean were eager to serve on the fleet. It was considered an honour to be allowed to serve the emperor. The disadvantages, such as the requirement to remain unmarried during the term of service, were taken in stride. Large numbers of young men, aged between 18 and 33, enlisted on the fleet, admired by their family and friends at home. A well-known story is that of Apion, a young Egyptian, who wrote a letter to his father from the naval base at Misenum relating his adventures:

Dear Father Epimachus,

First of all I hope that you are in good health and will remain so and that my sister, her daughter and my brother are well. I thank the god Serapis who saved me when during my journey I was in danger. When I arrived here in Misenum I was given three gold coins as travelling money on behalf of the emperor. I am well. I ask you, father, please write to me a short letter telling me how you, my brother and my sister are. I also want to thank you for giving me such a good education and for that reason I hope to be promoted soon, if the gods allow it. Greet Capito on my behalf and my brother and my sister and Serenilla and my friends. Euktemon will bring you a small portrait of me. I am now called Antonius Maximus. I hope that you will remain in good health. From the centuria Athenonike.

Apion

Whether Apion was, in fact, promoted, we do not know. He does seem to have remained in good spirits. A second letter informs us that he is happy, has married (either against the rules or the letter must be dated after AD 166, when marriage during the term was allowed) and has three children. He probably never went back to Egypt, as most oarsmen never returned to their native lands but stayed in the ports of Italy. While in service they had children with their wives or concubines and lost touch with their homeland. They did remain faithful to their religion. Many gods were honoured in Italy; in this way the Egyptian gods Serapis and Isis appeared in the Italian ports at the side of Neptune. The eastern god Mithras, so popular among the soldiers of the legions, was hardly worshipped by the sailors, no more than Castor and Pollux, the traditional patron saints of seamen.

The distance separating the oarsmen and the commanders was enormous. The highest post a rower could ever attain was *trierarchos*. Those who commanded the various fleets knew little about naval tactics. Fleet admirals came from the equestrian class, a practice originating in the naval command of Agrippa, Augustus' friend, who was a knight and the first non-senator to command a fleet. Moreover, the emperors were rather hesitant to appoint senators to high and powerful positions within Italy. The senators did not mind this at all; they still looked upon the fleet with some contempt and concentrated on the army. Admirals had usually started their military career as prefect of an auxiliary cohort, then became tribune of a legion or prefect of an auxiliary squadron of cavalry, and finally *procurator* in one of the provinces. Thereafter they could become prefect of a small fleet and work their way up to the highest naval position: *praefectus classis praetoriae Misenensis*, a post which ranked directly below the three great prefectures, of the food supply, of Egypt and of the watch in Rome.

The prefect's responsibilities were manifold. He and his staff took care of the administration and organisation of the fleet, such as supplies, replacing old ships and recruiting and training oarsmen. The question remains to what extent the prefect and his direct subordinates were responsible for navigation and other naval activities. Due to the fact that prefects had not served on the fleets their knowledge of strategy and naval tactics was limited. At sea they were usually advised by the *navarchus princeps*, who was a capable seaman. Furthermore, Roman fleet commanders could afford a mistake or two. In the first two centuries of the empire there were no fleets, in the Mediterranean or on the frontiers, which were a match for the Romans.[3]

Trade and Tourism

Now that order and safety had been firmly established both at sea and in the countries surrounding the Mediterranean trade was greatly stimulated. A network of trade routes criss-crossed the Mediterranean. Beside grain, Egypt exported papyrus, glass, cotton and precious stones; Syria supplied exclusive wines, dried fruits, woollen garments and whatever products the caravans of the Arabian tribes of the Syrian desert brought to the harbours of Antiochia and Seleuceia. From Asia Minor olive oil, expensive wines, *garum* (fish sauce), wood, copper and wool were shipped. Greece played a minor role during the empire. Only exclusive wines, ceramics and copies of bronze sculptures of the heyday of Athens were exported.

This pattern was a direct continuation of the trade situation as it had developed during the late republic. Significant changes occurred when Gaul and Spain appeared on the market and began to export large quantities of goods. Gaul produced wines and, much more important for the Romans, corn. As a grain producing region it was second only to Egypt and northern Africa. Lugdunum (Lyon) became a centre where, besides corn and wine, textiles, ceramics and glass were traded. Farther to the west Spain developed into a major exporting nation; gold, silver, lead, copper, tin and iron were sold in great quantities all over the Mediterranean, as were Spanish olive oil and *garum*. Products from Africa such as corn, oil and wild animals for the arenas, found a ready market. Even from outside the Roman empire goods were imported: silk and other luxury goods from India and China, slaves and amber from northern Europe. Most of the commodities mentioned above were shipped to Italy and, particu-larly, to Rome. Italy's own export had practically disappeared and from the middle of the first century AD onwards the deficits on the trade balance continually increased. In the second century AD Italy, the political centre of the Roman empire, became more and more dependent upon the provinces.[4]

The emperor Claudius was very much aware of the importance of trade, especially that in grain. In AD 42 he ordered the construction of a large round harbour at Ostia, a few miles north of the mouth of the Tiber. At the site of a small bay a harbour of more than 80 hectares was dug, protected by two piers of over 700 m in length. Canals connected the harbour to the Tiber. It was, however, far from perfect, because the currents deposited large amounts of silt and insufficient protection was offered against storms due to the enormous size of the harbour. This became evident in AD 62, when 200 ships, laden with grain, sunk inside the harbour. The emperor Trajan constructed a new, smaller and hexagonally shaped, harbour of *c*. 33 hectares between Claudius' harbour and the mouth of the Tiber (Fig. 14.3). In Ostia the cargoes were stored in large silos or transferred on to smaller ships, which were then towed up the Tiber to Rome. A special type of ship had been designed for this purpose, the *codiciaria*, which had a sturdy, round hull. The mast was stepped forward and may have been used for a spritsail fore and aft (see p. 225), so that optimal use could be made of the wind. Its capacity is estimated at 60 tons at the most, which means that the annual grain imports of 200,000 tons required at least 3400 of these transports. In addition, there were transports of heavy loads, luxury products and consumption goods, so that the routes of the Tiber often became congested, especially near the quays of the river port at Rome. Ostia developed into an international trade centre and attracted large numbers of merchants, trade agents, bankers, shipbuilders, sail-makers, caulkers, loaders and dock-hands. On the quays galleries were built with offices and warehouses. The harbour quarter was full of hotels, taverns and brothels. Further inland residential districts were built for all those who were permanently employed in the harbour.[5]

Trade mostly remained in private hands. Senators and knights were involved through widespread organisations (*societates*), which were made up of people from all classes, each working in his own field. Senators did not actively participate in the trading process but did often supply finances. For an aristocrat it was acceptable to invest in trade, but to be a trader was humiliating. The wealthy elite of the eastern provinces were less strict: there councillors often owned ships, but active trading remained in the hands of people of lower status.[6] As for grain imports, it is difficult to determine the extent of state involvement. On the face of it, the emperors seemed to control the grain supply meticulously. The *praefectus annonae*, appointed by the emperor himself, was a

Figure 14.3 Harbour of Ostia

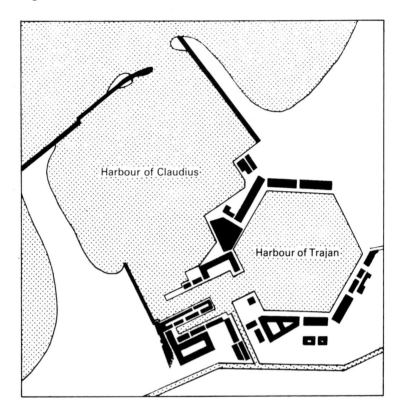

token of their involvement. His task was, however, limited to paying the *navicularii*. They are presumably not to be seen as public employers who were forced by the state to transport grain as members of self-perpetuating corporations, but probably were private entrepreneurs who voluntarily concluded contracts, stimulated by the prices offered by the state. Their participation in the grain imports was not much different from that of the *negotiatores*, who as dependent captains or participants in corporate activities leased space in a ship in order to transport grain for the state or the free market.[7]

The expansion and professionalisation of trade also affected the ships. More, and larger, ships sailed the seas. The basic principles of ship construction were not changed, but the variety of types increased (Fig. 14.4). Numerous representations, mostly on reliefs and mosaics, and the results of underwater archaeology, primarily in the western Mediterranean, show that the round, symmetrical type with similarly curved prow and stern, of which the *corbita* is best known, remained the most common. In addition, on the south

Figure 14.4 Mosaic from Althiburus with Different Kinds of Craft

coast of Gaul a new type made its appearance: the stern was round but the prow protruded sharply due to elongation of the keel.

Representations of ships from the empire illustrate that ships were no longer exclusively square-rigged. Vessels with one or more square sails could not easily tack. The shape of the sail and the rig prevented them from sailing sharply into the wind, probably no more than seven points into the wind. The small triangular topsail, specially constructed to catch higher winds during calm weather, was of little use, no more than the small foresail (*artemon*), a small square sail on a mast which stooped over the

Figure 14.5 Reconstruction of a Merchant Vessel with Fore and Top-Sail

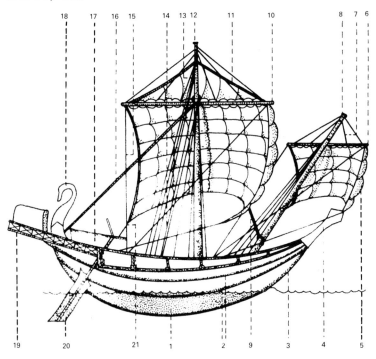

1 keel   2 wale   3 cutwater   4 sternpost   5 foresail   6 yard   7 lifts
8 foremast   9 forestay   10 yard   11 topsail   12 masttop   13 mast
14 halyards   15 braces   16 backstay   17 cabin   18 goose headed
sternpost ornament   19 staffrail   20 steering oar   21 sheets

bow (Fig. 14.5). On some ships, therefore, fore- and aft-rigs were constructed, so that two or more sails were set in line with the keel. While sailing before the wind these sails were less useful, but with a half wind or at an even sharper course they served their purpose. Best known is the spritsail. The mast is stepped far in the bows, the sail is loosely attached to it and the sprit, a long spar running diagonally across the windward side of the ship, supports the peak, and a double-ended vang allows the peak to be trimmed. Less frequent was the lateen, a quadrangular or triangular sail, set and lowered with a sloping yard attached to the head on either side of the mast (Fig. 14.6). For large freighters, however, square sails continued to be preferred (Fig. 14.7).[8]

Figure 14.6 Lateen and Spritrig

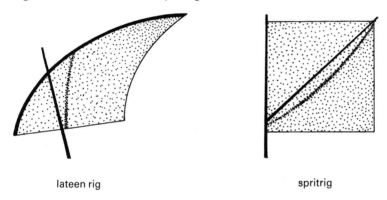

lateen rig   spritrig

In view of the steady expansion of trade in various commodities and the important position of grain transport it may be supposed that freighters, particularly those used for transporting grain and heavy loads, became heavier. Yet, it would be wrong to assume that there were many ships with a tonnage of over 400 tons. The ship built by the emperor Caligula in AD 40 in order to transport an obelisk of 322 tons and its pedestal of 174 tons from Alexandria to Rome remained an exception. The elder Pliny wrote that this ship was the most astonishing vessel ever seen at sea. After arriving in Rome it was taken out of service and sunk, finally to serve as a foundation for one of the moles of the new harbour at Ostia. One century later, according to the writer Lucian, there was an exceptionally large grainship. Lucian relates how he himself has seen this ship, when during a voyage from Alexandria it had been

Figure 14.7 Mosaic with Two Freighters (*c.* AD 200). One has a Rounded Bow and a Standard Rig, the other a Projecting Cutwater and Three-masted Rig

driven off course and moored at Athens. He is filled with admiration by this superfreighter, the dimensions of which he had been told by the ship's carpenter. Its total length was 55 m, the width more than a quarter of that (*c.* 13.75 m) and from the deck to the deepest point in the bilge 13.25 m. Lucian was equally impressed by the other aspects of the ship. He describes the high prow, decorated with a goose head, and the slightly lower stern with statues of the goddess Isis on both ends, the enormous mast, the red sails, the anchors lying on the deck and the cabins on the after deck. Modern scholars have tried to determine the capacity of this mammoth vessel. Estimates range from 1000 to 6400 tons, the most widely accepted one being 1200 tons. This ship, too, should be considered an exception. Lucian's amazement was caused by its uniqueness. If this had been a current type he would not have described it at such length. Many smaller ships were used, also for grain transports, as appears from information from the first and second centuries AD. During a period of food shortage Claudius offered inducements to shipbuilders and owners of ships with a capacity of more than 10,000 *modii* (70 tons), so that these ships might be used for grain transports. Similarly during the reigns of Hadrian and Antoninus Pius ships with a capacity over 50,000 *modii* (350 tons) were requested.[9]

About the costs of transportation by sea very little is known. The most informative source is Diocletian's edict on maximum prices issued in AD 301. Prices of transport by sea are mentioned 44 times, but they are widely different, due to several variable factors: distance, kind of cargo, type of ship, predictability of the weather and prevailing winds. The last factor was particularly important. During the summer a journey from Rome to Alexandria took up 20 to 25 days, but to go back against the north-westerly wind 55 to 75 days were required. This ratio of 1:2.5 also holds for other destinations. It turns out that under favourable circumstances ships were able to attain an average speed of 3.5 to 6 knots, while unfavourable conditions reduced this speed to 1.6 to 2.4 knots, as is shown in the tables below.[10]

Table 14.1: Favourable Wind

	distance (miles)	duration (days)	mean speed (knots)
Rome/Ostia-Africa	270	2	6
Puteoli-Alexandria	1000	9	4.6
Rome/Ostia-Gibraltar	935	7	5.6
Rhodes-Alexandria	325	33	3.9
Corinth-Puteoli	670	4.5	6.2
Byzantium-Gaza	855	10	3.6
Ibiza-Gibraltar	400	3	5.5

The sailing season was from March to October. During summer the weather was generally stable and shippers could safely reckon with the average speed listed in the table above. In March, April and May and in September and October the weather was more uncertain and possible delays had to be taken into account. This was even more true during winter, when navigation was not stopped completely but certainly reduced to an absolute minimum. As far as commercial shipping is concerned motives for

Table 14.2: Unfavourable Wind

	distance (miles)	duration (days)	mean speed (knots)
Alexandria-Massilia	1500	30	2.5
Alexandria-Cyprus	250	6.25	1.6
Rhodes-Gaza	410	7	2.4
Puteoli-Ostia	120	2.5	2
Caesarea-Rhodes	400	10	1.7

sailing in winter are obvious. Pursuit of gain was probably one of the major reasons for traders to put out, since the higher risks allowed them to raise their prices. Food shortages sometimes led the state to force shippers to sail during winter. When in AD 51 the grain imported during summer proved insufficient and the stores on hand would feed the population only for another 15 days, Claudius granted the request of the people and ordered extra imports of food. The supplies did, in fact, arrive, according to Tacitus, 'thanks to the mild winter'. For military and political reasons, too, winter voyages were sometimes undertaken. The emperor's messengers and political officials often preferred the risks of a journey by sea to one over land, especially in urgent cases.[11]

Maritime peace and safety brought about an entirely new industry: tourism. Many distinguished Romans wished to see the places where the Greek and oriental civilisations had left their marks. Athens was a popular destination, often combined with visits to Marathon, Salamis and Chaeronea. Other regions of Greece attracted many visitors, such as the islands in the Aegean and Olympia, where every four years the Olympic Games drew large crowds. Alexandria with its famous lighthouse was also popular among the Romans, who also made excursions on the Nile to the pyramids. Troy, too, was visited by large numbers of tourists from Italy. As Christianity became increasingly popular many people sailed to Antiochia, Caesarea or Alexandria to visit from there the holy places in Palestine. Since passenger ships did not exist in antiquity tourists had to travel on freighters. Travel agents, too, were lacking, so that they had to go around the ports in order to find a place on a ship, which in most cases would not sail directly to the desired destination. Only passengers travelling from Rome or Massilia to Alexandria could be sure of a direct journey on one of the many grain ships. The others had no way of planning the duration of their trip. They probably went about this in the same way as the apostle Paul, when he had to travel from Caesarea in Palestine to Rome to stand trial. First he booked a place on a ship to Asia Minor. Having arrived there he was lucky and found a ship bound for Italy. Sometimes, however, travellers arrived in a port so late in the season that they were compelled to spend the winter there.

Accommodations on board were by no means the same on all ships. Large grain ships could take more than 600 passengers. Stewards and pursers were unknown. Passengers had to provide their own meals and clean their cabins themselves. Some were accompanied by slaves who did everything they could to make their masters as comfortable as possible. They brought along baskets filled with food and at every port they went on shore to replenish their supplies. No entertainment was provided on board.[12]

Not all journeys were prosperous. Delays were among the less bothersome problems, though long spells of calm were far from pleasant. Storms, however, could cause trouble of the worst kind, as one may learn from the *Acta Apostolorum*, which contain a description of Paul's journey from Caesarea to Puteoli. It is the best preserved account of a voyage by sea that has come down to us. An interesting aspect of this journey is the fact that it was made in a north-north-westerly direction, against the prevailing winds. On a merchant galley Paul travelled to Myra along the coast of Asia Minor. There he embarked on another ship, presumably a large sailing ship, and sailed via Cnidus to the south coast of Crete, to the port of Kaloi Limenes. But the steersman and the owner of the ship preferred the harbour of Phoenix as a possible place to pass the winter, and continued. A storm, however, prevented the ship from reaching Phoenix and drove it, with 276 paying passengers, to the west. For 14 days the ship was thus driven on by the winds, until on the fifteenth day it was thrown on to the cliffs of Malta, in spite of the four anchors cast aft and attempts to also cast anchors from the fore end. All passengers and crew members were rescued. For three months they wintered on Malta and were picked up by a freighter from Alexandria and taken to Puteoli.[13]

In the first centuries AD navigation extended far beyond the limits of the Mediterranean. The discoveries of Pytheas had opened up the waters of the North Sea and presumably also the

Baltic to Mediterranean seafarers. Further explorations were, however, hardly undertaken. Trade with northwest Europe stopped at the borders of the empire in the middle of Holland and at the rivers Tyne and Solway in Britain, and the seas farther to the north were sailed by Roman seafarers only occasionally. One of the few people known to have undertaken an exploration journey to the north is the geographer Philemon. In the first century AD he visited Jutland, the coasts of the Baltic, Heligoland, Ireland and the Shetland Islands.

Of much greater significance for Roman seafaring was the route to India. Around 500 BC the Persian king Darius had already constructed the 'Suez Canal', connecting the Nile and the Red Sea. In the fourth century BC this canal had fallen into disuse but had been reopened in the third century BC by Ptolemy II. From then on it was possible to reach the Indian Ocean from the Mediterranean via the Red Sea. The trade routes to the east were, however, not controlled by Greeks or Egyptians. Products from India were shipped to Arab ports by shippers from India and Arabia and then transported to Egypt over sea along the coast or over land through southern Syria. The sea lanes to India remained a secret for Greeks and Egyptian sailors. They did not find out about the monsoon winds, which facilitated navigation. It was thanks to a stroke of luck — an Indian seaman was found half-dead on a grounded ship and revealed the well-kept secret out of gratitude to his rescuers — that around 120 BC the seasons of the monsoon winds became known. The Egyptians learnt that from May to September there was a constant south-westerly wind; a ship could thus sail before the wind all the way from Bab el Mandeb on the mouth of the Red Sea to India. The return journey could be made during the period from November to March, when the monsoon blows from the north-east. Eudoxus, a Greek seaman from Cyzicus who was in Alexandria when the Indian sailor's story became known, was ordered to open up the route to India. Guided by the Indian he reached India from the Red Sea and returned with a rich cargo of spices and other valuable commodities, all of which, to Eudoxus' disappointment, the Egyptian king confiscated for his own use. A second journey, shortly afterwards, again took him to India and, on the way back, to Ethiopia. At the Egyptian border, however, the valuable cargo was again confiscated by the guards of the Egyptian king. Seriously disappointed, Eudoxus attempted to find a route to India around

Africa, encouraged by stories he had heard in Ethiopia about seafarers who had come from the south-west. In this way he would avoid the Egyptian customs. His expedition failed. Due to mutinies and shipwreck Eudoxus did not get any farther than the Atlantic coast of Morocco. Sixteen centuries would pass before the Portuguese explorer Vasco da Gama discovered the southerly passage to India. For the Romans the route from the Red Sea was enough. From the first century AD onwards large freighters sailed to India on the monsoons and brought back precious cargoes of cotton, cinnamon, nard and pepper. Trade agencies were established in India and conducted business with the Far East, acquiring exclusive silk. How intensive these trade contacts were is unknown.[14]

The End of Ancient Seafaring

The peace on and around the Mediterranean lasted for about two centuries. The first signs of change appeared during the reign of the emperor Marc Aurelius (AD 161–80). Both on the frontiers and in the Mediterranean itself unrest increased. Marc Aurelius and his successors restored order, albeit with great efforts. Yet, tribes such as the Marcomanni on the Danube, the Costoboci in the Aegean and the Mauretanians in the western Mediterranean had caused the Romans a great deal of trouble, and the aura of invincibility that had surrounded Roman military power was gone for ever.

In the third century AD the fleet played only a minor role. The fall of the empire was decided on the frontiers, where the legions could hardly withstand the hordes of barbarians. The ever decreasing state revenues — due to inflation, monetary crises and stagnating tax revenues — were spent almost entirely on the maintenance of the armies at the borders. Hardly anything was left for the fleet. The Roman rulers, whose reigns became increasingly shorter, limited the role of the fleet to offering support to the army. The seas were no longer patrolled. War fleets were mainly used for rapid troop transports to threatened regions. As a result, the Romans gradually lost control of the situation at sea. Piracy reappeared, initially on a small scale, but when no countermeasures were taken, rapidly spreading. Maritime trade, already reduced by the collapse of the economy, was seriously disturbed.

The dismantling of the war fleet became evident during the invasions by the Goths in the second half of the third century AD. In AD 254 the Goths, having crossed the Danube, appeared at sea. Since they had no ships of their own, they forced the inhabitants of the regions around the Bosporus to construct ships for them in order to cross over to Pontus on the Black Sea. Hardly any resistance was offered. They plundered the coasts of Moesia and Thrace down to Byzantium and Bithynia. Unfortunately, we have so little information about these invasions that it is not known why these plundering expeditions came to an end in AD 257. To what extent the Roman fleets were involved is uncertain, because it is difficult to determine whether during the third century AD units of the Italian, Syrian or Pontian fleets permanently patrolled the Aegean and Black Seas, or whether parts of the fleet based at Ravenna and Misenum were sent out only in threatening situations. However, in view of the fact that during the Gothic invasions new crews had to be levied in order to call a halt to the Goths, it may be assumed that the permanent fleets no longer existed.

Before long the Goths returned. In the years AD 267 to 269 they must have caused the Aegean cities a great deal of trouble. Near the mouth of the Danube, in AD 267, they constructed a fleet of 500 light galleys and sailed into the Aegean. The Roman fleet temporarily checked their advance and drove them back. Two years later, however, they returned and met with no resistance at all. The Roman fleet was not there to prevent them from passing through the Hellespont. The Goths ransacked the coasts of the Aegean and were finally defeated by a fleet commanded by the Egyptian prefect Probus and by an army led by the emperor Claudius, who was awarded the title 'Gothicus'.[15]

During the last decades of the third century AD Italy itself was defended by a permanent fleet. At the time of Diocletian's reign (AD 284–305), mention is made of the *classis praetoria Misenensis*, which, after Diocletian's voluntary abdication, was taken over by his successor Maxentius. It is uncertain whether this fleet is a direct continuation of the old fleet of Misenum; it is also possible that Diocletian, having realised that a good fleet was indispensable, had revived the old fleet. If the latter was the case, Diocletian did not make the new fleet large enough. Maxentius' opponent Constantine, who was declared anti-emperor by the army in Britain, hurriedly constructed a fleet in Arles and

Marseille and had no trouble gaining control of the Tyrrhenian Sea.

With Constantine (AD 306–37) a period begins during which pretenders to the throne did all they could to assemble a strong fleet as well as an army. The late republic seemed to have been revived. In AD 324 both Constantine and his opponent Licinius began the construction of a gigantic fleet. At Adrianopolis Constantine defeated Licinius on land, who then retreated with his fleet to Byzantium, confident that his 350 triremes would get the better of Constantine's fleet of 200 triaconters and several penteconters. He was proved wrong. The triaconters, which almost 1000 years earlier had been brought into action as the warships *par excellence* and had since been replaced by triremes, were victorious. The superiority of these one-level, 30-oared vessels to Licinius' triremes was a great surprise and contrary to the laws of naval warfare. It may perhaps be explained by the fact that due to lack of money and capable crews the triremes were undermanned. In a regular naval battle the triaconters would not have stood a chance against the much faster triremes. Now the triremes got a bad reputation. They gradually disappeared from the seas and according to the writer Zosimus no more triremes were constructed from the beginning of the fifth century AD.[16]

In the middle of the fourth century AD the anonymous writer of the treatise *De rebus bellicis* posed the problem of the lack of trained oarsmen and proposed a unique solution. According to this resourceful man, large *liburnae* should be built which were not propelled by manpower but by means of an ingenious contraption. On either side of such a *liburna* a paddle-wheel would be constructed; these paddle-wheels would be powered by oxen on the deck, thus giving the ship a speed never attained by any other type. This plan was, however, never carried out (Fig. 14.8).[17]

The definitive division of the Roman empire after Theodosius' death in AD 395 also affected naval matters. In the west the fleets lost much of their significance. In AD 397 Stilicho, the emperor Honorius' general, still made use of a fleet against the Goths, but after he had been sent away from the court the situation changed rapidly. This may be deduced from a passage of Jordanes (*c.* AD 550) in which he complains about the decline of Ravenna and relates how Alaric, king of the Visigoths, advanced to the harbour, which had been filled with fruit trees rather than ships. Zosimus (*c.* AD 500) mentions that in AD 410 Honorius himself fled from

Figure 14.8 Oxen Used to Propel a Ship

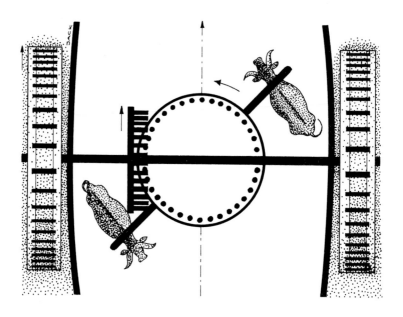

Ravenna. Italy and a large part of the western Roman empire suffered from invasions by the Germans. These tribes penetrated far into the empire. The Visigoths settled in Spain and south-west Gaul, the Bourgonds took possession of south-east Gaul in the basin of the rivers Rhône and Saône. The Vandals, who had crossed the Rhine together with the Bourgonds in AD 406, occupied Africa and built up a maritime empire in the western Mediterranean with strong bases on Corsica and Sardinia. Italy, no longer entitled to the support of the fleets of the east, was no match for the Vandals, who even plundered Rome in AD 455.

The east, on the other hand, continued the rich traditions of the Aegean world. Unhindered by invasions the rulers in Constantinople could direct their attention to the sea. While Italy was being ransacked, the eastern emperors constructed a new fleet with new types of ship. Constantine's successful triaconters served as a model for the *moneres* and the *galea*, patrol vessels rowed at one level. The favourite ship of the Byzantines was the *dromon*, a very fast ship with two levels of rowers. About the *dromon* not much is known. Representations and descriptions are from the tenth century AD. Three variations existed: the *ousiakos*, the *pamphylos* and the *dromon* 'proper'. Though the two former types were lighter the dimensions were more or less similar. The length of all types is estimated to have been 40 m, the width 5.20 to 5.50 m, the draught 1.50 to 1.80 m. The largest type may have been slightly longer. Each *dromon* had at least 100 oars, so that some ships had 50 rowers on each side at two levels. The largest ships had a minimum complement of 200 men. Of these, 50 occupied the lowest benches on the port and starboard sides, each with his own oar, while the upper benches were occupied by 150 men, three per oar. Possibly the upper benches accommodated only 100 rowers and the remaining 50 men served as special marines. The largest *dromon* known to us had a crew of 300, 230 oarsmen and 70 marines. Its oarage is unknown. Though the *dromon* did have a ram, boarding tactics were presumably more frequently applied. Flame-throwers and catapults were used to intimidate the enemy.

Only once did an emperor from the east attempt to restore the empire to its former glory. In AD 535 Justinian destroyed the empire of the Vandals in Africa, Sardinia and Corsica and also conquered Italy, then occupied by the Ostrogoths. But the new unity did not last. In AD 568, just before Justinian's death, the recently acquired regions were lost to the Longobards who invaded Italy from the north-east. East and west were now split up for good. The extent and nature of trade and commerce in east and west differed considerably. Traders in the east carried on as they had done earlier. Constantinople was dependent on Egypt for its grain supplies. Many large grain ships moored at the quays of Constantinople, as well as freighters carrying prestigious valuable commodities from all parts of the empire and from beyond its frontiers. The war fleet provided protection. In the western Mediterranean organised long-distance trade decreased considerably in favour of coasting trade with smaller ships. The centre of trade moved to the north. New routes came into existence, between Britain and northern Gaul, and between the nations on the Rhine and Danube and northern Italy. Several centuries would pass until the Mediterranean became, once again, the centre of international trade.[18]

Notes

1. CLASSIS MISENENSIS AND CLASSIS RAVENNAS: Starr, 1941, pp. 11–29; Kienast, 1966, pp. 48–81.
2. AUXILIARY FLEETS: Starr, 1941, pp. 106–66; Kienast, 1966, pp. 82–123. PROVINCIAL ROMAN SHIPBUILDING IN GERMANIA AND GAUL: Ellmers, 1971, pp. 73–122.
3. ORIGIN AND STATUS OF THE ROWERS: Kienast, 1966, pp. 9–47. DEGRADATION OF A LEGIONARY SOLDIER: Cass. Dio 79.3.5; cf. Flav. Jos. 17.12.2. LETTER OF APION: *BGU* 432; *BGU* 632. MARRIAGES OF SAILORS: *CIL* 16. 122; cf. *P. Mich.* 4703. CAREER OF NAVAL PREFECTS: Plin. Min. *Ep.* 6.16.4.
4. PRODUCTS FROM THE PROVINCES: Roztovtzeff, 1957, pp. 153–70; cf. D'Arms and Kopff (eds.), 1980, *passim*.
5. HARBOUR OF OSTIA: Meiggs, 1973, pp. 149–71. SHIPWRECK OF 200 SHIPS: Tac. *Ann.* 15.18.3. CODICIARIA: Casson, 1971, p. 332.
6. STRUCTURE OF TRADE: D'Arms, 1981, pp. 149–71; Pleket, 1983, pp. 131–44.
7. NAVICULARII AND NEGOTIATORES IN GRAIN TRADE: Rougé, 1966, p. 233–57 and 274–94; Rickman, 1980, p. 72–93; Garnsey, 1983, pp. 118–30.
8. TYPES OF SHIP: Rougé, 1966, pp. 47–50. RIGGING: Casson, 1971, pp. 243–5; White, 1984, pp. 143–5.
9. SHIP OF CALIGULA: Plin. *Nat. Hist.* 16.201; Casson, 1971, p. 189. ISIS: Lucian, *Nav. Isid.* 5. TONNAGE OF THE ISIS: Casson, 1950, pp. 43–56; Pomey and Tchernia, 1978, pp. 235–51 give various estimates; cf. Rougé, 1966, pp. 69–70. CONTRACTS WITH NAVICULARII AND NEGOTIATORES: Suet. *Claud.* 18.3–4; 19; Gaius *Inst.* 1.32c; *Dig.* L. 6.6.5; *Dig.* L 6.6.8.; *Dig.* L. 6.6.9.
10. PRICES OF TRANSPORT: Duncan Jones, 1974, pp. 366–9; Hopkins, 1983, pp. 102–5. SPEED OF THE SHIPS: Casson, 1951, pp. 136–48; Casson, 1971, pp. 281–96; Viereck, 1975, p. 29.
11. SEAFARING IN WINTER: De Saint Denis, 1947, pp. 196–214; Meijer, 1983, pp. 2–20. SHIPPING IN 51 AD: Tac. *Ann.* 12.43; Suet. *Claud.* 18.
12. CURIOSITIES: Liv. 45.27–8; cf. Friedländer, 1922, pp. 408–63; Casson, 1974, pp. 229–37. CHRISTIAN CURIOSITIES: Hunt, 1984. TRAVELLING BY SEA: Casson, 1974, 152–8.
13. VOYAGE AND SHIPWRECK OF PAUL: *Act. Ap.* 27–28.13; Wallinga, 1978, pp. 265–87.
14. EXPLORATIONS OF PHILEMON: Plin. *Nat. Hist.* 4.95; 37.33 and 36; Ptolem. 1.11.7; cf. Pédech, 1976, pp. 174–5. EXPLORATIONS OF EUDOXUS: Strabo 2.3.4. C98–C100; cf. Thiel, 1966; cf. Casson, 1974, pp. 118–27; Dilke, 1985, pp. 61–2.
15. DISTURBANCE OF THE MEDITERRANEAN DURING THE REIGN OF MARC AURELIUS: Starr, 1941, pp. 190–7 suggests that the permanent fleets had disappeared; Kienast, 1966, pp. 116–19 stresses that there were still permanent *stationes*.
16. MENTION OF THE CLASSIS PRAETORIA MISENENSIS: *CIL* 10.3343. CONSTANTINE'S CONTROL OF THE TYRRHENIAN SEA: *Pan. Lat.* 12.25.2. STRUGGLE OF CONSTANTINE AND LICINIUS: Zos. 2.22–5. DISAPPEARANCE OF TRIREMES: Zos. 5.20.3.
17. Thompson, 1952, pp. 50–4, p. 102 and pp. 119–20.
18. DECAY OF RAVENNA: Jord. *Getica* 29.147; Zos. 6.8; cf. Kienast 1966, pp. 124–8. BYZANTINE FLEET: Dolley, 1948, pp. 47–53. Dolley, 1953, pp. 324–39. TRADE IN LATE ANTIQUITY: Whittaker, 1983, pp. 163–80.

Abbreviations

AJA	*American Journal of Archaeology*
AJP	*American Journal of Philology*
Anc. Soc.	*Ancient Society*
BCH	*Bulletin de Correspondance Hellénique*
BGU	*Berliner Griechische Urkunden (Aegyptische Urkunden aus den Königlichen Museen zu Berlin)*
CIL	*Corpus Inscriptionum Latinarum*
Class. Phil.	*Classical Philology*
Class. Quart.	*Classical Quarterly*
CRAI	*Comptes rendus de l'académie des Inscriptions et Belles-Lettres*
ESAR	T. Frank *et al.*, *An Economic Survey of Ancient Rome*
FGrH	F. Jacoby, *Die Fragmente der Griechischen Historiker*
IG	*Inscriptiones Graecae*
IGRR	*Inscriptiones Graecae ad Res Romanas Pertinentes*
IJNA	*International Journal of Nautical Archaeology and Underwater Exploration*
JHS	*Journal of Hellenic Studies*
JRS	*Journal of Roman Studies*
JS	*Journal des Savants*
MM	*The Mariner's Mirror*
OGIS	*Orientis Graecae Inscriptiones Selectae*
P. Mich	*Michigan Papyri*
RE	*Realencyclopädie der Klassischen Altertumswissenschaft*
REG	*Revue des Études Grecques*
REL	*Revue des Études Latines*
SEG	*Supplementum Epigraphicum Graecum*
TAPA	*Transactions and Proceedings of the American Philological Association*
Tod	M.N. Tod, *A Selection of Greek Historical Inscriptions*

237

Bibliography

Amit, M. (1962) 'The Sailors of the Athenian Fleet', *Athenaeum, 60*, 157–78
—— (1965) *Athens and the Sea: A Study in Athenian Sea-Power*, Coll. Latomus, vol. 74, Brussels
Anderson, R. (1962) *Oared Fighting Ships; From Classical Times to The Coming of Steam*, Percival Marshall, London
D'Arms, J. H. (1981) *Commerce and Social Standing in Ancient Rome*, Harvard University Press
D'Arms, J. H. and E. C. Kopff (eds) (1984) *The Seaborne Commerce of Ancient Rome: Studies in Archaeology and History*, American Academy in Rome
Austin, M. M. and P. Vidal-Naquet (1977) *Economic and Social History of Ancient Greece, An Introduction*, Batsford, London
Basch, M. L. (1969) 'Phoenician Oared Ships', *MM, 55*, 139–62; 227–46
—— (1977) 'Trières Grecques, Phéniciennes et Egyptiennes', *JHS, 97*, 1–10
—— (1980) 'M. le Professeur Lloyd et les trières: Quelques remarques', *JHS, 100*, 198–9
Bass, G. F. (1967) *Cape Gelidonya: A Bronze Age Shipwreck*, Transactions of the American Philosophical Society, New Series, 57, 8, Philadelphia
—— ed. (1972) *A History of Seafaring Based on Underwater Archaeology*, Thames and Hudson, London
——, D. A. Frey and C. Pulak (1984) 'A Late Bronze Shipwreck at Kas, Turkey', *IJNA, 13*, 271–9
Berthold, R. M. (1984) *Rhodes in the Hellenistic World*, Cornell University Press, Ithaca and London
Bengtson, H. (1968) *The Greeks and the Persians from the Sixth to the Fourth Centuries*, Weidenfeld and Nicolson, London
Biers, J. C. and S. Humphreys (1977) 'Eleven Ships from Etruria, *IJNA, 6*, 153–6
Blackman, D. J. (ed.) (1973) *Marine Archaeology*, Butterworths, London
Boardman, J. (1964) *The Greeks Overseas*, Penguin, Harmondsworth
Brulé, P. (1978) *La piraterie crétoise hellénistique*, Les Belles Lettres, Paris
Burn, A. R. (1962) *Persia and the Greeks. The Defence of the West 546–478 BC*, Arnold, London
Cargill, J. (1981) *The Second Athenian League*, California University Press, Berkeley
Cartledge, P. (1983) 'Trade and Politics Revisited: Archaic Greece' in Garnsey *et al.* (1983), pp. 1–15
Cary, M. and E. H. Warmington (1929) *The Ancient Explorers*, Methuen, London
Casson, L. (1950) 'The Isis and her Voyage', *TAPA, 81*, 43–56
—— (1951) 'Speed under Sail of Ancient Ships', *TAPA, 82*, 136–48
—— (1954a) 'The Sails of the Ancient Mariner', *Archaeology, 7*, 214–9
—— (1954b) 'The Grain Trade of the Hellenistic World', *TAPA, 85*, 168–87
—— (1959) *The Ancient Mariners: Seafarers and Seafighters of the Mediterranean in Ancient Times*, Macmillan, New York
—— (1966) 'Galley Slaves', *TAPA, 97*, 35–44
—— (1969) 'The Super-galleys of the Hellenistic Age', *MM, 55*, 185–93
—— (1971) *Ships and Seamanship in the Ancient World*, Princeton University Press
—— (1974) *Travel in the Ancient World*, Allen and Unwin, London

—— (1975) 'Bronze Age Ships. The Evidence of the Thera Wall Paintings', *IJNA*, *4*, 3–10

—— (1979) 'Traders and Trading', *Expedition*, *21*, 25–32

Chadwick, J. (1976) *The Mycenaean World*, Cambridge University Press

Charlesworth, M. P. (1924) *Trade Routes and Commerce of the Roman Empire*, Cambridge University Press

Davison, J. A. (1947) 'The First Greek Triremes', *Class. Quart.*, *41*, 18–24

Dell, H. J. (1967) 'The Origin and Nature of Illyrian Piracy', *Historia*, *16*, 344–58

Dilke, O. A. W. (1985) *Greek and Roman Maps*, Thames and Hudson, London

Dolley, R. (1953) 'Naval Tactics in the Heyday of the Byzantine Thalassocracy', *Atti dell' VIII congresso di studi Byzantini I*, Rome

Duncan Jones, R. (1974) *The Economy of the Roman Empire*, Cambridge University Press

Ellmers, D. (1971) *Keltischer Schiffbau*, Jahrbuch des Römisch-Germanischen Zentralmuseums Mainz

Evans, J. A. S. (1969) 'Notes on Thermopulae and Artemision', *Historia*, *18*, 389–406

Erxleben, E. (1974) 'Die Rolle der Bevölkerungsklassen im Aussenhandel Athens in 4 Jahrhundert Vu. Z.' in E. Welskopf (ed.), *Hellenische Poleis*, Wissenschaftliche Buchgesellschaft, Darmstadt, I, 460–520

Finley, M. J. (1968) *Ancient Sicily to the Arab Conquest*, Chatto and Windus, London

—— (1973) *The Ancient Economy*, University of California Press, Berkeley

—— (1977) *Early Greece: The Bronze and Archaic Ages*, Chatto and Windus, London

Fraser, P. M. (1972) *Ptolemaic Alexandria*, Clarendon Press, Oxford

Friedländer, L. (1922) *Darstellungen aus der Sittengeschichte Roms in der Zeit von Augustus bis zum Ausgang der Antonius*, Leipzig (repr. (1979): Scientia, Aalen)

Frost, F. (1968) 'Scyllias: Diving in Antiquity', *Greece and Rome, second series*, *15*, 180–5

Garnsey, P. D. A., K. Hopkins and C. R. Whittaker (eds) (1983) *Trade in the Ancient Economy*, University of California Press, Berkeley

Garnsey, P. D. A. (1983) 'Grain for Rome' in Garnsey *et al.* (1983), pp. 118–30

Gianfrotta, P. A. and P. Pomey (1981) *Archeologia subacquea*, Mondadori, Milan

Gille, P. (1965) 'Les navires à rames de l'antiquité. Trières grecques et liburnes', *JS*, *63*, 36–72

Gillmer, T. C. (1978) 'The Thera Ships; A Re-Analysis', *MM*, *64*, 125–34

Gomme, A. W. (1933) 'A Forgotten Factor in Greek Naval Strategy', *JHS*, *53*, 16–24

—— (1937) 'Traders and Manufacturers in Greece' in A. W. Gomme, *Essays in Greek History and Literature*, Blackwell, Oxford

—— (1944) 'Athenian Notes', *AJP*, *65*, 321–9

Göttlicher, A. (1985) *Die Schiffe der Antike. Eine Einführung in die Archäologie der Wasserfahrzeuge*, Mann Verlag, Berlin

De Graeve, M. C. (1981) *The Ships of the Ancient Near East (c. 2000–500 BC)*, Departement Orientalistiek, Louvain

Graham, A. J. (1964) *Colony and Mother City in Ancient Greece*, Manchester University Press

Gras, M. (1972) 'A propos de la "bataille d' Alalia"', *Latomus*, *31*, 698–716

Green, P. (1970) *The Year of Salamis 480–479 BC*, Weidenfeld and Nicolson, London

—— (1971) *Armada from Athens. The Failure of the Sicilian Expedition, 415–413 BC*, Hodder and Stoughton, London

Gruen, E. S. (1984) *The Hellenistic World and the Coming of Rome*, University of California Press, Berkeley

Guglielmi, M. (1971) 'Sulla navigazione in età micenea', *Parola del Passato*, *26*, 418–35

Haas, J. (1985) 'Athenian Naval Power Before Themistocles', *Historia*, *34*, 29–46

Hägg, R. and N. Marinatos (eds) (1984) *The Minoan Thalassocracy. Myth and Reality*, Paul Aströms Förlag, Göteborg

Hammond, N. G. L. (1956) 'The Battle of Salamis', *JHS, 76*, 32–54

—— (1968) 'The Campaign and Battle of Marathon', *JHS, 88*, 13–57

Harris, W. V. (1979) *War and Imperialism in Republican Rome, 327–70 BC*, Clarendon Press, Oxford

Hasebroek, J. (1928) *Staat und Handel im alten Griechenland*, Mohr, Tübingen

Hauben, H. (1976a) 'The Expansion of Macedonian Seapower under Alexander the Great', *Anc. Soc., 7*, 79–205

—— (1976b) 'Fleet Strength at the Battle of Salamis (306 BC)', *Chiron, 6*, 1–5

Hawkes, C. F. C. (1975) *Pytheas: Europe and the Greek Explorers*, The eighth J. L. Myres Memorial Lecture, Oxford

Heubeck, A. (1974) *Die Homerische Frage*, Wissenschaftliche Buchgesellschaft, Darmstadt

Hignett, C. (1963) *Xerxes' Invasion of Greece*, Clarendon Press, Oxford

Höckmann, O. (1985) *Antike Seefahrt*, Beck Verlag, Munich

Hope Simpson, R. and J. F. Lazenby (1970) *The Catalogue of the Ships in Homer's Iliad*, Clarendon Press, Oxford

Hopkins, K. (1983) 'Models, Ships and Staples' in Garnsey *et al.* (1983), pp. 84–109

Humphreys, S. C. (1978) *Anthropology and the Greeks*, Routledge and Kegan Paul, London

Hus, A. (1980) *Les Etrusques et leur destin*, Picard, Paris

Hunt, E. D. (1984) *Holy Land Pilgrimage in the Later Roman Empire*, Clarendon Press, Oxford

Jeffery, L. H. (1976) *Archaic Greece. The City States c. 700–500 BC*, Ernest Benn, London

Jenkins, N. (1980) *The Boat Beneath the Pyramid. King Cheops' Royal Ship*, Thames and Hudson, London

Jordan, B. (1975) *The Athenian Navy in the Classical Period*, University of California, Berkeley

Kagan, D. (1971) *The Outbreak of the Peloponnesian War*, Cornell University Press, Ithaca

—— (1974) *The Archidamian War*, Cornell University Press, Ithaca

—— (1981) *The Peace of Nicias and the Sicilian Expedition*, Cornell University Press, Ithaca

Kapitän, G. (1973) 'Greco-Roman Anchors and the Evidence for the One-armed Wooden Anchor in Antiquity' in D. J. Blackman (1973), pp. 383–96

Kienast, D. (1966) *Untersuchungen zu den Kriegsflotten der Römischen Kaiserzeit*, Rudolf Habelt Verlag, Bonn

Larsen, J. A. O. (1932) 'Sparta and the Ionian Revolt: A Study of Spartan Foreign Policy and the Genesis of the Peloponnesian League', *Class. Phil., 27*, 136–150

Lateiner, D. (1982) 'The Failure of the Ionian Revolt', *Historia, 31*, 129–60

Lehmann-Hartleben, K. (1923) 'Die Antiken Hafenanlagen des Mittelmeeres', *Klio*, Beiheft 14, Leipzig

Lenardon, R. J. (1978) *The Saga of Themistocles*, Thames and Hudson, London

Lintott, A. (1982) *Violence, Civil Strife and Revolution in the Classical City*, Croom Helm, London

Littmann, R. J. (1974) *The Greek Experiment. Imperialism and Social Conflict 800–400 BC*, Thames and Hudson, London

Lloyd, A. B. (1975) 'Were Necho's Triremes Phoenician', *JHS, 95*, 45–61

—— (1980) 'M. Basch on Triremes: Some Observations', *JHS, 100*, 195–8

Marinatos, S. (1933) 'La Marine Créto-Mycénienne', *BCH, 57*, 170–235

Meiggs, R. (1972) *The Athenian Empire*, Clarendon Press, Oxford

—— (1973) *Roman Ostia*, Clarendon Press, Oxford

—— (1982) *Trees and Timber in the Ancient Mediterranean World*, Clarendon Press, Oxford

Meijer, F. J. (1983) 'Mare clausum aut mare apertum. Een beschouwing over zeevaart in de winter', *Hermeneus, 55*, 2–20

Morrison, J. S. (1941) 'The Greek Trireme', *MM, 27*, 14–44

—— (1974) 'Greek Naval Tactics in the 5th Century BC', *IJNA, 3*, 21–6

—— (1979) 'The First Triremes', *MM, 65*, 53–63

—— (1980a) *The Ship. Long Ships and Round Ships*, National Maritime Museum, London

—— (1980b) 'Hemiolia, Trihemiolia', *IJNA, 9*, 121–6

—— (1984) '*Hyperesia* in Naval Contexts in the Fifth and Fourth Centuries BC', *JHS, 104*, 48–59

Morrison, J. S. and R. T. Williams (1968) *Greek Oared Ships 900–322 BC*, Cambridge University Press

Muhly, J. D. (1977) 'The Copper Ox Hide Ingots and the Bronze Age Metals Trade', *Iraq, 39*, 73–82

Myres, J. L. (1954) 'The Battle of Ladè, 494 BC', *Greece and Rome, 1*, 50–4

Ormerod, H. A. (1924) *Piracy in the Ancient World*, University Press of Liverpool

Owen, D. (1971) 'Excavating a Classical Shipwreck', *Archaeology, 24*, 118–29

Parker, A. J. (1980) 'Roman Wrecks in the Western Mediterranean' in K. Muckelroy (ed.), *Archaeology Under Water. An Atlas of the World's Submerged Sites*, McGraw Hill Book Company, New York-London, pp. 50–1

Pédech, P. (1976) *La géographie des Grecs*, PUF, Paris

Pekáry, Th. (1976) *Die Wirtschaft der Griechisch-Römischen Antike*, Steiner Verlag, Wiesbaden

Pleket, H. W. (1983) 'Urban Elites and Business in the Greek Part of the Roman Empire' in Garnsey *et al.* (1983), pp. 131–44

Pomey, P. and A. Tchernia (1978) 'Le Tonnage maximum des navires de commerce Romains', *Archaeonautica, 2*, 233–51

Pomey, P. (1982) 'Le navire Romain de la Madrague de Giens', *CRAI*, 133–54

Poznanski, I. (1979) 'Encore le *corvus* de la terre à la mer', *Latomus, 38*, 652–61

Pulak, C. and D. A. Frey (1985) 'The Search for a Bronze Age Shipwreck', *Archaeology, 38*, 18–24

Raban, A. (1984) 'The Thera Ships: Another Interpretation', *AJA, 88*, 11–19

Rickman, G. (1980) *The Corn Supply of Ancient Rome*, Oxford University Press

Robertson, N. (1980) 'The Sequence of Events in the Aegean in 408 and 407 BC', *Historia, 29*, 282–99

Rodgers, W. L. (1937) *Greek and Roman Naval Warfare*, United States Naval Institute, Annapolis

Roztovtzeff, M. (1941) *The Social and Economic History of the Hellenistic World*, Clarendon Press, Oxford

—— (1957) *The Social and Economic History of the Roman Empire*, Clarendon Press, Oxford

Rougé, J. (1966) *L'organisation du commerce maritime en Mediterranée sous l'empire Romain*, SEVPEN, Paris

—— (1975) *La marine dans l'Antiquité*, PUF, Paris

De Saint Denis, E. (1935) *Le vocabulaire des manoeuvres nautiques en Latin* (diss), Mâcon

—— (1947) 'Mare Clausum', *REL, 25*, 196–214

—— (1975) 'Nostrum Mare', *REL, 53*, 62–85

De Ste Croix, G. E. M. (1972) *The Origins of the Peloponnesian War*, Duckworth, London

Sandars, N. K. (1978) *The Sea Peoples. Warriors of the Ancient Mediterranean*, Thames and Hudson, London

242   Bibliography

Sargent, R. (1927) 'The Use of Slaves by the Athenians in Warfare', *Class. Phil.*, *22*, 264–79

Schmitt, J. M. (1974) 'Les premières Tetrères à Athènes', *REG, 87*, 80–90

Schuller, W. (1974) *Die Herrschaft der Athener im ersten Attischen Seebund*, Walter de Gruyter, Berlin

Sealey, R. (1976) *A History of the Greek City States 700–338 BC*, University of California Press, Berkeley

Seibert, J. (1972) *Alexander der Große*, Wissenschaftliche Buchgesellschaft, Darmstadt

Smart, J. D. (1967) 'Kimon's Capture of Eion', *JHS, 87*, 136–8

Snodgrass, A. M. (1983) 'Heavy Freight in Archaic Greece', in Garnsey *et al.* (1983), pp. 16–26

Starr, Ch. G. (1940), 'The Ancient Warship', *Class. Phil.*, *35*, 353–74

—— (1941) *The Roman Imperial Navy 31 BC–AD 324*, Cornell University Press, Ithaca

—— (1977) *The Economic and Social Growth of Early Greece 800–500 BC*, Oxford University Press, New York

Swiny, H. W. and M. Katzer (1973) *The Kyrenia Shipwreck: A fourth-century BC Greek Merchant Ship* in D. J. Blackman (1973), pp. 339–60

Tarn, W. W. (1905) 'The Greek Warship', *JHS, 25*, 137–56; 204–24

—— (1907) 'The Fleets of the First Punic War', *JHS, 27*, 48–60

—— (1910) 'The Dedicated Ship of Antigonus Gonatas', *JHS, 30*, 209–22

—— (1930) *Hellenistic Military and Naval Developments*, Cambridge University Press

—— (1931) 'The Battle of Actium', *JRS, 21*, 173–99

Thiel, J. H. (1946) *Studies on the History of Roman Sea Power in Republican Times*, North Holland Publishing, Amsterdam

—— (1954) *A History of Roman Sea Power in Republican Times*, North Holland Publishing, Amsterdam

—— (1966) *Eudoxus of Cyzicus. A Chapter in the History of the Sea-route to India and the Route round the Cape in Ancient Times*, Wolters, Groningen

Thompson, E. A. (1952) *A Roman Reformer and Inventor: Being a New Text of the Treatise De Rebus Bellicis with a Translation and Introduction*, Clarendon Press, Oxford

Thomson, J. O. (1948) *History of Ancient Geography*, Cambridge University Press

Topham-Meekings, D. (1976) *The Hollow Ships. Trade and Seafaring in the Ancient World*, Macmillan, London

Torr, C. (1895) *Ancient Ships*, Cambridge University Press

Viereck, H. D. L. (1975) *Die Römische Flotte. Classis Romana*, Koehler, Herford

Wachsmann, S. (1981) 'The Ships of the Sea Peoples', *IJNA, 10*, 187–220

Wallinga, H. T. (1956) *The Boarding Bridge of the Romans: Its Construction and its Function in the Naval Tactics of the First Punic War*, Wolters, Groningen

—— (1964) 'Nautika, I: The Limit of Capacity for Ancient Ships', *Mnemosyne, 17*, 1–40

—— (1965) *De Griekse Kolonisatie in Zuid-Italië en Sicilië*, Wolters, Groningen

—— (1969–70) 'De slag bij Salamis', *Lampas, 2*, 127–48

—— (1978) 'Paulus' zeereis naar Rome', *Lampas, 11*, 265–87

—— (1982) 'The Trireme and its Crew' in J. Den Boeft and A. H. M. Kessels (eds), *Actus. Studies in Honour of H. L. W. Nelson*, Utrecht, pp. 463–82

—— (1984) 'The Ionian Revolt', *Mnemosyne, 37*, 401–37

Ward-Perkins, J. (1984) 'The Marble Trade and Its Organization; Evidence from Nicomedia' in J. H. D'Arms and E. C. Kopff (1984), pp. 325–38

White, K. D. (1984) *Greek and Roman Technology*, Thames and Hudson, London

Whittaker, C. R. (1983) 'Late Roman Trade and Traders' in Garnsey *et al.* (1983), pp. 163–80

Will, E. (1972) *Le monde Grec et l'orient*, PUF, Paris

Index

243

246 *Index*